D1797206

The Splintered Glass

CROSS
CULTURES

Readings in Post / Colonial
Literatures and Cultures in English

136

SERIES EDITORS

Gordon Collier   Bénédicte Ledent   Geoffrey Davis
(Giessen)   (Liège)   (Aachen)

CO-FOUNDING EDITOR
†Hena Maes–Jelinek

The Splintered Glass

Facets of Trauma in the Post-Colony and Beyond

Edited by
Dolores Herrero and Sonia Baelo-Allué

Amsterdam - New York, NY 2011

Cover image:
Bea Maddock
born 1934 Australia
Four-finger exercise for two hands 1982
photo-etched linocut, printed in process colour, from four blocks
printed image 53.4cm x 46.9cm
sheet 76.6 x 58.4 cm
National Gallery of Australia, Canberra
Gordon Darling Fund 1984

Cover design: Pier Post

The paper on which this book is printed meets the requirements of "ISO
9706:1994, Information and documentation - Paper for
documents - Requirements for permanence".

ISBN: 978-90-420-3388-7
E-Book ISBN: 978-94-012-0083-7
© Editions Rodopi B.V., Amsterdam – New York, NY 2011
Printed in The Netherlands

Table of Contents

Acknowledgements

The research carried out for the following contributions is part of a research project financed by the Spanish Ministry of Science and Innovation (MICINN) and the European Regional Fund (ERDF) (code HUM2007–61035). The authors are also grateful for the support of the Government of Aragón and the University of Zaragoza.

Dolores Herrero and Sonia Baelo–Allué, "Introduction";

Susana Onega, "Trauma, Madness, and the Ethics of Narration in J.M. Coetzee's *In the Heart of the Country*";

Maite Escudero, "'Softer than Cotton, Stronger than Steel': Metaphor and Trauma in Shani Mootoo's *Cereus Blooms at Night*";

Bárbara Arizti, "Personal Trauma/Historical Trauma in Tim Winton's *Dirt Music*";

Isabel Fraile, "Inside Out in the Land Down Under: Reading Trauma through Janette Turner Hospital's *Oyster*."

::

Introduction

T HE ESSAYS SELECTED FOR THIS BOOK tackle the topic of
cultural and personal trauma and the blurring of the two terms in
postcolonial narrative in English. To put it differently, they show
how individual trauma in literature has become one of the most common
ways of expressing and representing collective and, by extension, cultural and
ethnic traumas. As is well known, trauma studies became prominent in the
early to mid-1990s as an important sub-strand of 'ethical criticism', whose
most defining feature was an intense concern with the demands of otherness.
This explicit commitment to ethics set these approaches apart from the poststructuralist criticism of the 1970s and 1980s from which they emerged. The
earlier formalist paradigm, so often accused of lacking any kind of serious
commitment to real-world issues such as history, politics, and ethics, was
eventually replaced by such historicist or culturalist approaches as the New
Historicism, cultural materialism, and cultural studies. Trauma studies could
therefore be regarded as "the reinvention in an ethical guise of this much
maligned textualism."[1] According to Cathy Caruth, one of the most outstand-
ing trauma theorists – together with Shoshana Felman, Geoffrey Hartman,
and Dominick LaCapra, to name but a few – a textualist approach, far from
detaching us from history, can grant us unique access to it. Caruth emphasizes
the ethical relevance of this formal scheme. As she sees it, the insights of
deconstructive and psychoanalytical criticism can help critics to better analyze
texts that bear witness to traumatic histories, thus rendering accessible to the
reader events and experiences that defy understanding and representation. In
"a catastrophic age" such as the one we are living in, Caruth goes on to argue,

---

[1] Stef Craps & Gert Buelens, "Introduction: Postcolonial Trauma Novels," *Studies
in the Novel* 40.1–2 (Spring–Summer 2008): 1.

X THE SPLINTERED GLASS ◄❖►

"trauma itself may provide the very link between cultures,"[2] since opening oneself up to the trauma of another can lead to cross-cultural understanding and to the possibility of new forms of community.

Even though Caruth mentions trauma as a link between cultures, in her own study of the subject she has not focused on the cultural effects of trauma but, rather, on its psychological consequences for the human mind. Her path-breaking work – based on psychoanalysis and deconstruction – has generated a mounting number of studies about psychological trauma and its effects on the individual. Caruth's theories are well-known and are used by our contributors in this volume. Trauma is a wound inflicted upon the mind that breaks the victim's experience of time, self, and the world, and that causes great emotional anguish in the individual.[3] It is a wound in the mind, not a wound in society; it is a personal experience, not a social one. The symptoms which trauma produces in the individual usually appear belatedly and may be suffered by those directly involved or by secondary victims. However, if trauma is to be seen as a link between cultures, there is a need to study cultural trauma and its effects, not just on specific individuals but on whole societies that have seen their sense of identity shattered by a traumatic experience. As Ron Eyerman claims in connection with the trauma of slavery in the USA, collective identity needs to be reconfigured through collective representation to repair "the tear in the social fabric,"[4] not just the tear in the individual mind.

The effects of trauma were labelled in the American Psychiatric Association's *Diagnostic Manual* 'Post-Traumatic Stress Disorder' (PTSD), and the term entered official diagnosis in the 1980s, after the effects of the Vietnam War on veterans had been observed in the 1970s. Post-traumatic stress disorder is a cluster of symptoms which include repeated hallucinations, nightmares and flashbacks, emotional numbing, somatic reactions, and an absence of recall of the traumatic event.[5] The types of trauma considered by the Amer-

---

[2] Cathy Caruth, "Trauma and Experience: Introduction," in *Trauma: Explorations in Memory*, ed. Cathy Caruth (Baltimore MD & London: Johns Hopkins UP, 1995): 11.

[3] Cathy Caruth, *Unclaimed Experience: Trauma, Narrative and History* (Baltimore MD & London: Johns Hopkins UP, 1996): 3–4.

[4] Ron Eyerman, *Cultural Trauma: Slavery and the Formation of African American Identity* (Cambridge: Cambridge UP, 2001): 4.

[5] American Psychiatric Association, *Diagnostic and Statistic Manual* (Washington DC: APA, 4th rev. ed. 2000): 467–68.

ican Psychiatric Association range from domestic abuse to iconic cultural traumas, such as the Holocaust and the Vietnam War. The Holocaust constitutes the pivot around which much of trauma studies have revolved, especially since Dori Laub and Geoffrey Hartman created the Fortuneoff Video Archive Project at Yale University, where survivors were interviewed, thus encouraging new interest in Holocaust research.[6] The Holocaust has been treated by many of these scholars as a unique, unprecedented atrocity, a "massive trauma,"[7] and, as we can see in books like Steven Katz's *The Holocaust in Historical Context*,[8] it has turned into the touchstone traumatic event with which other historical traumas have been systematically compared.

If historical traumas such as the Holocaust have played an important role in the extension of trauma studies in the humanities, the effects of trauma have been specially studied as a set of symptoms that specific individuals, rather than communities, suffer in their minds and bodies. This focus on an individual/psychological perspective may pose the danger of separating facts from their causes, thus blurring the importance of the historical and social context, which is particularly relevant in postcolonial trauma narratives. As Judith Butler has claimed, "isolating the individuals involved absolves us of the necessity of coming up with a broader explanation for events."[9] In postcolonial literature, the personal and the social are inextricably linked, and trauma should be studied in a specific context. In the field of sociology, the focus has turned from the individual to the collective, creating a different conception of trauma, where it affects whole societies and generations.

The present book on postcolonial trauma draws both on the psychological conception of trauma as defined by Caruth and on the sociological definition

---

[6] See Shoshana Felman & Dori Laub, *Testimony: Crises of Witnessing in Literature, Psychoanalysis, and History* (New York & London: Routledge, 1992); Geoffrey H. Hartman, *The Longest Shadow: In the Aftermath of the Holocaust* (Bloomington: Indiana UP, 1996); Dominick LaCapra, *Representing the Holocaust: History, Theory, Trauma* (Ithaca NY: Cornell UP, 1994); and Michael Rothberg, *Traumatic Realism: The Demands of Holocaust Representation* (Minneapolis: U of Minnesota P, 2000).

[7] Felman & Laub, *Testimony: Crises of Witnessing in Literature, Psychoanalysis, and History*, 57.

[8] Steven T. Katz, *The Holocaust in Historical Context: The Holocaust and Mass Death Before the Modern Age* (New York & Oxford: Oxford UP, 1994).

[9] Judith Butler, *Precarious Life: The Powers of Mourning and Violence* (London: Verso, 2004): 5.

of cultural trauma as described by prominent sociologists[10] who have dealt
with cultural traumas such as the Great Depression, the slavery of African
Americans in the USA, and the assassination of Indira Gandhi in India, to
give but three representative examples. For Alexander,

> Cultural trauma occurs when members of a collectivity feel they have
> been subjected to a horrendous event that leaves inedible marks upon
> their group consciousness, marking their memories forever and changing
> their future identity in fundamental and irrevocable ways.[11]

Thus, the victims are collectivities that see not only their individual sense of
identity but also their group identity shattered.

Cultural and individual trauma have a lot in common but work in different
ways, since post-traumatic stress disorder cannot be straightforwardly applied
to whole societies and, as Dominick LaCapra has claimed, "historical trauma
is specific, and not everyone is subject to it or entitled to a subject position
associated with it."[12] The cultural construction of trauma begins with a series
of carrier groups broadcasting claims of an injury and demanding reparation
to an audience that needs to understand the nature of the pain, of the victim,
and of those responsible for it. This process is often articulated in several in-
stitutional arenas, such as the mass media, state bureaucracy, the legal system,
and even the aesthetic domain through narratives of trauma. The result of this
process is a revision of collective identity and, after a period of calming down,
the representation and institutionalization of the lessons of the trauma. Jeffrey
Alexander criticizes the way psychoanalytic theories of trauma defend the
view that trauma should be resolved by introspection and 'working through',[13]
setting things right in the self, thus downplaying the importance of setting

---

[10] See Arthur G. Neal, *National Trauma and Collective Memory: Major Events in
the American Century* (Armonk NY & London: M.E. Sharpe, 1998); Ron Eyerman,
Cultural Trauma: Slavery and the Formation of African American Identity; Michael
Roth & Charles Salas, *Disturbing Remains: Memory, History, and Crisis in the Twentieth Century* (Los Angeles: The Getty Research Institute, 2001); and Jeffrey C. Alexander, Ron Eyerman, Bernhard Giesen, Neil J. Smelser & Piotr Sztompka, *Cultural
Trauma and Collective Identity* (Berkeley: U of California P, 2004).

[11] Jeffrey C. Alexander, "Toward a Theory of Cultural Trauma," in *Cultural Trauma
and Collective Identity*, 1.

[12] Dominick LaCapra, *Writing History, Writing Trauma* (Baltimore MD & London:
Johns Hopkins UP, 2001): 78.

[13] Alexander "Toward a Theory of Cultural Trauma," 5.

them right in the world. Another important issue to take into account is that events are not inherently traumatic, since the effect of trauma depends on the socio-cultural context of the society affected and, for an event or situation to acquire the dimension of trauma, it must have destabilized the structures of meaning of a collectivity. As Neil Smelser further argues, an event may also be traumatic at a specific moment and change its status at a later stage. In any case, the event must be associated with a strong negative affect, and be remembered in a culturally relevant way.[14]

Both cultural and psychological trauma produce a sense of negative affect and can only be understood in retrospect; the similarities between the two cannot be overstated. Comparing cultural and psychological trauma, Arthur Neal claims:

> Just as the rape victim becomes permanently changed as a result of the trauma, the nation becomes permanently changed as a result of a trauma in the social realm.[15]

Comparing the suffering of a rape victim with the suffering of a society is probably a dangerous exaggeration, since the effects of trauma on the individual may differ from those on society at large. For example, whereas the mechanisms that constitute the individual trauma are "the intrapsychic dynamics of defence, adaptation, coping, and working through," those on the cultural level are established and sustained by power structures, social agents, and contending groups.[16] Unlike psychological trauma, which may 'disappear' through psychic work, in cultural traumas there is a constant, recurrent struggle that stirs up the troubling memory. Roth and Salas consider that one of the best ways in which collective trauma can be coped with is by overcoming the polarity between perpetrator and victim in order to reach a social consensus that may reconstruct the sense of collective identity.[17] In addition to psychological work, social consensus and reparation are also necessary.

In postcolonial trauma studies, the original psychological approach to trauma needs to be enriched with the social context that the notion of cultural trauma provides. However, cultural trauma on its own is not enough to permit

---

[14] Neil J. Smelser, "Psychological Trauma and Cultural Trauma," in *Cultural Trauma and Collective Identity*, 36.

[15] Neal, *National Trauma and Collective Memory*, 4.

[16] Smelser, "Psychological Trauma and Cultural Trauma," 39.

[17] Roth & Salas, *Disturbing Remains*, 11.

an understanding of postcolonial trauma, since, according to Rapport and
Overing,

> individuals personalize discourses within the context of their discrete
> perspectives on life, using them to make and express a personal con-
> struction of the world, a possibly original language-world, a sense par-
> ticular to them at a particular time.[18]

An event becomes a cultural trauma when it reaches many individuals, who
preserve the memory of the event and pass it on to the next generation. It is
only by combining personal and cultural trauma that one can fully grasp the
complex dynamics of postcolonial trauma, although even then these concepts
are not without problems. Some academics have criticized the concept of cultural trauma for having become a new master-narrative. To give one example,
in an essay entitled "Against the Concept of Cultural Trauma," Wulf Kansteiner and Harald Weilnböck have positioned themselves against what they
consider to be a "narrow and aestheticized concept of trauma."[19] However,
despite the title of their essay, these critics do not establish the distinction between psychological and cultural trauma, and claim mainly that trauma critics
in general speculate in abstract terms about the concept of trauma, thus ignoring empirical studies and the experiences of real people, and insulting
those who actually suffer from PTSD. When dealing with postcolonial
trauma fiction, it stands to reason that theoretical abstractions should be combined with facts, the psychological with the cultural, in an interdisciplinary
approach that draws on psychoanalysis, sociology, philosophy, and history in
the study of the aesthetic representation of trauma.

Some critics have also shown reticence about the assumptions put forward
by certain theories of cultural trauma and their relevance in the non-Western
world. Alexander, for example, has defended the universal relevance of
trauma theory and its freedom from geographical or cultural limitations.[20] He
argues that the non-Western regions of the world have suffered the most
recent terrifying traumas: the Hutu massacre of Tutsis in Rwanda, the

[18] Nigel Rapport & Joanna Overing, *Social and Cultural Anthropology: The Key
Concepts* (New York & London: Routledge, 2000): 124.

[19] Wulf Kansteiner & Harald Weilnböck, "Against the Concept of Cultural Trauma
(or How I Learned to Love the Suffering of Others without the Help of Psychotherapy)," in *Cultural Memory Studies: An International and Interdisciplinary Handbook*, ed. Astrid Erll & Ansgar Nünning (Berlin: De Gruyter, 2008): 229.

[20] Alexander, "Toward a Theory of Cultural Trauma," 24–27.

ethnocide of Mayan Indians in Guatemala in the 1980s, and the revolutionary Khmer Rouge purges in Cambodia in the 1970s, among others. Even in the case of Western cultural traumas, the victims have often been members of marginalized groups, such as Jews, homosexuals, and 'reds' in Nazi Germany. By contrast, other critics like Allan Young have objected that a related term like PTSD is a cultural construction, not a universal truth, an historical product that originated in the nineteenth century and is based on a Western conception of the world.[21] Along similar lines, Hanna Kienzler believes that "the globalization of Western ideas about suffering and its remedies become problematic in the context of other cultural and societal settings,"[22] and this imposition can even destabilize local forms of healing in the aftermath of a traumatic experience. Other critics, such as Michael Rothberg, believe that, in addition to the fact that the narrow eurocentric framework of trauma studies may distort the histories it addresses, the West/non-West binary is essentially reductive, since it ignores the heterogeneity of the West itself and the colonization of indigenous peoples within Western hegemony.[23]

Although literary criticism may run the risk of homogenizing trauma, especially when applying trauma theory to a postcolonial context, it is undeniable that it can shed light on the interpretation of postcolonial traumatic fiction. After all, trauma fiction and postcolonial fiction are, more often than not, closely related. According to Anne Whitehead, trauma fiction actually borrows from postcolonial fiction in its use of stylistic devices, its concern with the recovery of memory, and its interest in bringing marginalized and silent or silenced stories to public awareness.[24] Trauma fiction has made use of experimental forms often used in some postcolonial narratives as a vehicle for communicating the unreality of trauma, while remaining faithful to the facts of history. In order that trauma criticism can preserve its fundamental ethical component, European and US-American traumatic histories can, and should, conversely, be regarded as closely tied up with histories of colonial trauma.[25]

---

[21] See Allan Young, *The Harmony of Illusions: Inventing Post-Traumatic Stress Disorder* (Princeton NJ: Princeton UP, 1995).

[22] Hanna Kienzler, "Debating War-Trauma and Post-Traumatic Stress Disorder (PTSD) in an Interdisciplinary Arena," *Social Science and Medicine* 67 (2008): 222.

[23] Michael Rothberg, "Decolonizing Trauma Studies: A Response," *Studies in the Novel* 40.1–2 (Spring–Summer 2008): 227–28.

[24] Anne Whitehead, *Trauma Fiction* (Edinburgh: Edinburgh UP, 2004): 82.

[25] We make specific reference to Europe and the USA because, as Craps and Bue-

In other words, colonization should be further theorized, as postcolonial critics such as Leela Gandhi, David Lloyd, Sam Durrant, Victoria Burrows, and Rebecca Saunders and Kamram Aghaie have already tried to do,[26] in terms of the infliction of a collective trauma, and the very postcolonial process as a post-traumatic cultural formation and condition. To give yet another relevant example, in *World Memory*, Jill Bennet and Rosanne Kennedy called for a transformation of the field of trauma studies from a monocultural discipline grounded in a psychoanalytic methodology to a "mode of enquiry that can inform the study of memory within a changing global context."[27] To

---

lens have put it, "the founding texts of the field [of trauma criticism] [...] are almost exclusively concerned with traumatic experiences of white Westerners and solely employ critical methodologies emanating from a Euro-American context," to the effect that they have often contributed to ignoring non-Western traumatic events and theoretical work, thus perpetuating Western notions and ideologies that maintain the barrier between the West and the rest of the world ("Introduction: Postcolonial Trauma Novels," 2). Although it is surely possible that there is much less articulated and published non-Western work on trauma, and this for a variety of reasons – cultural reticence (Japan, Korea); state suppression of 'dissent' (China, Burma, Indonesia); repressive dictatorship (Uganda, parts of East Africa, the Maghreb); or state corruption (Nigeria), etc – it is also true that, even in the West, there have, in the postwar world, been phases and places where the articulation of massive trauma has been efficiently prevented or forced into allegory (Eastern Europe), or sanctioned into arranged amnesia (Belgium, Spain, Portugal), not to mention the USA, where, despite the successful lobbying for articulation of the traumatology of the Holocaust, what Toni Morrison has said about black trauma still obtains. Despite its civil-rights achievements, the USA eternally creeps back inside its truly 'colonial' shell: the amnesiac denial of the country's slavery past and its near-annihilation of the so-called First Nations.

[26] Leela Gandhi, *Postcolonial Theory: A Critical Introduction* (New York: Columbia UP, 1998); David Lloyd, "Colonial Trauma/Postcolonial Recovery?" *Interventions: International Journal of Postcolonial Studies* 2.2 (2000): 212–28; Sam Durrant, *Postcolonial Narrative and the World of Mourning: J.M. Coetzee, Wilson Harris, and Toni Morrison* (Albany NY: State U of New York P, 2003); Victoria Burrows, *Whiteness and Trauma: The Mother–Daughter Knot in the Fiction of Jean Rhys, Jamaica Kincaid and Toni Morrison* (New York & London: Palgrave Macmillan, 2004); Rebecca Saunders & Kamram Aghaie, "Introduction: Mourning and Memory," *Comparative Studies of South Asia, Africa and the Middle East* 25.1 (2005): 16–29.

[27] Jill Bennet & Rosanne Kennedy, "Introduction" to *World Memory: Personal Trajectories in Global Time*, ed. Jill Bennet & Rosanne Kennedy (New York & London: Palgrave Macmillan, 2003): 5.

make this transformation possible, they demanded that trauma critics should engage with "the multicultural and diasporic nature of contemporary culture,"[28] and that postcolonial critics should engage with trauma studies to develop frameworks that might help to analyze the traumatic legacies of colonialism. Their concern was not simply that trauma studies was unfortunately failing to address non-Western memories of trauma and loss, but also that opportunities for understanding the historical traumas and sufferings of other cultures were being denied by the monolithic orientation of trauma studies. If, as Caruth proposed, "trauma's address beyond itself" was to function "as a means of moving out of a 'historical isolation',"[29] then it would be necessary for literary and cultural critiques to deal with different testimonial practices and cultural languages of trauma. It is true that certain writers and intellectuals have recently tried to articulate the connections between traumas within Europe and traumas in colonial and postcolonial space. Collections such as *Trauma and Dissociation in a Cross-Cultural Perspective* and *Honoring Differences: Cultural Issues in the Treatment of Trauma and Loss*[30] are good examples of this attempt. However, despite these efforts, much work remains to be done so that the project of 'worlding' or 'postcolonializing' trauma studies can be fully accomplished.

As the essays that follow show, trauma theory can prove to be very useful in analyzing and understanding colonial traumas such as forced migration, sexual, racial and political violence, dispossession, segregation, genocide, and the intergenerational transmission of trauma, to mention but some. The authors in this collection rely on Western theoretical models, but only to make it clear that they must be necessarily questioned and modified so that they can tackle other contexts and cultures. They thus corroborate Laura S. Brown's main conviction: namely, that trauma scholars must expand their understanding of trauma from sudden catastrophic events that disrupt the lives of people enjoying good social and living conditions to what she labels "insidious trauma," and which she defines as "the traumatogenic effects of oppression

---

[28] Bennet & Kennedy, "Introduction," 5.

[29] Caruth, "Trauma and Experience: Introduction," 11.

[30] *Trauma and Dissociation in a Cross-Cultural Perspective: Not Just a North American Phenomenon*, ed. George F. Rhoades, Jr. & Vedat Sar (Binghamton NY: Haworth, 2006); *Honoring Differences: Cultural Issues in the Treatment of Trauma and Loss*, ed. Kathleen Nader, Nancy Dubrow & Beth Hudnall Stamm (Philadelphia PA: Brunner/Mazel, 1999).

that are not necessarily overtly violent or threatening to bodily well-being at the given moment but that do violence to the soul and spirit."[31]

One of the first charismatic 'colonial' voices to tackle the lethal effects of 'insidious trauma', thus cutting the Gordian knot of European self-absorption, was, without any doubt, that of Frantz Fanon. A linchpin at the precise angle between the historical trauma of personal ethnic origin (he was a Martinican bred out of the slave past) and the then present-day racial/racist trauma of European colonialism, neo-colonialism, and decolonization (North Africa), Fanon managed, as did Senghor and Césaire – one of his teachers – and Memmi and Derrida, to tactically employ and bind together the modes of Western discourse (psychoanalytical, epistemological, ontological, and socio-economic) to analyze the impact of colonialism and its deforming effects. In his seminal work *Peau noir, masques blancs* (1952)/*Black Skin, White Masks*, which, together with *Les damnés de la terre* (1961)/*The Wretched of the Earth*, had a major influence on civil rights, anticolonial, and black-consciousness movements around the world, Fanon explains how he suffered in his own flesh the shock of confronting racial prejudice, which he ineluctably experienced as both psychic splitting and physical amputation.[32] Fanon brings to light the lethal effects that the constant exposure to negative images and stereotypes can have upon marginalized peoples, who, more often than not, end up assuming and internalizing them as a result of having eventually lost their self-esteem and confidence. Fanon argued that white colonialism imposed on its mostly black victims an existentially false and degrading existence that demanded that they should blindly conform to its distorted values. The colonized are not seen by the colonizers as human beings, and this is the picture that the colonized are made to accept. Fanon argues that the problem of race, of colour, is inextricably linked with language. For him, being colonized by language has serious implications for one's consciousness. As he put it, "to speak [...] means above all to assume a culture, to support the weight of a civilization."[33] Speaking French means that one accepts, or is forced to accept, the collective consciousness of the French, which identifies blackness

[31] Laura S. Brown, "Not Outside the Range: One Feminist Perspective on Psychic Trauma," in *Trauma: Explorations in Memory*, ed. Cathy Caruth (Baltimore MD & London: Johns Hopkins UP, 1995): 107.

[32] Frantz Fanon, *Black Skin, White Masks*, tr. Charles Lam Markmann (*Peau noire, masques blancs*, 1952; New York: Grove, 1967): 112.

[33] Fanon, *Black Skin, White Masks*, 17–18.

with evil and sin. In a desperate effort to dissociate blackness from evil, the black man wears a white mask, and thinks of himself as a universal subject equally participating in a society that advocates an equality supposedly abstracted from personal appearance. Cultural values are internalized, 'epidermalized' into consciousness, which creates a fundamental disjuncture between the black man's consciousness and his body. In this way, the black man is inevitably alienated from himself. Following Fanon's arguments, the contributors to this volume often claim that trauma studies must necessarily try and account for this phenomenon, thus corroborating one of Craps and Buelens's main contentions:

> Routinely ignored or dismissed in trauma research, the chronic psychic suffering produced by the structural violence of racial, gender, sexual, class, and other inequities has yet to be fully accounted for.[34]

Moreover, this collection of essays will draw attention to the fact that, although the study of trauma has often focused on individuals and individual psychology, colonial/cultural trauma is, over and above everything, a collective experience, something that can affect whole communities, even nations. As was stated above, too narrow a focus on the individual psyche runs the risk of ignoring the actual historical and material conditions that made that abuse possible, thus enforcing the idea that it is exclusively up to the individual to work through her/his colonial/cultural trauma, mainly by becoming able to organize her/his traumatic memories into a coherent traumatic narrative. Individual psychological recovery would therefore be given priority at the expense of neglecting material restitution, with the result that the pernicious social, political, and economic conditions that enabled that collective trauma would remain unchanged. As Fanon warned decades ago,

> There will be an authentic disalienation only to the degree to which things, in the most materialistic meaning of the word, will have been restored to their proper places.[35]

Individual/psychological healing can only be fully possible when the wrong social/political/economic structures are radically questioned and transformed. Without the latter, the former is, more often than not, an impossible task.

On the other hand, consideration of these general conditions should not distract the critic from, conversely, accounting for the "divided legacies"[36] of

---

[34] Craps & Buelens, "Introduction: Postcolonial Trauma Novels," 2–3.

[35] *Black Skin, White Masks*, 11–12.

those traumatic histories and losses: i.e. it should always be taken into account that traumatic historical events affect different groups and individuals differently. No matter how collective a trauma may be, individual responses to it will always vary. In order to negotiate a balanced equation between the individual and the collective dimensions of cultural trauma, LaCapra's discussion of working through traumatic events can be particularly useful. As is well known, two of LaCapra's most significant binarisms are 'loss'/'absence' and 'historical trauma'/'structural trauma'. Loss "is situated on a historical level and is the consequence of particular events,"[37] whereas absence is a product of structural trauma, such as absence of ultimate foundations. Loss can be mourned and worked through; absence can only be lived with. As for the second pair, LaCapra understands historical trauma in relation to specific events, while structural trauma is not an event but an "anxiety-producing condition of possibility."[38] With regard to racism, although it cannot be considered to be an event, it is undeniable that racism is concomitant with a colonial environment. Unlike structural traumas such as entry into the symbolic, to give but one emblematic example, the concept of colonial environment, while inexorably 'anxiety-producing', is, in addition, historically specific. The problem here is whether the recurrent humiliations and negative effects of colonial and postcolonial racism can be understood in terms of notions such as 'traumatic event' and 'loss'. As Rosanne Kennedy argues,

> Although traumatic memory is atemporal in its structure, the concept of 'event' presumes a temporality of 'before' and 'after.' That very temporality, however, tends to obscure those ongoing investments in racialized discourses and positionings that are constitutive of identity and of a social and political environment. The colonial war is an 'event' that ends, but [...] racism continues to shape the present and the future in damaging ways.[39]

Since the concept of 'loss', like that of 'event', focuses on losses that can be clearly specified and enumerated, it is difficult to articulate the persistent psychological damage of racism by relying exclusively on terms such as 'loss'

---

[36] LaCapra, *Writing History, Writing Trauma*, 45.

[37] *Writing History, Writing Trauma*, 64.

[38] *Writing History, Writing Trauma*, 82.

[39] Rosanne Kennedy, "Mortgaged Futures: Trauma, Subjectivity, and the Legacies of Colonialism in Tsitsi Dangarembga's *The Book of Not*," *Studies in the Novel* 40.1–2 (Spring–Summer 2008): 103.

and 'mourning'. Other terms are definitely required to address such thorny issues, and individual and collective traumas get conflated in all sorts of ambivalent ways. Last but not least, the aforementioned considerations in turn lead us to maintain, following one of Stuart Hall's main convictions, that "the traumatic character of the 'colonial experience'" can only be properly tackled and understood when identity is regarded as a matter of "becoming" as well as "being." To quote Hall's words again, as "a matter of becoming [...], [i]t belongs to the future as much as to the past. It is not something which already exists, transcending place, time, history and culture."[40] Identity therefore becomes a site not only of contestation and change but also of future possibility. Postcolonial subjects can be seriously traumatized by colonialist/racist discourses of identity, but they can also work through these traumas in order to rewrite themselves into existence.

Furthermore, it should be noted that, while the question of representing and working through trauma is particularly indebted to certain strands of psychoanalysis and psychoanalytic literary criticism, there are also other aspects that are not directly accounted for in psychoanalysis, and which therefore transcend the discursive parameters of such work, while also bearing witness to other critical schemes and discourses. There is, for instance, a tendency to read history and its representations differently in relation to trauma, as Cathy Caruth states.[41] Whether or not history should be seen as *always* or *only* a history of trauma, some aspects of Caruth's complication of the notion of history are worth considering. To begin with, there is the question of referentiality, of the signs, traces or marks by which we try to recover or reconstruct history. In this account, history is clearly comprehended as textual, which by no means suggests that historical events do not actually happen. Instead, as Caruth goes on to explain, the materiality of the historical event is only ever available through the deferral that the materiality of signifiers inexorably entails. In other words, what we call 'history' always comes down to a matter of reading and writing and, similarly, of rereading and rewriting in as ethical and responsible a manner as possible, for subjectivity will always and inevitably play an important role in the process. Moreover, since the historical occurrence is neither fully perceivable in the event nor subsequently accessible after the fact

---

[40] Stuart Hall, "Cultural Identity and Diaspora" (1990), in *Colonial Discourse and Post-Colonial Theory: A Reader*, ed. Patrick Williams & Laura Chrisman (New York: Columbia UP, 1994): 394.

[41] See Caruth, *Unclaimed Experience: Trauma, Narrative and History*.

of its occurrence, the work of reading becomes an imperative, albeit also impossible, task. LaCapra claims that empathy is fundamental in responding to traumatic events, providing it does not entail inappropriate identification with the victim. "Empathic unsettlement" is understood as

> a kind of virtual experience through which one puts oneself in the other's position while recognizing the difference of that position and hence not taking the other's place.[42]

By encouraging empathic unsettlement: i.e. by allowing the reader to identify with the subject-positions and experiences of a variety of characters while also becoming aware of their difference and distance, narratives like the ones that will be analyzed in this collection contribute not only to bridging the gap between past and present and different cultures but also, and more importantly, to healing traumatic wounds and paving the way for a better future. LaCapra also suggests that empathy may affect narrative form. As he sees it, empathy should always be looked for and enforced, since it alone makes the reader question and put to the test "fetishized and totalizing narratives that deny the trauma that called them into existence" and that rewrite the past "in terms of uplifting messages or optimistic, self-serving scenarios."[43]

Following LaCapra's caveat, the following essays will focus on different and 'empathic' representations, negotiations, and articulations of trauma associated with colonialism or, rather, will analyze the multifarious ways in which such traumatic experiences have been inscribed in postcolonial narrative. As is well known, a certain number of trauma critics have insistently upheld the idea that only experimental works can partly manage to represent the profound psychic, and often also physical, disruption that trauma inevitably entails. The authors in this collection will counter this hypothesis by analyzing  the different representational practices used by various postcolonial writers to bear witness to variegated colonial/cultural traumas. Not only will they consider texts that, to a lesser or greater extent, rely on fragmentation and anti-linearity, but will also tackle rather more realistic narratives, which, contrary to what less broad-minded critics have affirmed, can also offer valid accounts of traumatic experiences. What is absolutely fundamental in all these cases is the need to take into serious consideration, or, rather, to adopt an 'ethical' attitude towards, the specific cultural and political contexts out of which these

---

[42] LaCapra, *Writing History, Writing Trauma*, 78.

[43] *Writing History, Writing Trauma*, 78.

texts emerged, in order that sweeping and categorical, hence unethical and biased, statements can be avoided.

This book offers a collection of essays that study the different ways in which postcolonial writers of several kinds have responded to both personal and cultural traumas in their fiction. It is divided into three thematic sections. Section I, "From Official History to Individual and Collective Trauma," deals with the close interaction between historical/official/cultural traumas and personal ones as reflected in texts pertaining to different cultures. The historical traumas dealt with are the violent history of Haiti and how it can only be 'represented' in the consequences it bears for the victims and their descendants in Edwidge Danticat's fiction (Aitor Ibarrola–Armendáriz); the famous Twenty-Eighth Maori Battalion and its role in the Second World War as seen in Patricia Grace's *Tu* (2004) through the traumatic story of three brothers who join the Battalion (Donna Coates); the 1987 total war waged by the Philippine government against communist insurgency as seen in the short story "Fish-Hair Woman" and the play adaptation "River, River" (Merlinda Bobis); and the traumatic violent events that took place in two Septembers – the terrorist attack on 11 September 2001 in New York, and the massacre of Muslims at the hands of Hindu fundamentalists on 11 September 2002 in Ahmedabad, India – as reflected, internalized, and 'translated' by the poet in her work (Meena Alexander). Section II, "Women and Cultural/Colonial Trauma," treats trauma as experienced particularly by women, in both the private/domestic and the public/national sphere. The essays included in this section analyze the ambivalent role of the white woman farmer in South Africa's apartheid as reflected in J.M. Coetzee's *In the Heart of the Country* (Susana Onega); the representation of trauma as a legacy of painful remembering and as an archive of colonial, racial, gendered, and sexualized violence in Shani Mootoo's first novel *Cereus Blooms at Night*, one of a growing cluster of works written by Indo-Canadian women in the diaspora (Maite Escudero); and autobiography as a means for African diasporic or afrosporic women authors to write experientially about the trauma brought about by genital operations such as excision and infibulation, and for male writers to also show how this resulting trauma can in turn be extended to male circumcision (Chantal Zabus). Finally, Section III, "The Australian Apology and Trauma of Unbelonging," offers four essays dealing with yet another contemporary polemical issue: namely, the Australian predicament, both as the outcome of the Aboriginal genocide and the nation's multicultural nature resulting from immigration. As is well known, the dark and traumatic side of Australian history, all the more so in today's problematic 'post-reconciliation era', is another specific historical trauma that has attracted the attention of many a scholar in the past decade or so. Trauma theory does not seem to travel easily to the settler colonies, where there is a risk that it might be called upon to perform the service of allowing the beneficiaries of conquest to masquerade as its victims. Besides, in Australia, such gesturing towards the dividends of suffering can never be wholly divorced from the felt (il)legitimacy of the settlers' occupation of stolen territories. It is the contradictory and polemical nature of this thorny historical issue that has led us to include four essays that analyze the way in which Australian literature copes with, on the one hand, 'white trauma envy' (Bárbara Arizti and Marc Delrez) and, on the other, the trauma that results from the clash and coexistence of different cultural traditions (Heinz Antor and Isabel Fraile).

As has been shown, each essay deals with specific examples of how different traumas have been represented in the literature of various formerly colonized territories, thus acknowledging a series of traumatic experiences in different non-Western settings and taking account of cultural differences in the treatment of trauma. The articles in this collection, therefore, go beyond purely theoretical sources in order to offer a current and coherent study of the connections between cultural and individual trauma in contemporary postcolonial literature in English.

WORKS CITED

Alexander, Jeffrey C. "Toward a Theory of Cultural Trauma," in *Cultural Trauma and Collective Identity*, Jeffrey C. Alexander et al. (Berkeley: U of California P, 2004): 1–30.
——, Ron Eyerman, Bernhard Giesen, Neil J. Smelser & Piotr Sztompka. *Cultural Trauma and Collective Identity* (Berkeley: U of California P, 2004).
American Psychiatric Association. *Diagnostic and Statistic Manual* (Washington DC: APA, 4th rev. ed. 2000).
Bennet, Jill, & Rosanne Kennedy. "Introduction" to *World Memory: Personal Trajectories in Global Time*, ed. Jill Bennet & Rosanne Kennedy (New York & London: Palgrave Macmillan, 2003): 1–15.
Brown, Laura S. "Not Outside the Range: One Feminist Perspective on Psychic Trauma," in *Trauma: Explorations in Memory*, ed. Cathy Caruth (Baltimore MD & London: Johns Hopkins UP, 1995): 100–12.

Burrows, Victoria. *Whiteness and Trauma: The Mother-Daughter Knot in the Fiction of Jean Rhys, Jamaica Kincaid and Toni Morrison* (New York & London: Palgrave Macmillan, 2004).

Butler, Judith. *Precarious Life: The Powers of Mourning and Violence* (London: Verso, 2004).

Caruth, Cathy. "Trauma and Experience: Introduction," in *Trauma: Explorations in Memory*, ed. Cathy Caruth (Baltimore MD & London: Johns Hopkins UP, 1995): 3–12.

——. *Unclaimed Experience: Trauma, Narrative and History* (Baltimore MD & London: Johns Hopkins UP, 1996).

Craps, Stef, & Gert Buelens. "Introduction: Postcolonial Trauma Novels," *Studies in the Novel* 40.1–2 (Spring–Summer 2008): 1–12.

Durrant, Sam. *Postcolonial Narrative and the World of Mourning: J.M. Coetzee, Wilson Harris, and Toni Morrison* (Albany NY: State U of New York P, 2003).

Eyerman, Ron. *Cultural Trauma: Slavery and the Formation of African American Identity* (Cambridge: Cambridge UP, 2001).

Fanon, Frantz. *Black Skin, White Masks*, tr. Charles Lam Markmann (*Peau noire, masques blancs*, 1952; New York: Grove, 1967).

——. *The Wretched of the Earth*, tr. Constance Farrington, preface by Jean–Paul Sartre (*Les damnés de la terre*, 1961; tr. 1963; New York: Grove, 1967).

Felman, Shoshana, & Dori Laub. *Testimony: Crises of Witnessing in Literature, Psychoanalysis, and History* (New York & London: Routledge, 1992).

Gandhi, Leela. *Postcolonial Theory: A Critical Introduction* (New York: Columbia UP, 1998).

Hall, Stuart. "Cultural Identity and Diaspora" (1990), in *Colonial Discourse and Post-Colonial Theory: A Reader*, ed. Patrick Williams & Laura Chrisman (New York: Columbia UP, 1994): 392–403.

Hartman, Geoffrey H. *The Longest Shadow: In the Aftermath of the Holocaust* (Bloomington: Indiana UP, 1996).

Kansteiner, Wulf, & Harald Weilnböck. "Against the Concept of Cultural Trauma (or How I Learned to Love the Suffering of Others without the Help of Psychotherapy)," in *Cultural Memory Studies: An International and Interdisciplinary Handbook*, ed. Astrid Erll & Ansgar Nünning (Berlin: De Gruyter, 2008): 229–40.

Katz, Steven T. *The Holocaust in Historical Context: The Holocaust and Mass Death Before the Modern Age* (New York & Oxford: Oxford UP, 1994).

Kennedy, Rosanne. "Mortgaged Futures: Trauma, Subjectivity, and the Legacies of Colonialism in Tsitsi Dangarembga's *The Book of Not*," *Studies in the Novel* 40.1–2 (Spring–Summer 2008): 86–107.

Kienzler, Hanna. "Debating War-Trauma and Post-Traumatic Stress Disorder (PTSD) in an Interdisciplinary Arena," *Social Science and Medicine* 67 (2008): 218–27.

LaCapra, Dominick. *Representing the Holocaust: History, Theory, Trauma* (Ithaca NY: Cornell UP, 1994).

——. *Writing History, Writing Trauma* (Baltimore MD & London: Johns Hopkins UP, 2001).

Lloyd, David. "Colonial Trauma/Postcolonial Recovery?" *Interventions: International Journal of Postcolonial Studies* 2.2 (2000): 212–28.

Nader, Kathleen, Nancy Dubrow & Beth Hudnall Stamm, ed. *Honoring Differences: Cultural Issues in the Treatment of Trauma and Loss* (Philadelphia PA: Brunner/Mazel, 1999).

Neal, Arthur G. *National Trauma and Collective Memory: Major Events in the American Century* (Armonk NY & London: M.E. Sharpe, 1998).

Rapport, Nigel, & Joanna Overing. *Social and Cultural Anthropology: The Key Concepts* (New York & London: Routledge, 2000).

Rhoades, George F., Jr., & Vedat Sar, ed. *Trauma and Dissociation in a Cross-Cultural Perspective: Not Just a North American Phenomenon* (Binghamton NY: Haworth, 2006).

Roth, Michael, & Charles Salas. *Disturbing Remains: Memory, History, and Crisis in the Twentieth Century* (Los Angeles: The Getty Research Institute, 2001).

Rothberg, Michael. *Traumatic Realism: The Demands of Holocaust Representation* (Minneapolis: U of Minnesota P, 2000).

——. "Decolonizing Trauma Studies: A Response," *Studies in the Novel* 40.1–2 (Spring–Summer 2008): 224–34.

Saunders, Rebecca, & Kamram Aghaie. "Introduction: Mourning and Memory," *Comparative Studies of South Asia, Africa and the Middle East* 25.1 (2005): 16–29.

Smelser, Neil J. "Psychological Trauma and Cultural Trauma," in *Cultural Trauma and Collective Identity*, Jeffrey C. Alexander et al. (Berkeley: U of California P, 2004): 31–59.

Whitehead, Anne. *Trauma Fiction* (Edinburgh: Edinburgh UP, 2004).

Young, Allan. *The Harmony of Illusions: Inventing Post-Traumatic Stress Disorder* (Princeton NJ: Princeton UP, 1995).

DOLORES HERRERO & SONIA BAELO-ALLUÉ

◄❖►

From Official History
to Individual and Collective Trauma

Broken Memories of a Traumatic Past and the Redemptive Power of Narrative in the Fiction of Edwidge Danticat[1]

AITOR IBARROLA–ARMENDÁRIZ

Introduction

T HERE ARE FEW PLACES around the globe where the memories of a traumatic past are so present in the everyday life of the population as in Haiti. From the very moment in which Columbus set foot on the island of Hispaniola to claim it for the Spanish Crown in 1492, the history of the place has been characterized by conquest, rigid stratification along racial lines, foreign interference, and violent exploitation. Édouard Glissant has noted that the cruel dislocation caused by the early introduction of the slave trade occasioned an initial disruption in the history of the Caribbean archipelago that cannot be easily repaired:

[1] I would like to express my gratitude to my colleague at Deusto Dr Claire Firth who first ignited my interest in this topic by inviting me to participate in her project "Landscapes of Exile, Dislocation and Loss." I am also grateful to some of the participants in the International Conference "Betweeen the 'Urge to Know' and the 'Need to Deny': Ethics and Trauma in Contemporary Narrative in English," held in Jaca (Spain) in March, 2009. Their comments on my paper were enlightening, especially those of Belén Martín–Lucas and Constanza del Río.

> Our historical consciousness could not be deposited gradually and con-
> tinuously like sediment […] but came together in the context of shock,
> contradiction, painful negation, and explosive forces.[2]

It goes without saying that slavery, with its abrupt displacements and systematic infliction of pain and punishment, is at the very origin of an historical
legacy plagued with traumata.[3] Given the abuses and the unspeakable crimes
that the plantation economy fostered, it is little wonder that Haiti's modern
history has been marked from its inception by the erasure of a collective
memory that could have given shape and sense to the events taking place in
the country. Actually, this 'nonhistory', as Glissant calls it,[4] greatly resembles
the "inherent forgetting" that Cathy Caruth and other trauma specialists have
said is common among traumatized individuals and groups, which are repeatedly disturbed by experiences and/or images of the past. A sort of interper-
sonal and transgenerational vicious circle is generated which impedes any
proper interpretation of historical events, if it is not as a mere reiteration and
return of earlier traumatic experiences that had remained unassimilated.

This grim picture may seem a bit paradoxical to those familiar with the
history of the country, for it is also true that it has had its periods of respite.
Although external intervention and economic dependency have been fairly
constant, there have been some outbursts of resistance and popular insurrec-
tions which could have radically altered the predicament of the country. Not
in vain, Haiti was the first colonized territory to win independence from its
colonial rulers in 1804 and, for several historians, the Haitian revolution
played a key role in the advancement of European modernity – especially in
what concerns the position of the proletariat. According to C.L.R. James, the
society on the island over two hundred years ago uncannily displayed a number of "the critical elements of a world system still in the early stages of its

---

[2] Édouard Glissant, *Poetics of Relation*, tr. Betsy Wing (*Poétique de la Relation*,
1990; Ann Arbor: U of Michigan P, 1997): 61–62.

[3] Among the authors who have referred to the slave trade as one of the severest col-
lective scars on the Caribbean unconscious, the following could be mentioned: Aimé
Césaire, *Toussaint Louverture: La Révolution française et le problème colonial* (Paris:
Club française du livre, 1960); Frantz Fanon, *Black Skin, White Masks*, tr. Charles L.
Markmann (*Peau noire, masques blancs*, 1952, New York: Grove, 1967); and, more
recently, Paul Gilroy, *The Black Atlantic: Modernity and Double-Consciousness*
(Cambridge MA: Harvard UP, 1993).

[4] Glissant, *Poetics of Relation*, 67.

evolution."[5] Unfortunately, however, the revolutionary movement soon got caught up in the characteristic complications of post-independence, Third-World states. General Jean J. Dessalines declared the independence of the new nation in January 1804, but soon after ordered the remaining Frenchmen slaughtered. Only two years later, he himself was brutally assassinated by conspirators among his closest advisors and the country was divided into two rival regimes. What had seemed for a short while exciting socio-political opportunities for freedom and equality soon became rapid cycles of invasion, violence, corruption, and dictatorships that have punctuated the history of the nation these past two centuries.[6] Little is said in today's history books of the significance of the revolution and the achievements of the world's oldest black republic, while, as Carole Sweeney's explains, "the traces of violence, rupture, and dislocation continue to possess and to haunt generations of Haitians, thereby producing a present that is played out as repetition and recurrence, endlessly circling around a central lacuna of loss and dispossession."[7]

There is little question that Edwidge Danticat's fiction is very much haunted by those episodes of "violence, rupture, and dislocation" that have doomed many of her compatriots to remain prisoners of a distressing past they find quite impossible to leave behind.

> Haiti is struggling to heal the wounds of its violent past as this legacy lingers and impedes Haiti's rehabilitative progress to eradicate social, political, and economic unrest.[8]

---

[5] Anna Grimshaw, "Introduction: C.L.R. James: A Revolutionary View," in *The C.L.R. James Reader*, ed. Anna Grimshaw (Oxford: Blackwell, 1992): 19. James's classic volume *The Black Jacobins: Toussaint L'Ouverture and the San Domingo Revolution* (New York: Vintage, 1963) is an invaluable source of information about the early stages of the aforementioned world system.

[6] For an illuminating discussion of Haiti's violent history, see Robert D. Heinl & Nancy G. Heinl, *Written in Blood: The History of the Haitian People* (Lanham MD: UP of America, rev. ed. 1996).

[7] Carole Sweeney, "The Unmaking of the World: Haiti, History, and Writing in Édouard Glissant and Edwidge Danticat," *Atlantic Studies* 4.1 (April 2007): 54.

[8] Dorsía Smith, "A Violent Homeland: Recalling Haiti in Edwidge Danticat's Novels," in *Narrating the Past: (Re)constructing Memory, (Re)negotiating History*, ed. Nandita Batra (Newcastle upon Tyne: Cambridge Scholars, 2007): 133.

Her short stories and novels are full of characters anxious to understand and to exorcize experiences that have crippled them for life, and which prevent them from building relationships and constituting identities that would permit them to lead an ordinary existence. Having been victims of rape, parental neglect, torture, mass execution, exile, and a long list of other horrors, they are faced with the arduous task of finding ways to recuperate from the traumas that have turned their lives into true nightmares. Hence the constant self-questioning pervading her fiction and making any all-round resolution quite impossible. Martin Munro points out that Danticat's works of fiction tend to present the effects of trauma on the individual and the community, and also identify "what is destroyed by trauma."[9] Nevertheless, as the following pages intend to demonstrate, this Haitian author is not happy with merely showing the gaps, lacunae, and traumatic black holes that prevail in the individual and collective memories of her characters. Probably because she sees the act of writing as an attempt to conjure up those ghostly absences and to deal with them in new and effective ways, her works may be said to represent an invaluable opportunity to reach a safe post-traumatic condition:

> I think a lot of creative work springs out of some place deeper in us, a place that maybe even the writer does not have access to until he or she begins writing. I grew up under a dictatorship. Maybe that's a bigger scar than even I realized when I was a child, or even now. Maybe I'll understand it finally when I am an old woman. […] Maybe I was traumatized and that trauma is now surfacing in this way.[10]

Although there is no doubt that both Danticat's collections of short stories and her novels are only very loosely structured and try to preserve the fractured quality of memories that have had a hard time surfacing into consciousness, her narratives also include a number of 'female' metaphors and redemptive features that can be seen to transform the otherwise disjointed and discontinuous fictional world. Since the author is mostly interested in documenting the poverty, crimes, anxiety, and internal unrest that govern life in her homeland, and the kind of psychological 'dis-eases' that result from them, it is only natural that she should be reticent about giving coherence to and fully domesticating those materials. Her solution is to let the two extremes

---

[9] Martin Munro, "Writing Disaster: Trauma, Memory, and History in Edwidge Danticat's *The Farming of Bones,*" *Ethnologies* 28.1 (2006): 83.

[10] Danticat (personal interview with Munro, January 2003), quoted in Munro, "Writing Disaster," 85.

meet halfway, with the crude experiential and psychological chaos being still represented but partly tamed by an effort to unearth its sources and alleviate its effects as much as possible. In a way, her work is best interpreted as a powerful quest for a new sensibility in fiction-writing and history-making that would manage, to some extent, to outgrow that 'fragile sky' that has kept her people speechless and paralyzed for long centuries. The female 'disembodied voice' in the Epilogue of *Krik? Krak!* is quite explicit about the key role played by storytelling in this quest,[11] which will endow the author with the protection and energy she needs to recover from all her grievances:

> You thought that if you didn't tell the stories, the sky would fall on your head. You often thought that without the trees, the sky would fall on your head. You learned in school that you have pencils and paper only because the trees gave themselves in unconditional sacrifice. There have been days when the sky was as close as your hair to falling on your head.[12]

Broken Memories of a Traumatic Past

> the historical power of trauma is not just that the experience is repeated after its forgetting, but that it is only in and through its inherent forgetting that it is first experienced at all. And it is this inherent latency of the event that paradoxically explains the peculiar, temporal structure, the belatedness, of historical experience: since the traumatic event is not experienced as it occurs, it is fully evident only in connection with another place, and in another time.[13]

In a review of Danticat's collection *The Dew Breaker*, the critic Michiko Kakutani explains:

> Haiti's bloody and bitter history of violence, corruption, and vengeance stalks all the characters in [this] remarkable new novel, infect-

---

[11] Danticat herself has underlined in several interviews the importance of the storytelling tradition in her culture and her fiction. Some of her ideas are reminiscent of 'talking cure' advocates, such us Freud, Klein, Irigaray, Lacan, Lear, and so on. See, for example, Bonnie Lyons, "An Interview with Edwidge Danticat," *Contemporary Literature* 44.2 (Summer 2003): 192–93.

[12] Danticat, *Krik? Krak!*, 223.

[13] Cathy Caruth, "Introduction" to *Trauma: Explorations in Memory*, ed. Cathy Caruth (Baltimore MD & London: Johns Hopkins UP, 1996): 8.

ing their dreams and circumscribing their expectations. It is a nightmare they are all trying in vain to rewind and erase.[14]

To a great extent, this description could be equally applied, with little quali-
fication, to all her earlier works of fiction, which, in various ways, also
portray people belatedly suffering from the mental – and sometimes physical
– traumata of previous experiences. Such is the case with Martine and Sophie
Caco in *Breath, Eyes, Memory*, which tells the story of a mother and her
daughter whose experiences of sexual violation took place, respectively, in
public by rape in a Haitian sugarcane field and in private by the cultural ritual
of virginity-testing in Brooklyn. Interestingly, although the immense sexual
pain leading to the trauma is inflicted in each case by a faceless *Tonton
Macoute*[15] and by Sophie's own mother, both acts of violence are repeatedly
experienced in dreams and hallucinations as not fully accepted and assimilated:

> Martine – herself a survivor of sexual abuse – contributes to the conti-
> nuous cycle of sexual violence against Haitian women as acknowl-
> edged by Sophie's pain during the tests.[16]

Ann Douglass and Thomas Vogler have rightly noted that

> the traumatic event bears a striking similarity to the always absent sig-
> nified or referent of the poststructuralist discourse, an object that can
> by definition only be constructed retroactively, never observed di-
> rectly.[17]

---

[14] Michiko Kakutani, "Books of the Times; Hiding from a Brutal Past Spent Shattering Lives in Haiti," *New York Times* (10 March 2004) [Review of *The Dew Breaker*],
http://query.nytimes.com/gst/fullpage.html?res=9400E6DE143EF933A25750C0A9629
C8B63&ref=edwidge_danticat (accessed 28 July 2010).

[15] The *Tonton Macoutes* were the bloodthirsty enforcers of Francois Duvalier's –
and later his son's – dictatorial regime in the late 1960s and 1970s. They were a vicious body of right-wing paramilitary thugs who took their name from a folkloric figure
in Haiti, 'the bogeyman', who would come at night and steal the children from their
homes.

[16] Smith, "A Violent Homeland," 137–38.

[17] Ann Douglass & Thomas A. Vogler, "Introduction" to *Witness and Memory: The
Discourse of Trauma*, ed. Ann Douglass & Thomas A. Vogler (New York & London:
Routledge, 2003): 5.

The novel shows Sophie's hopeless endeavours to rebuild a daughter–mother relationship that has been torn apart by the recurring trauma of the violent rape and the distance created by Martine's subsequent exile to the USA.[18] As Caruth sees it, traumatized individuals "carry an impossible history with them, or they become themselves the symptoms of a history they cannot entirely possess."[19] This is certainly the case with Sophie and her mother, who are alienated from their bodies by experiences that are deliberately pushed out of consciousness, but keep returning to them in the form of nightmares and ghastly visions:

> Later that night, I heard the same voice screaming as though someone was trying to kill her. I rushed over, but my mother was alone thrashing against the sheets.[20]

When Martine finally confides to Sophie the story of her rape in a cane field, her attempts at establishing a distance between herself and the harrowing event are quite apparent:

> She did not sound hurt or angry, just like someone who was stating a fact. Like naming a color or calling a name. Something that already existed and could not be changed. It took me twelve years to piece together my mother's entire story. By then, it was already too late. (61)

Martine's dispassionate retelling of the traumatic episode should not surprise us, though, because, as Judith Herman observes, the afflicted individual "may experience intense emotion but without clear memory of the event, or may remember everything in detail but without emotion."[21] Mother and daughter in this novel present us with clear instances of these extreme reactions to distressing experiences, for, whereas the former is constantly reliev-

---

[18] Expatriation and exile are, of course, among the most common consequences of politically oppressive regimes. It is no coincidence that many of Danticat's characters – like the author herself, who was taken to the USA as a child – should decide to abandon their native land in an attempt to escape their painful memories and start from scratch. Curiously, though, many of them feel compelled to return to Haiti to make peace with their past and themselves.

[19] Caruth, *Trauma*, 231.

[20] Edwidge Danticat, *Breath, Eyes, Memory* (New York: Random House, 1994): 48. Further page references are in the main text.

[21] Judith Herman, *Trauma and Recovery: From Domestic Abuse to Political Terror* (New York: HarperCollins, 1992): 47.

ing the trauma in her night-time visions – even as she tries to erase those memories by negating their influence on her current life – the latter feels floods of intense emotion every time she recalls the obnoxious trial of having her purity tested. Like her mother, Sophie also tries to set some distance between her body and her mind every time the unpalatable ritual is performed:

> In my mind, I tried to relive all the pleasant memories I remembered from my life. My special moments with Tante Atie and with Joseph and even with my mother. (84)

Nevertheless, and somehow predictably, her strained efforts to forget that insidious cultural practice are invariably countered by involuntary flashbacks of memory that make her aware of the psychological wound that her mother has inflicted upon her.[22] As Sophie soon realizes, her mother is right when she declares after each test that *"there are secrets you cannot keep"* (85; emphasis in original) – although the reasons for each of them to be convinced that this is so are, of course, quite different. Following Herman, one could argue that both Martine and Sophie are deeply marked by traumatic events that prevent them from leading a normal existence and building healthy relationships.[23] In this sense, the latter's dream at the beginning of the novel proves quite premonitory,[24] for her mother will try to *frame* Sophie within the same story of violence and suppressed sentiments that have driven her to a mostly sterile and tormented existence:

> I sometimes saw my mother in my dreams. She would chase me through a field of wildflowers as tall as the sky. When she caught me, she would try to squeeze me into the small frame so I could be in the picture with her. I would scream and scream until my voice gave out, then Aunt Atie would come and save me from her grasp. (8)

In Danticat's second novel, *The Farming of Bones*, we are transported to what Pierre Nora has termed a *"lieu de mémoire,"* a mental place recurrently

---

[22] See Donette A. Francis, "'Silences too horrific to disturb': Writing Sexual Histories in Edwidge Danticat's *Breath, Eyes, Memory*," *Research in African Literatures* 35.2 (Summer 2004): 80–83.

[23] Herman, *Trauma and Recovery*, 51.

[24] Dreams and nightmares repeatedly appear in Danticat's fiction as conveyors of those meanings – often fears or phobias – that her characters try to repress. Trauma theory has actually devoted significant efforts to the study of the connections between the shattering external incidents and the victim's psychosomatic internal responses.

revisited, rather than a real landscape.[25] The massacre of Haitian migrant
workers living in the Dominican Republic in 1937 has become one of the
most potent sources of discomfort for the collective consciousness of the
nation.[26] Danticat had already visited this psychic site in one of the stories in
Krik? Krak!, tellingly entitled "Nineteen Thirty-Seven," in which the narrator
and a whole other group of women are haunted by the dismal memories of the
human slaughter. As one of the anonymous female voices tells the protagonist, "I am a child of that place […]. We come from that long trail of
blood."[27] *The Farming of Bones* could be said to elaborate on some of the
themes already hinted at in the earlier micro-narrative as its protagonist–
narrator, Amabelle, a young Haitian maid working for an affluent Dominican
family, needs to come to grips with the guilty feelings arising in her as a result
of her parents' drowning in the Massacre River. Like most of Danticat's characters, she shows all the classic signs of a traumatized individual who seems
to be trapped in a spiral of recollections that doom her attempts at building a
full-fledged selfhood:

> It's either be in a nightmare or be nowhere at all. Or otherwise simply
> float inside these remembrances, grieving for who I was, and even
> more for what I've become.[28]

Not unlike Martine's account of her brutal rape, Amabelle's narration of her
reactions to her parents' death is also characterized by a language deprived of
emotion that reflects her desire to detach herself from the traumatic episode.
But, of course, it soon becomes evident that the historical suffering that came
to a climax with the sacrifice of the innocent labourers – and which is represented in the novel by the mythic figure of the 'sugar lady' – is far from being
over. Amabelle is just one of the numerous victims – Sebastien Onius, her

---

[25] Pierre Nora, "Between Memory and History: *Les Lieux de Mémoire*," tr. Marc
Roudebush ("Entre mémoire et histoire," 1984), *Representations* 26 (Special Issue:
"Memory and Counter-Memory," Spring 1889): 7–9.

[26] The Massacre River received its name originally when a group of Spanish colonists slaughtered some French pirates in the area in 1728. However, in today's Haitian
national imaginary, the place is immediately associated with the mass murder of thousands of cane workers – estimates range from 20,000 to 30,000 – by Trujillo's forces.

[27] *Krik? Krak!*, 44.

[28] Edwidge Danticat, *The Farming of Bones* (London: Abacus, 2000): 2. Further
page references in the main text.

lover, and Father Romain being among the most deeply stricken – of an event
that binds them together, and to a great extent hinders their chances of ac-
quiring a stable selfhood and living their lives normally. Munro contends that
this incapacity becomes evident in that "there is in the novel no one single
flowing narrative, but a deliberately disjointed juxtaposition of the traumatizing past and the traumatized present."[29] As happens in much of Danticat's
fiction, the reader needs to look into the freighted silences, the unnerving
dreams, and the broken memories in order to identify those component parts
of the self that have been most seriously damaged or utterly destroyed by the
trauma.

Of course, since it is Amabelle's voice that we see primarily represented in
the text, it is only natural that her tortuous inner journey should capture most
of the reader's attention. Furthermore, she exhibits a special ability to draw all
kinds of original and revealing correlations between her permanently exci-
table state of mind and the natural phenomena on the island – heavy rains,
deserts, hurricanes – all of which are presented as cruel companions to human
violence. Nevertheless, it would be incorrect to assume that it is the protagonist's premature loss of her parents and her subsequent remorse that cause
the narrative to remain so spasmodic and incomplete.[30] As pointed out above,
the Massacre River represents a collective 'memory-site' in the book that
leaves visible psychic scars on most of the other characters, too. Father
Romain, the Haitian priest in the Dominican town of Alegría, is very likely
the clearest instance of a traumatized individual in the novel, since he suffers
from a chronic state of amnesia that has wiped away the last traces of lucidity
and mental balance. The protagonist describes him as a "badly wound
machine" (260) whose communicative skills are reduced to a repetition of
some of Trujillo's catchphrases:[31] "'We, as Dominicans, must have our sepa-
rate traditions and our own ways of living. If not, in less than three generations, we will all be Haitians'" (61). Like Amabelle, he is another victim of

---

[29] Munro, "Writing Disaster," 91.

[30] See Amy Novak, "'A Marred Testament': Cultural Trauma and Narrative in Danticat's *The Farming of Bones,*" *Arizona Quarterly* 62.4 (Winter 2006): 118.

[31] Rafael L. Trujillo Molina (1891–1961) ruled the Dominican Republic from 1930
to 1961, when he was killed. His years in power ('the Trujillo era') are remembered
today as one of the darkest periods in the history of the country. He was a megalo-
maniac and a racist (despite his never-mentioned mixed-blood heritage) who contributed greatly to exacerbating the animosity between Haiti and his country.

the mental *sequelae* of the massacre, although in his case these are further aggravated by his later experiences in a Dominican prison. Other characters such as Kongo and Sebastien are also haunted by terrifying images of the traumatic event, which quite often make them behave in dysfunctional ways. Lambek and Antze have stressed that

> personal memory is always connected to social narrative as is social memory to the personal. The self and the community are the imagined products of a continuous process.[32]

The Farming of Bones perfectly illustrates this commonplace in trauma studies: i.e. that the individual can hardly be separated from the collective, especially when specific events seem to absorb so much of the traumatic energy present in particular national narratives. This fact becomes most evident when Amabelle finally realizes that she is nothing but a prolongation of the folkloric figure of the sugar woman; the voice that comes out of her mouth "is the voice of the orphaned child at the stream, the child who from then on would only talk to strange faces" (133).

The Dew Breaker is in all likelihood Danticat's most accomplished work of fiction so far, since it manages to capture in pristine prose the unbounded character and hardly foreseeable aftermath of violence. The title of the book refers to a torturer employed by the ruthless government of François 'Papa Doc' Duvalier (1957–71) to kidnap, maim, and murder people – they often came "before dawn, as the dew was settling on the leaves, and they'd take you away."[33] Nevertheless, it is only in the last chapter of the collection that we meet this detestable creature face to face, while the rest of the book is dedicated to his victims and their descendants, whose lives have been violently damaged by his unspeakable crimes. As Kakutani explains,

> they all find themselves haunted by the long events that left them with broken bodies, fractured families or smashed hopes. For these characters the dead are not merely ghosts; they are palpable, intimately felt presences in their lives.[34]

---

[32] Michael Lambek & Paul Antze, "Introduction: Forecasting Memory," in *Tense Past: Cultural Essays in Trauma and Memory,* ed. Paul Antze & Michael Lambek (London: Routledge, 1996): xx.

[33] Edwidge Danticat, *The Dew Breaker* (New York: Vintage, 2005): 189. Further page references in the main text.

[34] Kakutani, "Books of the Times."

Some try to appease their ancestors' hunger for justice and recognition by
contriving little rituals aimed at memorializing their sacrifice, others consider
a more literal revenge against the perpetrator. *The Dew Breaker* turns out to
be a priceless casebook for illuminating trauma theory, because it brings to
the fore such critical concerns of the discipline as: how to deal with atrocities;
how to respond ethically to them; the problems of forgetting or forgiving;
what kind of accounts outlive the victims and witnesses; and how to move
from individual voices to a collective consciousness.[35] These are by no means
easy questions to tackle, as the fact that there are whole volumes fully engrossed in trying to unravel them shows. Sometimes, however, the indirect and
more intuitive approaches that literary texts take to these prickly issues may
prove at least as enlightening and rewarding as the more learned discussions.
Very much in line with this view, I have remarked elsewhere that

> the evocative imagery and prevailingly lyrical language that Danticat
> employs to portray the unstable and remorse-ridden lives of her char-
> acters seem appropriate to reveal the serious wounds that a violent en-
> vironment has inflicted upon them.[36]

As also happens in *Krik? Krak!*, the fact that what we hold in our hands
here is a collection of short stories provides the author with more leeway in
terms of the time-frame she may want to set and, also, the variety of locations
that she may want to visit in her narrative.[37] This is particularly important in
The Dew Breaker because the structure of the collection is reminiscent of
Caruth's ideas on the necessity of an "inherent forgetting" of the original
event for the ghost of trauma to become visible. As the first epigraph above
explained, "it is this inherent latency of the event that paradoxically explains
the peculiar, temporal structure, the belatedness, of historical experience."[38] It
is no coincidence in this regard that most of the stories in the collection – with

---

[35] See Douglass & Vogler, "Introduction," 4.

[36] Aitor Ibarrola–Armendáriz, "Edwidge Danticat's *The Dew Breaker*: Another Instance of a (Secretive and) Composite Novel by an Ethnic Writer," paper presented at
the eighth SAAS Conference, A Coruña, March 2007 (MS).

[37] For an illuminating discussion of this diversification of times and places, see
Brinda J. Mehta, "Diasporic Trauma, Memory, and Migration in Edwidge Danticat's
The Dew Breaker," in her *Notions of Identity, Diaspora and Gender in Caribbean
Women's Writing* (London: Palgrave Macmillan, 2009): 63–88.

[38] Caruth, *Trauma*, 8.

the exception of "Night Talkers," "Monkey Tails," and of course "The Dew Breaker" – should take place in the USA over thirty years after the events that set the trauma machine going occurred in Haiti. The protagonists of the tales are at least one generation and many miles away from the political terror that caused endless pain to their relatives and friends; yet they are a constituent part of the psychological shrapnel deriving from that terror. Be they men or women, nurse, janitor or funeral singer, they are all similarly in thrall to the past and all suffering from varying degrees of trauma. At first, the reader is quite confounded, because, while there are some characters and incidents that seem to link the different stories, there is also a manifest element of disjunction, as other aspects are frustratingly difficult to place. According to Ron Charles, these structural complications may bear a thematic significance:

> the effort to draw connections between characters and events in these chapters reflects, in some mercifully small degree, the challenge faced by victims of torture to render their lives whole.[39]

Much has been written of late about the validity and status of secondary and tertiary witnessing in trauma analyses; so, it would be quite unforgivable not to see how Danticat's texts contribute decisively to this debate by allowing important reflections on how the victims' descendants live up to their task and how readers are also compelled to make important ethical decisions to study the stories in the most appropriate interpretative light. Of course, the reader's position is not so difficult and agony-laden as that of the dew breaker's wife in the closing chapter of the collection; and yet, we do not feel utterly estranged from her troubling ruminations, either:

> There was no way to escape this dread anymore, this pendulum between regret and forgiveness, this fright that the most important relationships of her life were always on the verge of being severed or lost, that the people closest to her were always disappearing. (242)

The Redemptive Power of Narrative

> This fragile sky has terrified you your whole life. Silence terrifies you more than the pounding of a million pieces of steel chopping away at your flesh. Sometimes, you dream of hearing only the beating of your

---

[39] Ron Charles, "A Spectrum of Lives Touched by Torture: Stories about the Legacy of Abuse in Haiti," review of *The Dew Breaker*, *Christian Science Monitor* (23 March 2004): 15.

own heart, but this has never been the case. You have never been able
to escape the pounding of a thousand other hearts that have outlived
yours by thousands of years. And over the years when you have
needed us, you have always cried "Krik?" and we have answered
"Krak!" and it has shown us that you have not forgotten us.[40]

There is widespread consensus among scholars in the field of memory and
trauma studies that the appearance of new, subaltern narratives exposing in-
stitutional crimes and the suffering they caused are among the most effective
instruments to counter official distortions of the events and accelerating the
healing process of the afflicted group. According to Jeffrey Alexander, this
retrieval of long-repressed memories can be said to be instrumental in the
recognition of the damage done to the individual and collective consciousness
and in the allocation of responsibility among the criminals.[41] But, of course,
this process is only possible if those new narratives ring true and authentic in
a given social milieu, and if audiences offer adequate responses to those
works. With regard to this point, Herman observes that

> the conflict between the will to deny horrible events and the will to
> proclaim them aloud is a central dialectic of psychological trauma.
> People who have survived atrocities often tell their stories in a highly
> emotional, contradictory, and fragmented manner which undermines
> their credibility and thereby serves the twin imperatives of truth-telling
> and secrecy.[42]

Although it may be contended that there are more practical ways to deal with
trauma – such as amnesty, establishing truth commissions and victim reparation, or bringing the violators to trial – there is little question that the representation of collective traumatic events in narrative through personal testimony has played a key role in the recovery and management of memories that
would otherwise have remained silent.[43] Some specialists in the fields of
literary studies, history, and narratology have come to the conclusion that,
apart from rehabilitating memory and renegotiating the past through the
investigation of new and existing sources, authors also need to restructure that

---

[40] Edwidge Danticat, *Krik? Krak!* (New York: Vintage, 1994): 223–24.

[41] Jeffrey C. Alexander, "Toward a Theory of Cultural Trauma," in *Cultural Trauma and Collective Identity,* ed. Jeffrey C. Alexander et al. (Berkeley: U of California P, 2004): 15–24.

[42] Herman, *Trauma and Recovery,* 1.

[43] See Douglass & Vogler, "Introduction," 31–35.

knowledge by means of narrative devices that will allow them to convey the desired type of meanings. As Paul Ricoeur and others have argued, the impulse towards narrativization is particularly urgent in the case of writers who, for various reasons, need to bring order and integrity to the exposition of experiences that would otherwise remain unfathomable.[44] In an article on Danticat's *The Farming of Bones*, Vega–González remarks on this point that

> since writing is an act of remembrance, when the past has been especially marginalized and marked by oppressive forces, then the literary discourse turns into a source of restoration and regeneration. Haitian-American writer Edwidge Danticat joins the number of contemporary authors who are determined to uncover and recover the forgotten and manipulated histories of the dead through memory and narrative.[45]

Indeed, it can be fairly argued that one of Danticat's main purposes in writing fiction about her homeland and people has been to document and testify to their traumata in order to fill in the gaps in the historical record and restructure the fragmented narrative of their oppression.[46] Her work is, therefore, a performative act which, by means of metaphor and various forms of storytelling, seeks to bring those memories to the public eye and produce some interpretative shifts that may free them from their earlier impenetrability. In Alexander's view, for trauma to be properly represented, a "compelling framework of cultural classification" needs to be established to articulate the complex and often ambivalent experiences of victims and witnesses. Likewise, this scholar holds the belief that this "new master narrative" can only be created if four critical elements are represented: the nature of the violence and the pain; the nature of the victimized collectivity; the relation of the trauma victims to the larger audience; and, finally, the attribution of responsibility to the perpetrators.[47] This checklist could be productively employed in analyses of Danticat's works of fiction in order to reveal how rigorous and com-

---

[44] See Paul Ricoeur, *La Mémoire, L'Histoire, L'Oubli* (Paris: Seuil, 2000).

[45] Susana Vega–González, "Sites of Memory, Sites of Mourning and History: Danticat's Insights into the Past," *Revista Alicantina de Estudios Ingleses* 17 (2004): 298.

[46] Danticat has declared in interviews that she feels a pressing responsibility to uncover and to make known certain chapters of her native country's history which are often underrepresented or obliterated in the historical record. See, for example, Mallay Charters, "Edwidge Danticat: A Bitter Legacy Revisited," *Publishers Weekly* (17 August 1998): 42–43.

[47] Alexander, "Toward a Theory of Cultural Trauma," 12, 12–15.

prehensive her efforts are to cover all the dimensions of trauma and memory that should be represented in narratives of this kind. Not only this but, as I argued earlier, she manages to engage the reader in a process of meaning-production that, to a certain extent, replicates the experience of those suffering the trauma firsthand.

Her collection *Krik? Krak!* offers nine stories of women who, against all odds, seem to continue loving and believing on derelict boats, behind prison walls, in enforced prostitution or, even, after committing infanticide. Obviously, these are not the most favourable conditions to foster the construction of female selfhood, and many of them do indeed present a rather pathetic picture. However, in the face of overwhelming brutality and incalculable loss, they – like the author herself – are able to use the power of their voices and imagination to revamp their female subjectivity against the horrors of the past and present.[48] In the words of Semia Harbawi,

> these female storytellers have constantly been positioning their tales of
> loss and recovery, trauma and survival, aslant the typically masculinist
> logic of senseless violence.[49]

This is the case with the narrator of "Night Women," a prostitute who tries to protect her son from the harsh reality around by funnelling stories into his dreams:

> I whisper my mountain stories in his ear, stories of the ghost women
> and the stars in their hair. I tell him of the deadly snakes lying at one
> end of a rainbow and the hat full of gold lying at the other end. I tell
> him that if I cross a stream of glass-clear hibiscus, I can make myself a
> goddess. I blow on his long eyelashes to see if he's truly asleep. My
> fingers coil themselves into visions of birds on his nose. I want him to
> forget that we live in a place where nothing lasts.[50]

---

[48] It is always recommendable to remind ourselves that women are generally the chief target of oppressive military regimes. Because their bodies are often perceived as the texts on which hierarchies, rules, or the key purposes of the system need to be inscribed, they become the most vulnerable segment of the population. Danticat's fiction is a remarkable showcase of the kind of abuses and violations that they have historically suffered.

[49] Semia Harbawi, "Against All Odds: The Experience of Trauma and the Economy of Survival in Edwidge Danticat's *Breath, Eyes, Memory*," *Wasafiri* 23.1 (March 2008): 38.

[50] Danticat, *Krik? Krak!*, 86.

As Danticat has explained in several interviews, this gift of storytelling is almost natural to Haitian women, who have needed to find ways to reconstitute their occluded female subjectivity from the silence imposed by the 'official' male histories.[51] In *Breath, Eyes, Memory*, Sophie seems able to gain the wisdom necessary to heal the deep wounds of her traumatic past only when she finally sees herself as the last link in a long female chain of affliction. It is only when she and her mother return to Haiti that their trauma of sexual violation comes to an end, since there the "nightmares are passed on through generation like heirlooms" (234). Sophie's healing process begins when she tells her mother about the insufferable pain caused by the purity tests and, later, learns to accept her explanations for that cruel practice:

> 'I did it [...] because my mother had done it to me. I have no greater excuse. I realize standing here that the two greatest pains in my life are very much related. [...] I live both every day.' (170)

After her mother's confession and, then, her demise, the protagonist is granted the information needed to look for some of the missing pieces in the incomplete puzzle her life had become:

> We did not call it a wake, but we played cards and drank ginger tea, and strung my wedding ring along a thread while singing a festive wake song: *Ring sways to mother. Ring stays with Mother. Pass it. Pass it along. Pass me. Pass me along.*
>
> Listening to the song, I realized that it was neither my mother nor my Tante Atie who had given all the mother-and-daughter motifs to all the stories told and all the songs they sang. It was something that was essentially Haitian. Somehow, early on, our song makers and tale weavers had decided that we were all daughters of the land. (230)

The process of self-recovery and self-acceptance is only fully completed when, in the closing pages of the novel, Sophie revisits the place where her mother had been raped. There, and with her grandmother and aunt as witnesses, the protagonist undergoes a catharsis that liberates her from all the sexual violence running in her family.[52] When the two elder women ask her

---

[51] Lyons, "An Interview with Edwidge Danticat," 192.

[52] The inclusion of these cathartic or epiphanic moments has been praised by several reviewers of Danticat's works of fiction. They contend that among all the anxieties and uncertainties readers experience in unravelling her stories, these moments of recognition – and self-recognition – are particularly welcomed.

"'*Ou liberé*' – Are you free?" she is not even allowed to reply, because, as her grandmother explains,"'Now, you will know how to answer'" (234).

Lambek and Antze, among several other scholars of trauma and memory, have claimed that

> the invocation of memory signals association as opposed to dissocia-
> tion, continuity over discontinuity. Hence it speaks, implicitly and ex-
> plicitly, to the temporal axis of personhood.[53]

Even though Danticat's works of fiction do exhibit the inevitable connection between intense suffering in the past and pathological symptoms now, some of the female metaphors she includes – such as hair-braiding, shrine-building or ethnic cooking – and the therapeutic language she uses signal in the direction of a certain continuity that permits contemporary Haitians to identify a number of basic pillars of their collective identity:

> You remember thinking while braiding your hair that you look a lot
> like your mother and her mother before her. It was their whispers that
> pushed you, their murmurs over pots sizzling in your head. A thousand
> women urging you to speak through the blunt tip of your pencil.
> Kitchen poets, you call them. Ghosts like burnished branches on a
> flame tree.[54]

Not only that, but, as several specialists have pointed out, she shares with Toni Morrison the idea that by revisiting a few factual episodes and using her imagination to refashion them into a fuller picture, she is able to recover some truths generally omitted in the historical record.[55] *The Farming of Bones*, for instance, is structured as an attempt at putting together and casting new light on the fragmented personal and collective memories of the 1937 massacre. It is arguable that Amabelle finally succeeds in recuperating meaning and producing a fully consistent representation of the event,[56] but what cannot be

---

[53] Lambek & Antze, "Introduction: Forecasting Memory," xxv.

[54] Danticat, *Krik? Krak!*, 222.

[55] See Jennifer C. Rossi, "'Let the words bring wings to our feet': Negotiating Exile and Trauma through Narrative in Danticat's *Breath, Eyes, Memory*," *Obsidian III* 6.2–7.1 (Fall 2005–2006), and Vega–González, "Sites of Memory, Sites of Mourning and History."

[56] See Munro, "Writing Disaster," 93. As this critic notes, the elements of suspension and incompletion are justified because "the 'writing of disaster' is not an attempt

denied is that she feels partly redeemed by the return to those memory-sites that have been torturing her for a long time. She has shown, moreover, that particular persons and institutions have continuing accountability and responsibilities towards victims indelibly marked by their crimes:

> It is perhaps the great discomfort of those trying to silence the world to discover that we have voices sealed inside our heads, voices that with each passing day, grow even louder than the clamor of the world outside.[57]

Like Sophie, Amabelle's inner journey can only be brought to its completion by a literal return to the location where her trauma originated: the Massacre River, which had swallowed her parents and, later, become an unmarked grave for the Haitian cane workers. When she enters the river near the end of the novel, she is not only ritually re-enacting some traumatic episodes of the past, but also memorializing those unfairly murdered and, then, historically silenced. It is not surprising that she should think of the task of recovering their story as her fundamental responsibility:

> The slaughter is the only thing that is mine enough to pass on. All I want to do is find a place to lay it down now and again, a safe nest where it will neither be scattered in the wind, nor remain forever buried beneath the sod.[58]

This unsealing of the vault containing long-silenced voices is a precondition not only to bring to public light the real hero(in)es and villains of the (hi)stories but also to consummate the atonement, reparation, and redemption that are necessary to get rid of those elongated shadows of the past that will keep preventing her people from seeing the sunshine.[59]

It could be argued that the achievement of *The Dew Breaker* grows in direct proportion to the difficult challenge that the writer has set for herself this time: how does one represent the cruelties perpetrated by a dreaded *Tonton Macoute* and his later transformation into a quiet barber and seem-

---

to arrive at a final understanding, but is a discourse that, again paradoxically, questions itself incessantly without offering any real, recuperative replies."

[57] Danticat, *The Farming of Bones*, 266.

[58] *The Farming of Bones*, 266.

[59] See Nick Nesbitt, "Voicing Memory: Maryse Condé, Edwidge Danticat," in *Voicing Memory: History and Subjectivity in French Caribbean Literature* (Charlottesville: UP of Virginia, 2003): 192–212.

ingly perfect father in Brooklyn? This is by no means an easy task, as the looping structure of interconnected stories and the immense lacunae that loom in and between them attest. We only get to learn about the title character through the eyes of others who have been directly or indirectly affected by his terrible deeds thirty years back:

> He liked questioning the prisoners, teaching them to play zo and bezik, stapling clothespins to their ears as they lost and removing them as he let them win, convincing them that their false victories would save their lives. He liked to paddle them with braided cowhide, stand on their cracking backs and jump up and down like a drunk on a trampoline, pound a rock on the protruding bone behind the earlobes until they couldn't hear the orders he was shouting at them, tie blocks of concrete to the end of sisal ropes and balance them off their testicles if they were men or their breasts if they were women.[60]

Of course, when we first meet this incredibly violent creature in the opening story of the book – told by his own daughter – he is utterly unrecognizable. Mr Bienaime, as the ex-torturer had renamed himself when he came to America, is travelling south in a car with his artist–daughter to deliver a sculpture of himself to a famous Haitian TV actress. The turning-point in the story occurs when, after inexplicably throwing the artwork into a lake, he reveals to her that, back in Haiti, "your father was the hunter, he was not the prey" (20), as she had always assumed because of the nasty scar on his face. In a state of shock, the daughter asks: "What are you talking about?"

> I immediately regret the question. Is he going to explain why he and my mother have no close friends, why they've never had anyone over to the house, why they never speak of any relatives in Haiti or anywhere else, or have never returned there or, even after I learned Creole from them, have never taught me anything else about the country beyond what I could find out on my own, on the television, in newspapers, in books? Is he about to tell me why Mama is so pious? Why she goes to daily mass? (20–21)

This intense moment of revelation, when everything in her earlier experience needs to be restructured and reinterpreted, is faced not only by the title character's daughter but also by most of the other characters in the book, who are forced to realign their entire concept of the person – and very likely of them-

---

[60] Danticat, *The Dew Breaker*, 198.

selves – when they realize the kind of 'monster' they have been sharing different spaces with. Since each of their traumas is multi-layered and multi-faceted, they resort to very different strategies and rituals to try to overcome the new pain they are suffering from.[61] The protagonist of "The Funeral Singer," for example, decides to share it with two Haitian classmates in Manhattan: "I thought exposing a few details of my life would inspire them to do the same and slowly we'd parcel our sorrows, each walking out with fewer than we'd carried in" (170). Dany, in "Night Talkers," who had seen his parents murdered by the dew breaker when he was still a child, is throughout a significant part of the story in favour of more radical retaliation. However, when the moment of vengeance comes, he is unable to put an end to the criminal's life:

> Looking down at the barber's face, which had shrunk so much over the years, he lost the desire to kill. It wasn't that he was afraid, for he was momentarily feeling bold, fearless. It wasn't pity, either. He was too angry to feel pity. It was something else, something less measurable. It was the dread of being wrong, of harming the wrong man, of making the wrong woman a widow and the wrong child an orphan. It was the realization that he would never know why – why one single person had been given the power to destroy his entire life. (107)

Less gendered than her earlier books, *The Dew Breaker* offers a more diverse and complicated set of strategies to combat the effects of trauma. Sometimes they are closely related to the initial wounds inflicted on the victims' psyches, but quite often they respond to the ulterior ramifications of the sorrow in other directions. After all, we have learned that

> imagination informs trauma construction just as much when the reference is to something that has actually occurred as to something that has not. It is only through the imaginative process of representation that actors have a sense of the experience.[62]

In fact, the closing section of the collection – which also bears its title – is likely to confuse readers further, because, while it is true that the main character proves to be the beastly torturer we had assumed him to be, we also meet somebody "more complex and disturbing, a man troubled by his work, a

---

[61] Richard Eder, "Off the Island," *New York Times* (21 March 2004): 5 (review of *The Dew Breaker*).

[62] Alexander, "Toward a Theory of Cultural Trauma," 9.

little bored with torturing, prone to errors, and afraid for his own safety."[63]
Little wonder, then, that in his case, redemption does not demand revisiting
the real settings where his disturbing "*lieux de mémoire*" originated. Evident-
ly, regeneration for victimizers is not so easily achieved.

Conclusion

My discussion of four works of fiction by the Haitian-American writer Edwidge Danticat has demonstrated that they are generally informed by an interest in the aftermath of violence and traumatic experiences. This is observable
not only in what concerns the themes that she chooses to cover in her stories
but also, and perhaps most importantly, in the narrative structures she uses to
represent and come to grips with these difficult issues. It has become evident
throughout my discussion that this writer finds it more important to show and
reflect on the consequences of individual or collective acts of violence than to
try to elucidate the conditions and causes underpinning them. Her novels and
short stories tell us, in fact, about people who, although often untouched by
the crimes that their elders suffered, are still deeply – and belatedly – marked
by those cruelties. This fact becomes particularly noticeable in their difficulties in rendering the traumatic experiences as narrative. Their voices are
fraught with remorseful feelings, unassimilated events, cognitive lacunae, and
uncertain purposes that turn the work of reading into a truly challenging – and
sometimes unnerving – experience. The author, however, does manage to provide these broken fragments of memory and experience, these "beautiful
shards of a broken vase,"[64] with a certain degree of continuity and cohesion.
In order to do so, she relies on certain cultural traditions and narrative devices
that are seen to help her characters and herself to redeem the chaos of emotions and uncertainties that invades them every time they look upon their past.
Not only this, but the often forgotten victims of a long history of political terror and social injustice are finally allowed to occupy their rightful place in the
collective consciousness of the island.

---

[63] Charles, "A Spectrum of Lives Touched by Torture," 15.

[64] "A Spectrum of Lives Touched by Torture," 15.

WORKS CITED

Alexander, Jeffrey C. "Toward a Theory of Cultural Trauma," in *Cultural Trauma and Collective Identity*, ed. Jeffrey C. Alexander et al. (Berkeley: U of California P, 2004): 1–30.

Caruth, Cathy. *Trauma: Explorations in Memory* (Baltimore MD & London: Johns Hopkins UP, 1996).

Césaire, Aimé. *Toussaint Louverture: La Révolution française et le problème colonial* (Paris: Club française du livre, 1960).

Charles, Ron. "A Spectrum of Lives Touched by Torture: Stories About the Legacy of Abuse in Haiti," *Christian Science Monitor* (23 March 2004): 15 [review of *The Dew Breaker*], http://www.csmonitor.com/2004/0323/p15s02-bogn.html (accessed 20 September 2010).

Charters, Mallay. "Edwidge Danticat: A Bitter Legacy Revisited," *Publishers Weekly* (17 August 1998): 42–43.

Danticat, Edwidge. *Breath, Eyes, Memory* (New York: Random House, 1994).

——. *The Dew Breaker* (New York: Vintage, 2005).

——. *The Farming of Bones* (London: Abacus, 2000).

——. *Krik? Krak!* (New York: Vintage, 1996).

Douglass, Ann, & Thomas A. Vogler. "Introduction" to *Witness and Memory: The Discourse of Trauma*, ed. Ann Douglass & T.A. Vogler (New York & London: Routledge, 2003): 1–53.

Eder, Richard. "Off the Island," *New York Times* (21 March 2004): 5 [review of *The Dew Breaker*], http://www.nytimes.com/2004/03/21/books/off-the-island.html (accessed 14 September 2010).

Fanon, Frantz. *Black Skin, White Masks*, tr. Charles L. Markmann (*Peau noire, masques blancs*, 1952; New York: Grove, 1967).

Francis, Donette A. "'Silences too horrific to disturb': Writing Sexual Histories in Edwidge Danticat's *Breath, Eyes, Memory*," *Research in African Literatures* 35.2 (Summer 2004): 75–90.

Gilroy, Paul. *The Black Atlantic: Modernity and Double-Consciousness* (Cambridge MA: Harvard UP, 1993).

Glissant, Édouard. *Poetics of Relation*, tr. Betsy Wing (*Poétique de la Relation*, 1990; Ann Arbor: U of Michigan P, 1997).

Grimshaw, Anna. "Introduction: C.L.R. James: A Revolutionary View," in *The C.L.R. James Reader*, ed. Anna Grimshaw (Oxford: Blackwell, 1992): 1–22.

Harbawi, Semia. "Against All Odds: The Experience of Trauma and the Economy of Survival in Edwidge Danticat's *Breath, Eyes, Memory*," *Wasafiri* 23.1 (March 2008): 38–44.

Heinl, Robert D., & Nancy G. Heinl. *Written in Blood: The History of the Haitian People* (Lanham MD: UP of America, rev. ed. 1996).

Herman, Judith. *Trauma and Recovery: From Domestic Abuse to Political Terror* (New York: HarperCollins, 1992).

Ibarrola–Armendáriz, Aitor. "Edwidge Danticat's *The Dew Breaker*: Another Instance of a (Secretive and) Composite Novel by an Ethnic Writer," paper delivered at the eighth SAAS (Spanish Association for American Studies) Conference, A Coruña, March 2007 (MS).

James, C.L.R. *The Black Jacobins: Toussaint Louverture and the San Domingo Revolution* (1938; New York: Vintage, 1963).

Kakutani, Michiko. "Books of the Times; Hiding from a Brutal Past Spent Shattering Lives in Haiti," *New York Times* (10 March 2004): 1 [review of *The Dew Breaker*], http://query.nytimes.com/gst/fullpage.html?res=9400E6DE143EF933A25750C0A 9629C8B63&ref=edwidge_danticat (accessed 28 July 2010).

Lambek, Michael, & Paul Antze. "Introduction: Forecasting Memory," in *Tense Past: Cultural Essays in Trauma and Memory*, ed. Paul Antze & Michael Lambek (London: Routledge, 1996): xi–xxxviii.

Lyons, Bonnie. "An Interview with Edwidge Danticat," *Contemporary Literature* 44.2 (Summer 2003): 183–98.

Mehta, Brinda J. "Diasporic Trauma, Memory, and Migration in Edwidge Danticat's *The Dew Breaker*," in *Notions of Identity, Diaspora and Gender in Caribbean Women's Writing*, ed. Brinda J. Mehta (London: Palgrave Macmillan, 2009): 63–88.

Munro, Martin. "Writing Disaster: Trauma, Memory, and History in Edwidge Danticat's *The Farming of Bones*," *Ethnologies* 28.1 (2006): 81–98.

Nesbitt, Nick. "Voicing Memory: Maryse Condé, Edwidge Danticat," in *Voicing Memory: History and Subjectivity in French Caribbean Literature* (Charlottesville: UP of Virginia, 2003): 192–212.

Nora, Pierre. "Between Memory and History: *Les Lieux de Mémoire*," tr. Marc Roudebush, *Representations* 26 (Special Issue: "Memory and Counter-Memory," Spring 1989): 7–24; repr. in *History and Memory in African-American Culture*, ed. Geneviève Fabre & Robert O'Meally ("Entre Mémoire et Histoire," 1984; New York & Oxford: Oxford UP, 1994): 284–300.

Novak, Amy. "'A Marred Testament': Cultural Trauma and Narrative in Danticat's *The Farming of Bones*," *Arizona Quarterly* 62.4 (Winter 2006): 93–120.

Ricoeur, Paul. *La Mémoire, L'Histoire, L'Oubli* (Paris: Seuil, 2000).

Rossi, Jennifer C. "'Let the words bring wings to our feet': Negotiating Exile and Trauma Through Narrative in Danticat's *Breath, Eyes, Memory*," *Obsidian III* 6.2–7.1 (Fall 2005–2006): 203–16.

Smith, Dorsía. "A Violent Homeland: Recalling Haiti in Edwidge Danticat's Novels," in *Narrating the Past: (Re)constructing Memory, (Re)negotiating History*, ed. Nandita Batra (Newcastle upon Tyne: Cambridge Scholars, 2007): 133–40.

Sweeney, Carole. "The Unmaking of the World: Haiti, History, and Writing in Édouard Glissant and Edwidge Danticat," *Atlantic Studies* 4.1 (April 2007): 51–66.

Vega–González, Susana. "Sites of Memory, Sites of Mourning and History: Danticat's Insights into the Past," *Revista Alicantina de Estudios Ingleses* 17 (2004): 297–304.

◄❖►

"When the World is Free"

Traumatized Soldiers in Patricia
Grace's Second World War Novel *Tu*

DONNA COATES

CCORDING TO RANGINUI WALKER, "the ancestors of the
Māori people [the indigenous population of New Zealand] settled
the land they named Aotearoa from Central Polynesia around 900
AD," but their largely agrarian way of life was forever altered when Captain
Cook arrived in 1769.[1] Although the Pakeha (people living in New Zealand of
British/European origin) provided the Māori with a "cornucopia of material
goods," the small population was nevertheless devastated by the introduction
of "strange diseases" in some coastal regions, the "undermining" of numerous
cultural symbols by missionaries and their church dogma, the "emascula-
t[ion]" of their ancient carvings, and the disappearance of the art of carving in
some areas.[2] Māori culture was further weakened when the missionaries, who
had become the Māori people's "trusted advisors," encouraged their chiefs to
sign the Treaty of Waitangi in 1840, which

> paved the way for British colonialism and the eclipse of Māori *mana*
> [power, authority] by British sovereignty. Pakeha dominion was

---

[1] R.J. Walker, "Māori Identity," in *Culture and Identity in New Zealand*, ed. David
Novitz & Bill Willmott (Wellington: GP Books, 1989): 37.

[2] Walker, "Māori Identity," 39.

> spread gradually over the land by the colonial techniques of extin-
> guishing native title to land by fair purchase and the transmigration of
> surplus population from industrial England.[3]

By 1858, Pakeha outnumbered Māori, and in spite of strenuous resistance, the
latter proved unable to prevent the British Crown from confiscating some
3,000,000 acres of land for "military settlers"; in a "matter of a hundred
years, Māori-owned land was reduced to 5.9 percent of the land of Aotearoa."[4] Since land constitutes the main basis of the cultural identity of the
Māori people,[5] its loss resulted in alienation, sickness, and demoralization,[6] to
the extent that, as Michael King observes, "at the turn of the century there was
a widespread belief among Europeans that the Māori race was doomed to ex-
tinction."[7]

Although Ian McGibbon notes that the Māori did not die out but, rather,
began to revive during the late 1890s – by 1939, their population had reached
about 90,000, and was about six percent of the total population of New Zealand – tension over land claims continued,[8] and Māori were still considered to
be racially and culturally inferior. King observes that the Māori, who had
"always placed a high value on prowess in battle," responded with patriotic
fervour to the Boer War, albeit to little avail,[9] as the 'Imperial masters' of
New Zealand declared that it was a 'white man's war' and would not accept
the participation of Māori warriors (especially as a native contingent).
Notwithstanding this, a few did manage to enlist individually. Furthermore, at
the outbreak of hostilities in the First World War, the Imperial Government
continued to oppose "the idea of native peoples fighting in a war among
Europeans":

---

[3] Walker, "Māori Identity," 40.

[4] "Māori Identity," 41.

[5] For more information on the importance of land to Māori culture, see Judith Dell
Panny, "A Cultural-Historical Reading of Patricia Grace's *Cousins*," *Kotare* 6 (2006)
http://www.nzet.org/tm/scholarly/tei-Whi06Kota-t1-g1l-t1.hmtl (accessed 20 September 2010).

[6] Walker, "Māori Identity," 41.

[7] Michael King, "Between Two Worlds," in *The Oxford History of New Zealand*,
ed. W.H. Oliver & B.R. Williams (Oxford: Clarendon, 1981): 303.

[8] Ian McGibbon, *New Zealand and the Second World War: The People, the Battles
and the Legacy* (Auckland: Hodder Moa Beckett, 2003): 18.

[9] Michael King, *Te Puea: A Biography* (Auckland: Hodder & Stoughton, 1977): 79.

Their loyalties might prove suspect; they might even turn on their colonial masters; they might have to be treated as the equals of European soldiers in circumstances where this could become an embarrassment.[10]

Once the British Government learned that Indian troops had been deployed along the Suez Canal in mid-1914, however, they were forced to relent,[11] and the first contingent of 505 Māori warriors sailed for Europe in 1915.[12] King writes that the Māori were eager to "show themselves to be the equals of Pakeha in recruitment, casualty rates, and fighting skills,"[13] and he further documents the fact that one of their popular leaders, the MP Maui Pomare, insisted that it was a matter of "racial pride that the Māori soldier should stand alongside others of the British Empire."[14] Pomare insisted that the Māori wished to "prove to the world that [they] were the equal of the Pakeha in the fullest sense – physically, mentally and spiritually."[15] Hence, the Māori recruits resisted the pressure to take on only garrison duties and demanded that the contingent be allowed to retain its own identity and operate as an independent unit known as the 'Pioneer Battalion'. According to Wira Gardiner, after the Māori courageously passed their baptism of fire alongside the Pakeha at Gallipoli, they became known (in October 1917), as the '28 (Maori) Battalion'.[16]

But King also cautions that Māori participation in the Great War was not without problems: although they had initially raised some 2,200 volunteers for combat duty – about twenty percent of the eligible age group – it became difficult to maintain reinforcements because members of the Waikato tribes, who, as James Cowan writes, "neither forgot nor forgave" the Crown's wholesale confiscation of their lands, refused to enlist.[17] The issue became

---

[10] King, *Te Puea*, 79.

[11] *Te Puea*, 79.

[12] *Te Puea*, 81.

[13] King, "Between Two Worlds," 303.

[14] King, *Te Puea*, 80.

[15] *Te Puea*, 80.

[16] Wira Gardiner, *Te mura o te ahi: The Story of the Maori Battalion* (Auckland: Reed, 1992): 21.

[17] James Cowan, *The Maoris in the Great War: A History of the New Zealand Contingent and Pioneer Battalion Gallipoli 1915, France and Flanders 1916–18* (Auckland: Whitcombe & Tombs, 1926): 17.

contentious when the resisters were conscripted towards the end of the war as
a form of punishment, and even more so when, according to P.S. O'Connor,
they were then imprisoned in Auckland for resisting conscription.[18] The First
World War also took a heavy toll: Cowan documents that 336 died and 734
were wounded, "making the total casualties 1,070, or nearly fifty percent of
the total number of men sent overseas."[19] Although King stresses that these
kinds of figures made it increasingly difficult after the war for "Pakeha
leaders to discriminate against Māori," he nonetheless concludes that

> the hopes of returning Battalion members that the conditions of war-
> time equality with Pakeha soldiers would continue were not fulfilled.
> There was not even an adequate rehabilitation program for Māori
> servicemen.[20]

In a similar vein, Jock Phillips attests that while the Māori obtained "a world-
wide reputation at an enormous cost in casualties," it is a myth that after the
First World War "Māori and Pakeha became one people."[21]

Although McGibbon argues that the Māori did not express loyalty to the
Crown at the outbreak of the Second World War, because the combination of
"imperial and colonial forces" which had resulted in the confiscation of Māori
land during the nineteenth century continued to rankle,[22] it is also true that
even before the declaration of the war, the well-known and popular Māori
MP Sir Apirana Ngata, an 1890s graduate of law and arts from Canterbury
University College, had begun to agitate for the formation of a Māori military
unit because he viewed participation in combat as "the price of citizenship."
Ngata perceived that "commitment in war might be viewed by government
and the nation at large as the price of winning citizenship – on "Māori
Terms."[23] Writing in *The Price of Citizenship*, Ngata asked:

---

[18] P.S. O'Connor, "The Recruitment of Māori Soldiers, 1914–18," *Political Science*
19.2 (1967): 52.

[19] Cowan, *The Māoris in the Great War*, 8.

[20] King, "Between Two Worlds," 303.

[21] Jock Phillips, "War and National Identity," in *Culture and Identity in New Zealand*, ed. David Novitz & Bill Willmott (Wellington: GP Books, 1989): 104.

[22] McGibbon, *New Zealand and the Second World War*, 18.

[23] Claudia Orange, "The Price of Citizenship? The Māori War Effort," in *Kia Kaha:
New Zealand in the Second World War*, ed. John Crawford (Auckland: Oxford UP,
2000): 237.

What is the gain for so much loss? Can the former [the gain] be gauged in clear terms of compensation? The Māori in the last war was denied a place in the forefront of the battle […]. In this war he asked to take his full share in the front line […]. Has he proved a claim to be an asset to his country? If so, he asks to be dealt with as such. An asset discovered in the crucible of war should have a value in the coming peace. The men of the New Zealand Division have seen it below the brown skins of their Māori comrades. Have the civilians of New England, men and women, fully realized the implications of the joint participation of Pakeha and Māori in this last and greatest demonstration of the highest citizenship?[24]

Ngata's arguments at the outbreak of the war proved persuasive, for, as Claudia Orange confirms, the government announced in 1939 that an "infantry battalion of Maori recruits would be formed," and "within three weeks nearly 900 men had enlisted."[25] However, so eager were Ngata and other Māori leaders to see their people have a say in the shaping of the future of the nation after the war that they paid little attention to the objection that, given the size of their population, Māori could not maintain a strong combat force, nor could they maintain "a constant flow of reinforcements" should casualties be high.[26] These leaders also ignored suggestions that dispersing Māori among Pakeha units might lessen the possibility of heavy losses, and paid no heed to the popular leader Te Puea Herangi's declaration that Māori should not fight for an Empire that had, "within living memory, invaded and occupied their lands."[27] Ultimately, even sceptical Māori elders resigned them-

---

[24] Apirana Ngata, *The Price of Citizenship* (Wellington: Whitcombe & Tombs, 1943): 18.

[25] Orange, "The Price of Citizenship? The Māori War Effort," 237.

[26] See "Response to War – Māori and the Second World War: The Māori Response to the Declaration of War," http://www.nzhistory.net.nz/war/Maori-in-second-world-war/response (accessed 2 April 2008).

[27] See "Response to War – Māori and the Second World War." According to King, Te Puea (1883–1952), who was "born into the Waikato kahui ariki (paramount family) rose to prominence when she led the campaign against the conscription of Waikato Māori in the First World War. Her hereditary claims to leadership were strengthened by a sharp intellect, quick wits, remarkable fluency in Māori, and a formidable determination […]. From the 1920s she was a national Māori figure." "Between Two Worlds," 296.

selves to the fact that they were obliged to allow their sons to serve, for, as
one of the volunteers in the Second World War later wrote,

> Their request could not be denied them by their elders and chieftains
> [because] all their long history had been steeped in the religion of war,
> and the training of the Māori child from his infancy to manhood was
> aimed at the perfection of the warrior-class, while to die in the pursuit
> of the War God Tumatauenga was a sacred duty and a manly death.[28]

Some Māori in favour of enlistment proposed naming the force "Treaty of
Waitangi" to draw the attention of both Māori and Pakeha to their respective
obligations under that treaty, which had granted the rights of British citizenship to Māori – "rights which [Sir Ngata argued] would not have been ac-
corded under any conqueror."[29] As British subjects, Ngata insisted, Māori
should be willing to contribute "their blood and their lives" in defence of the
Empire, and he further stressed that if the Māori were to have a say in shaping
the future of the nation after the war, they needed to participate fully during it:

> We are of one house, and if our Pakeha brothers fall, we fall with
> them. How can we ever hold up our heads, when the struggle is over,
> to the question, 'Where were you when New Zealand was at war?'[30]

Accordingly, 3,500 volunteers, who rapidly became "known for their trucu-
lence, especially in close quarter combat, and sometimes for their unsparing
vengeance,"[31] joined the legendary 28 (Maori) Battalion. But, as predicted,
they suffered far higher losses than other infantry battalions: of the more than
3,600 men who volunteered with the Maori Battalion, which served in Egypt,
Greece, Crete, North Africa, and then Italy,

> 618 were killed, 1,710 were wounded, and 267 were taken prisoner or
> reported as missing: This casualty rate was almost fifty percent higher
> than the average for the New Zealand infantry battalions.[32]

---

[28] "Māori and the Second World War," Ministry for Culture and Heritage.
http://www.history.nzhistory.net.nz/Maori-in-second-world-war (accessed 21 August
2009).

[29] See "Response to War – Māori and the Second World War."

[30] See "Response to War – Māori and the Second World War."

[31] Patricia Grace, *Tu* (Auckland: Penguin, 2004): 283. Further page references are
in the main text.

[32] See "Impact – Māori and the Second World War," Ministry for Cultural and Heritage, http://www.nzhistory.net.nz/war/Maori-and-the-second-world-war/impact (accessed
20 October 2007).

Given the high rate of casualties in the Second World War, it is surprising
that Patricia Grace should be, according to Otto Heim, one of the few to have
made war a "prime topic of concern in Māori fiction."[33] Both her short story
"Going for the Bread" (1987) and her novel *Cousins* (1992) depict the devastating impact of the war on women and children, and in her sixth novel, *Tu,*
she tells the story of three brothers[34] who join the Maori Battalion, although at
different times and for different reasons. All three participate in the fierce
battles at Monte Cassino, where about 350 Māori are killed. The struggle over
the southern Italian town, which is overshadowed by a mountain-top monastery, forms the core of the action. In writing *Tu,* Grace drew her inspiration
from her father, who enlisted in 1944, served in Italy with the Maori Battalion, and left behind a brief notebook of his experiences, which Grace did not
read until some twenty years after his death in 1983. However, since the notebook consisted of a mere twenty-five pages, it failed to satisfy her curiosity
about why the Māori had been so committed to the war, what they had taken
as their cause, and what the war had been like "for this band of volunteers"
(283). In order to fill in the gaps, Grace pored over official historical records,
memoirs, letters, photographs, newspapers, and magazines, and conducted
interviews with returned soldiers and their families.

Although Grace's father apparently returned from the war relatively un-
scathed, her central characters do not: all three brothers are victims of trauma,
which she recounts through two parallel and interweaving storylines[35] that Tu,
the youngest and sole survivor, records in a notebook, much as Grace's father
had done. Tu narrates his story in the first person, primarily from the battlefield, and tells the eldest brother Pita's story in the third person, mostly from
the home front; he explains that "when I write down Pita's stories I like to fill

---

[33] Otto Heim, *Writing Along Broken Lines: Violence and Ethnicity in Contemporary
Māori Fiction* (Auckland: Auckland U P, 1998): 136.

[34] Grace's *iwi* (tribe), as well as that of most of her characters in her fiction, is loca-
ted in the lower east and west coastal areas of the North Island.

[35] The structure of both *Tu* and *Cousins*, which also focuses on three characters,
calls to mind the Māori art of *whiri* or plaiting, wherein several strands come together,
overlap intermittently, and often move back and forth in time before moving apart. In
Turning the Eye: Patricia Grace and the Short Story (Christchurch: Lincoln U P,
1997), Judith Dell Panny writes that this three-way structure "is found in the Māori art
of *kowhaiwhai*, which features on the rafters of many meeting houses" and uses "the
traditional colours red, white, and black" (4).

them out by putting in my own descriptions and observations, my own slant here and there. Sometimes I think that I find the right words and create just the right feeling" (150). Tu's notebook also includes a few letters which Rangi, the middle brother, sends from overseas,[36] and the novel is framed by letters Tu sends to his niece Rimini and nephew Benedictine after they have sought information from him about their father(s). Grace also contends that the personal experiences of all of three characters – two of whom die in combat – reflect a much larger, societal trauma that followed the events of the Second World War.

In *Worlds of Hurt*, Kalí Tal suggests that "the clearest point of access for untraumatized readers to the [literature of trauma] is through an understanding of clinical analysis of the effects of trauma on survivors."[37] It therefore seems appropriate to begin with a working definition of trauma, followed by an analysis of Grace's central characters, in order to establish an understanding of their individual experiences before extending these experiences to suggest a societal phenomenon. I shall begin with the psychiatrist Judith Herman, who explains that "trauma events overwhelm ordinary human adaptations of care that give people a sense of control, connection, and meaning."[38] Tal expands that definition by suggesting that trauma is any event that shatters "personal myth."[39] Every person, Tal goes on to explain, generates a "particular set of explanations and expectations [...] to account for his or her circumstances and actions."[40] Tal then cites Daniel Goleman's view that "personal myths take the form of schemas – assumptions about experience and the way the world works."[41] What individuals perceive, Goleman adds, is determined largely

---

[36] Rangi, the first to enlist, is the most aggressive, highly skilled warrior of the three. But Grace minimizes his story because, as she tells Sue Kedgley, she writes about the "types of men" she has experienced in her life – "the quiet and gentle type of family man." She confesses that she would not feel comfortable basing a story on a "macho hearty type because it wouldn't come from inside [her]. It would be outside of [her] upbringing and experience." Quoted in *Our Own Country: Leading New Zealand Women Writers Talk About Their Writing and Their Lives*, ed. Sue Kedgley (Auckland: Penguin, 1989): 66.

[37] Kalí Tal, *Worlds of Hurt* (New York: Cambridge UP, 1996): 134.

[38] Judith Herman, *Trauma and Recovery: From Domestic Abuse to Political Terror* (New York: HarperCollins, 1992): 33.

[39] Tal, *Worlds of Hurt*, 116.

[40] *Worlds of Hurt*, 116.

[41] *Worlds of Hurt*, 116.

unconsciously, by the scheme of assumptions they apply in a given situation. Such personal frames of understanding inevitably mean that individuals 'skew' perceptions of much of what goes on around them, but this is a useful "coping strategy, if a properly interpreted event threatens important, foundational schemas."[42]

Grace's Pita develops a personal myth heavily influenced by childhood events. When he is two years old (and his brother Rangi not yet born), his cheerful, happy-go-lucky father volunteers for World War I's Maori Pioneer Battalion; shot, his body riddled with shrapnel, and then gassed at Messines, he is eventually shipped to a hospital in Wellington, where he undergoes a lengthy recuperation. But once he is discharged from the hospital, the family, who live at the base of Mount Taranaki (then known as Mount Egmont), soon realize that, while his physical wounds are gradually healing, he remains severely wounded in mind, subject to fits of murderous rage which result in his trying to "choke [Pita's] mother, break their house to pieces, attempt to kill them all" (55). When this "roaring, threshing man" (55), whose room has become a "dead space in their house and in their lives" (51), goes on the rampage, Pita in particular undergoes enormous emotional strain, because he is the one sent to find Pita's uncles, who live nearby and can help calm his father. When the uncles find employment out of the city, Pita assumes the role of 'Little Father': fearful of what might happen to his mother in his absence, he rarely attends school or plays with friends or siblings. When his father (often referred to as an "old man") mercifully dies at the age of thirty-nine, however, Pita's mother decides there is no future for her family – which has by now swollen to include five children – in the country and, with the help of an uncle who has a good job in Parliament, moves the family to Wellington. Pita and Rangi, who are by this time young men, pool their meagre wages earned at seasonal part-time jobs, and manage to keep the family afloat.

In moving her fictional family to the city at that time, Grace records the pattern of urban migration that had begun prior to the outbreak of war. According to King, "in 1936, only 11.2 percent of the Māori population lived in urban areas; by 1945 this had risen to 19 percent."[43] Agnes Broughton et al. observe that, as a result, many Māori experienced "dislocation and profound

---

[42] Quoted in Tal, *Worlds of Hurt*, 117.
[43] King, "Between Two Worlds," 289.

loneliness [...] and culture shock,"[44] hence found it difficult to adjust to urban life, circumstances reflected in Grace's novels *Cousins* and *Tu.* In the latter, Pita encounters problems because his personal myth – that only he, as 'Little Father,' can provide for and safeguard his family – is severely challenged. His affable mother no longer requires his protection, for she operates a kind of 'open house' where the 'backhome' Māori in need are always welcome, and his siblings succumb to urban temptations: Rangi begins to drink heavily[45] and gives up going to church, and his sisters, whom Pita will not allow to work, wander the streets aimlessly. But in 1939, when Rangi's enlistment places financial stress on the family, Pita reluctantly permits his sisters to enter the industrial labour force. He steadfastly refuses, though, to let Tu, the youngest, become a paper boy, in part because he considers the work demeaning, but also because Tu represents the hope of the family. All of them make sacrifices so that he can attend boarding school and eventually become a cadet in a law office. However, Pita, unable to overcome his fears that the dangers to his family "might return at any moment" (51), lives as if on what Herman refers to as "permanent alert" or "hyperarousal."[46] He also continues to be haunted by memories of his father's brutality, thus suffering from the kind of symptom called "intrusion,"[47] because traumatized people (like Pita) tend to re-live events as though they were recurring in the present. These types of traumatic memories are "preserved in an abnormal state, set apart from ordinary consciousness" and, unlike normal memories, "lack verbal narrative and context; rather, they are encoded in the form of vivid sensations and images."[48] Pita's memories, which consist of "rage, hunger, hiding in trees, waiting, lying awake and listening in the dark; from dreams of finding his mother dead, chopped in the hall with an axe" (139–40), adhere to this pattern. Herman further argues that while "the ordinary response to atrocities is to banish

---

[44] Agnes Broughton et al., *The Silent Migration: Ngati Poneke Young Māori Club 1937–48: Stories Told to Patricia Grace, Irihapeti Ramsden, and Jonathan Dennis* (Wellington: Huia, 2001): 1.

[45] As with First Nations peoples the world over, genetically predetermined alcoholism is a problem endemic among the Māori, a problem aided and abetted by a colonialist/masculinist Pakeha (and generally Australasian) tradition of 'hard drinking'.

[46] Herman, *Trauma and Recovery*, 35.

[47] *Trauma and Recovery*, 35.

[48] *Trauma and Recovery*, 34, 38.

them from consciousness," they tend not to stay buried for long.[49] Correspondingly, Pita attempts to either repress or avoid re-living these traumatic memories, a common strategy also connected with the periods of numbness and dissociation Herman calls "constrictive cycles" because they serve to "keep the traumatic experience walled off from ordinary consciousness[50] and, as Abram Kardiner confirms, may "allow only a fragment of the memory to emerge as an intrusive symptom."[51] Thus trauma victims (like Pita) may look to the past by forcing themselves through a regimented series of thoughts that their shattered personal myths may be still able to explain.

Accordingly, Pita often reflects upon his life beneath Mount Taranaki; although his exposure to extreme violence had prevented him from developing any social skills, he had nevertheless felt comfortable in the countryside because most of the people he associated with were Māori. However, in Pakeha-dominated Wellington, where he is "unknown" and "knows no one" (69), he fears entering a shop or getting on a bus because he feels racially inferior, as if he is being watched by a "thousand eyes that made the colour of his skin a shame" (140).[52] He also laments that he is "too backhome and ignorant to understand" conversations, "too-in-a-tree waiting and not enough school. So he [keeps] himself quiet and work[s] hard, hardly opening his mouth because he always [feels] conspicuous" (140). Here again, Pita resembles a typical trauma victim, for, as Herman notes, a traumatized person's attempts "to avoid reliving the trauma too often result in a narrowing of consciousness, a withdrawal from engagement with others, and an impoverished life."[53] Furthermore, Tal observes, trauma victims are "forever changed" by their experiences: "many are transformed into liminal figures who must remain like ghostly Cassandras, on the fringes of society."[54] Moreover, Tal notes,

> If a trauma victim perceives [himself] as suffering alone, and has no
> sense of belonging to a community of victims, [he] will remain silent,
> imagining that [his] pain has no relevance to the larger society.[55]

---

[49] Herman, *Trauma and Recovery*, 1.

[50] *Trauma and Recovery*, 45.

[51] Quoted in Tal, *Worlds of Hurt*, 45.

[52] References to eyes, particularly in terms of racial discrimination, abound in the novel.

[53] Herman, *Trauma and Recovery*, 42.

[54] Tal, *Worlds of Hurt*, 122.

[55] *Worlds of Hurt*, 124.

Through most of the novel, Pita is a 'ghostly' figure who reveals none of his misery to anyone.

While Pita feels the most displaced in the urban environment, he is not the only family member to feel 'othered', as Grace's fiction underscores how institutionalized racism was in New Zealand at the time. Pita's widowed mother receives only half of a Pakeha woman's pension (74), and Pita's sisters protest that they are manpowered into low-paying jobs that Pakeha women do not want (185). Rangi complains bitterly that, while Pakeha and Chinamen can drink in pubs, Māori cannot (91); and he resents the fact that the Māoris' invisibility prevents them from being served, even at casual re-freshment counters (70). Both Pita and Rangi are unable to find well-paying permanent jobs (75), a circumstance that fuels Rangi's determination to enlist, and when Pita finally lands a full-time position in a government office, he merely pushes a broom. Even though he is now twenty-eight, his boss never-theless refers to him as "boy,"[56] a particularly demeaning insult, given that Pita has ostensibly been a man all his life. Eventually taking on a dangerous but better-paying job at a munitions factory, he resents being regarded as either a thief or a physical threat to the "the old guys" (171), and his uncle's words – that "the brown man has to be twice as good as the white man in order to be equal" (105) – ring in his ears.[57]

Although Pita feels estranged in the city, at the same time he also realizes that it offers his family a decent future: they can "pay their bills, get their meat and groceries, buy wood" to heat a cold house, and purchase decent clothes

---

[56] In *Cousins* (Auckland: Penguin, 1992): 185, Māori children are put into the "bot-tom" or "dumb" classes at school, and then ignored thereafter. The Māori were not taught their own language until the 1970s, when they (and progressive Pakeha) deman-ded that it be taught in schools. Moreover, Tu remarks that he learned only the history of England and Europe, a history that only starts to make sense once he is on the other side of the world (214). After he returns from war, Tu vows to study the history and geography of his own country. For more information on the insufficient education of-fered to Māori children, see King, "Between Two Worlds," 288–90, and the classic autobiographical novel *Spinster* by the educational pioneer Sylvia Ashton–Warner: *Spinster: a novel*, intro. Fleur Adcock (1958; Virago Modern Classics; London: Virago, 1980).

[57] Other nationalities display similar racist tendencies: Māori soldiers are initially not allowed to disembark in Cape Town, and the Yanks kill several Māori in drunken brawls in Wellington. Rangi also fights with an American soldier who tells him, "We don't drink with no darkies here, boy" (207).

(141). Yet Pita cannot envisage any prospects for himself, because the types of 'constrictive symptoms' Herman deems typical of trauma victims interfere with his abilities to anticipate or plan for the future. These symptoms also prevent Pita from developing successful relationships with his family members, who resent his constant vigilance and desire to control their lives, and mistakenly assume, as Herman suggests often happens, that these are "enduring characteristics" of his personality. Ultimately, Herman concludes, trauma victims (like Pita) whose symptoms go undetected alternate between cycles of numbness and intense feelings that are somehow removed from normal experience, and are thus "condemned to a diminished life, tormented by memory and bounded by helplessness and fear."[58]

Arguably, these undetected symptoms prevent Pita from forming a permanent relationship with Jess, a beautiful, working-class Pakeha woman with whom he has fallen in love, and she with him. Described by Pita's brothers as the "loveliest," most "beautiful, bright, warm and generous" young woman (271), Jess also possesses what Grace often refers to as 'disappearing eyes' – they crinkle up when she laughs, which seems to signify her willingness to overcome racial barriers. However, Pita's feelings for her tend to fluctuate; whenever victims of trauma attempt to "create some sense of safety and to control [their] pervasive fear,"[59] they restrict their lives. Furthermore, such oscillations often "occur in the regulation of intimacy," since "trauma impels people both to withdraw from close relationships and to seek them desperately."[60] Frantic to, but unable to, profess his love for Jess, Pita consoles himself with the belief that Jess could never be anything but his "dream," "not even when the world was free" (38), a phrase which runs like a refrain through the novel (60, 119, 160, 185), perhaps because "every traumatized member of an oppressed community is aware of the potential for repeated victimization."[61] Having lost trust in himself and in other people and, as a typical trauma sufferer who avoids "any initiative that might involve future planning and risk," Pita thus "deprive[s himself] of those new opportunities for successful coping that might mitigate the effect of the traumatic experience; the quality of life for trauma victims like Pita is "narrow" and "deplete[d]."[62]

---

[58] Herman, *Trauma and Recovery*, 49.

[59] *Trauma and Recovery*, 46.

[60] *Trauma and Recovery*, 56.

[61] Tal, *Worlds of Hurt*, 9.

[62] Herman, *Trauma and Recovery*, 47.

Pita's life takes a turn for the better, however, when he joins the Ngati
Poneke Club, which Fred, a man who has fought with Pita's father and is instrumental in forming the club, describes as a "home away from home for our
people coming to the city," where country folk can "keep their customs and
traditions" alive, and "practise the songs and dances and arts of the Māori,
learn from each other and be a comfort to each other in this new and different
world" (42). Pita throws himself into club events and almost immediately
feels as though "belonging to the Club [is] like an end of starvation": it offers
him a place where he does not feel "so backward" and "ignorant," so afraid of
"breaking rules" in this "unknown" world (88). Prior to joining the club, he
had kept himself "quiet, afraid of making mistakes, of breaking codes. It was
as though his voice had gone" (89), but now he enjoys singing at public performances. Moreover, in 1940, when the nation celebrates the centenary of
the signing of the Waitangi Treaty by building an imposing Centennial Exhibition Hall,[63] where Māori from all regions come to display their carvings and
weavings at the Māori Court and perform traditional dances and songs for
Māori and Pakeha, Pita is elated "because suddenly a place had been moulded
to fit [him]. [He] didn't have to be aware of a thousand eyes, because the eyes
were [his] own" (141). Pita thus begins to build a new personal myth shaped
by his reinvigorated pride in Māori culture and his place in it.

Tragically, however, Jess inadvertently shatters Pita's still-fragile personal
myth when she attends the opening celebration and makes disparaging remarks about the performances, which make Pita feel as if he is merely a "performing monkey" (154) in a kind of "sideshow" (153). Although he continues
to seek "the acceptance and approval of those of the thousand eyes" (155), he
also worries that the Pakeha regard Māori as "exhibits" or "attraction[s]"
(152). After vacillating for some weeks, Pita resolves to drop out of the con-
certs because he has a sense of being "owned" (154). Pita thus becomes
caught in what the anthropologist Arnold Van Gennep terms a liminal space,
or a disjunctive social world which situates trauma victims between "states,
places, or conditions."[64] Ultimately, recognizing that he is irrelevant to his

---

[63] Grace appears to juxtapose the 'backhome' Māoris' witnessing of the building of
the tower-like Centennial Exhibition Hall with the Māori soldiers' attempts to storm
the fortress-like setting of the monastery at Monte Cassino, which was, for the defen-
ders, a dream but, for the attackers, a nightmare. Frequent assaults on the mountain result only in dreadful loss of life and failure.

[64] Quoted in Tal, *Worlds of Hurt*, 117.

family, regarded as a shirker by his co-workers at the munitions factory, wanting to help end the war, "not just expect others to do it on his behalf" (37), and emboldened by his uncle's words that "Maybe fighting in their war will make the brown man equal to the white man" (155–56), Pita reluctantly enlists. Before he departs, he forsakes Jess and, as she predicted he would, marries a good Catholic Māori named Ani Rose.

Because the platoon groupings were organized along regional and tribal lines (as they had been in the First World War), Pita soon meets up with his brothers on the Italian battlefront, where, with the aid of much *vino*, he surprises Tu by talking constantly about "personal matters," including references to Jess (36, 137). Tu, who has only known his "big brother" as a taciturn man who has "never spoken to [him] in all [his] life except to correct or command [him]," is distressed by these emotional outpourings, which fail to generate sympathy or understanding, partly because, lacking verbal context, they are difficult to put into words, or, to use Tal's words, they can often "only invoke the incomprehensible."[65] Tu is unable to be his brother's "confessor" (210), because it is vital that the listener should know "'the lay of the land' – the landmarks, the undercurrents, and the pitfalls in the witness and in himself."[66] Tu has no way of understanding Pita's stories. Even though they had grown up "in the same household," he reflects,

> our lives have been so different. When [Pita] talks about the past, the backhome days, our father, what he has to say hardly ever matches up with my own feelings, memories and understandings of our early lives. (150)

His brother's outbursts serve only to embarrass Tu, who regards them as unintelligible, incoherent, and "none of his business" (36). Tu has no means of understanding that Pita has

> on some level prefer[red] silence so as to protect [himself] from the fear of being listened to – and of listening to [himself]. That while silence is defeat, it serves [him] both as a sanctuary and a place of bondage. (58)

Accordingly, Tu can be neither "a guide [nor] an explorer, a companion in a journey onto an uncharted land, a journey the survivor cannot traverse or

---

[65] *Worlds of Hurt*, 16.

[66] Dori Laub, "Bearing Witness or the Vicissitudes of Listening," in *Testimony: Crisis of Witnessing in Literature, Psychoanalysis, and History*, ed. Shoshana Felman & Dori Laub (New York & London: Routledge, 1992): 58.

return from alone."[67] Moreover, as Martin Buber suggests, "'testimony without acknowledgement' may paralyze the will, inhibiting action and speech."[68] Although cause and effect are not clear, it is possible that, without any 'acknowledgement' of his 'testimony', Pita may have lost his will to live, for shortly after he receives word that Ani Rose has given birth to a son, thereby making him the 'Little Father' he so longed to be, he is blown to bits on the battlefield.

During these troubling conversations with his brother, Tu dimly recognizes that he has "been fortunate, unaffected by some of the hardships that [his] family has suffered" (150), but remains largely unaware of the extent to which he has been shielded from his traumatized father's explosively aggressive behaviour. Taken to stay with relatives at the first sign of trouble and then sent to his uncles' farm during school holidays, Tu has, like Pita, formed a personal myth shaped by childhood experiences. A brilliant scholar and superb athlete, he might readily have fulfilled the family dream that he should succeed in the Pakeha world, had his uncles not imbued him with the warrior spirit: not only did they encourage him to live up to his full name, Tu Hokowhitu-a-Tu, and ancestrally to the Many Fighting Men of Tumatauenga, the patron of war, but they also taught him the "arts of the taiaha," the "skills of weaponry that came from the olden times" (94), which called for a high degree of muscular and visual coordination and entailed a drill perhaps even more precise than was demanded by military training. Tu is further predisposed by his Uncle Dave's claim (which clearly echoes Sir Apirana Ngata's words) that Māori should celebrate at the Centennial Exhibition Hall "the signing, the signing [...]. Of becoming a nation. Of becoming one people. You know, the Treaty. We are all one people. He iwi kotahi tatou. One people, one law, one language'" (131). When the one hundred members of the Maori Battalion, who had practised for "many extra hours" their "action songs, haka, poi and stick routines" (133), march into the new Māori Court Building, the fourteen-year-old Tu joins the people's pride in "their own Battalion" (142). After witnessing the ways in which the soldiers were "lauded and applauded by hundreds as they formed their guard of honour" (258), and taking much pride in his brother Rangi's enlistment (258), Tu thereafter listens for words of "triumph and glory" (259) from Mt Olympus, Tobruk, Gazala, and Alamein. Key battle sites, he attests,

---

[67] Laub, "Bearing Witness or the Vicissitudes of Listening," 59.
[68] Quoted in Tal, *Worlds of Hurt*, 126.

were on our lips, in our hearts, as we listened to news reports, or heard
the stories told by friends who had been invalided home. So in my
mind there was never a question of not going to war, even though I
knew so little of its causes, so little of what it was really about, so little
of what men are capable of doing to one another. (259)

The 28 (Maori) Battalion, he believes, are his "new mountain," his "home-
place" (258). Although Tu lists many reasons why Māori volunteered (they
were "running away from monotony"; or "were off to see the world"; or
"abscond[ing] from marriage or difficult family situations"; or "in trouble
with the law"; or had a "desire to belong to something, be part of what was
going on, perhaps be important and smart in a uniform, or to have excitement
and to test ourselves"; or did it simply for "comradeship"), he concludes that
most enlisted for "the honour of the people" (259–60). Given Tu's training,
his pride in the warrior culture, and the pressure on Māori to excel on the
battlefield, he aspires only to be a soldier, and in 1943, he runs away to war.

Even before he sets sail, however, Tu encounters several challenges to his
personal myth that fighting overseas will prove to be "the biggest adventure
of [his] life" (34). The military ignore the fact that he is under-age – he is
seventeen – because casualties are extremely high and they are "desperate to
fill the gaps" (33). On the other hand, Māori politicians request that the remaining volunteers be recalled, arguing that they have "done enough already"
and "there have been too many losses from such a small population" (34). Tu
reaches the battle zone and takes part in several disastrous attempts to "open
up the way to Rome" – a refrain which eventually takes on Chekhovian proportions (77). Although, during a major assault, he witnesses the deaths of one
hundred and fifty-four troops out of two hundred (many of them his relations), and then learns that both his brothers have been killed, Tu's boyish,
wild-eyed enthusiasm for war scarcely diminishes. Seemingly unaware that
the combat missions were either untenable or foolhardy, he blames "a river,
the weather, the moon, a mountain of many eyes" (130), and continues to take
pride in not having fallen "short of the job" he set out to do, in having "earned
membership [in his] Battalion, and in having done some of what Twenty-
eighth is known for" (184). "Our enemy," he writes, will "think that we […]
are a force that cannot be scorned" (182). Even when losses continue to esca-
late, Tu is rarely downhearted, and continues to reiterate the lyrics from the
Battalion's famous marching song, which stress that the warriors are brave
and true, and will fight right to the end for their country. When Rangi wounds
him seriously enough to put him out of the fighting (as he and Pita had pre-

viously agreed to do), Tu is ashamed, wrongly assumes that his brothers have decided that he is not "man enough" (237) to fight, and is furious that Rangi's actions have deprived him of being a member of his "beloved Battalion," a "man of [his] Battalion" (237). Although he spends the last months of the war recuperating in hospitals, getting to know the people (occasionally by engaging in several serious and not-so-serious affairs), and touring the magnificent Italian countryside, he frets that he will be treated "like a hero" when he returns home (238). Like Pita, who could never envisage a future for himself, Tu cannot "think of a life beyond life with my Battalion, a life with men who know what it's been like" (256). At the end of the war, he writes in his notebook, "There was a war. I had to go. It's over. I'm glad I went" (258).

Tu's inability to recognize the extent to which he has been mentally scarred by combat is not unusual; according to the social scientist Gregory Bateson, "people have many mechanisms to avoid assimilating disturbing information."[69] Tal adds:

> there is a sort of subconscious but intentional ignorance in operation in human beings. We do not notice a great deal of what we do not want to notice. What is disturbing can be ignored until (and often well after) it becomes dangerous to continue to ignore it.[70]

Tu therefore becomes the kind of warrior who has "rejected, repressed, and revised most of [his] war experiences until the parts that [he] can recall seem to be consonant with the greater body of national [or collective] myth"[71] which, according to Tal, is "propagated in textbooks, official histories, popular culture documents, public schools, and the like. This myth belongs to no one individual, though individuals borrow from it and buy into it in varying degrees."[72] Although Tal's definition of national myth refers to "textbooks" and "official histories" from which Māori were excluded, Phillips confirms that national myths – in particular that "racial distinctions" would be overcome in the "crucible of war" – were clearly circulating within the culture.[73]

Tu retains his belief in his personal and national myths long after it is dangerous to ignore them, perhaps because, as Gerald Linderman asserts, the

---

[69] Quoted in Tal, *Worlds of Hurt*, 133.

[70] Tal, *Worlds of Hurt*, 133–34.

[71] *Worlds of Hurt*, 130.

[72] *Worlds of Hurt*, 115.

[73] Phillips, "War and National Identity," 96.

soldier who remembers "correctly" is "forced to recognize that he has been a victim of a government and a social order that had exploited him."[74] Moreover, as Tal observes,

> grand revision of a personal myth must always spring from a traumatic experience, for the mechanism that maintains those foundational schemas will automatically distort or revise all but the most shattering revelations.[75]

Tu's traumatic experience does not occur until some years later, however. Initially unable to find work, not wanting to be a burden on his family, uncomfortable in his family's "house of heroes, with its photographs, its medals, its shrines and, most of all, its expectations," and "not wanting to make [his family members] his confessors" (271), he spends his time travelling aimlessly between small towns and cities, and drinking in pubs[76] with his "Battalion pals" (272) at Returned Services clubrooms.[77] The reason why he feels so comfortable among them is that they were men "whose eyes [he] could look into and find understanding, where [he] could detect a kind of knowing reflected back to [him]" (272). These were the men, he goes on to write, who "understood how misshapen we had become [...]. This had become our belonging now, with each other" (272).[78] After many years of working at temporary jobs, drinking heavily, and being unable to form lasting relationships with women, several of whom he treats badly, Tu reaches rock bottom and signs himself into a lunatic asylum, where his rants and raves are drowned out by the noise of the other inmates. Unlike the other "greatly insane," however, Tu takes advantage of his "new place of residence" to discover the meaning

---

[74] Tal, *Worlds of Hurt*, 119.

[75] *Worlds of Hurt*, 116.

[76] For more information on the problems faced by returned soldiers' "excessive alcohol consumption," see Gardiner, *Te mura o te ahi: The Story of the Maori Battalion*, 183.

[77] The war veterans' organization RSA, known popularly as the Returned Services' Association but properly designated as the Royal New Zealand Returned and Services' Association, is a national institution, its presence, proud or inconspicuous, felt ubiquitously (in meeting-halls and monuments) from city to the smallest township.

[78] Tu thanks "God" that he "had no treatment. The so-called cures [...] were many times worse than being struck down by madness" (274). Grace implies, though, that, like his father, Tu could certainly have benefitted from professional counselling and medical attention to help him overcome his many symptoms of trauma.

of his war experiences by reading history, for, as he states, "I had put myself in a war, in a place, in a time. There had to be a legacy" (274).

Although Tu fails to locate any kind of legacy, at least one historical account suggests, somewhat unproblematically, that the Second World War served to improve Māori–Pakeha relations:

> The contribution and reputation of the Māori Battalion was a source of great pride to the wider New Zealand community. It was seen by many as a positive step forward for race relations in this country. Apirana Ngata had argued that Māori participation in the First World War was the price of citizenship – after the Second World War it was clear that Māori had paid in full.[79]

That same source further suggests that Māori migration to urban centres, which continued in great numbers after the war, "brought Māori and non-Māori into closer contact, helping to shape modern New Zealand society." On the other hand, King argues that, although a number of the members of the Maori Battalion completed university degrees and declared that, having "shed [their] blood in two world wars," they "had at least purchased the right to equality,"[80] they were nonetheless only able to effect minor improvements in Pakeha–Māori relationships; it took the "country's legislators" at least another generation to address crucial areas of concern such as poverty, housing, educational inequality, and pay equity.[81] In keeping with King's argument, Orange states that, although the Labour government took steps to "eradicate blatant paternalism and inequalities" by replacing the word 'Native' with 'Māori', by equalizing drinking laws, by attempting to make state rental housing more accessible, and by making allocation of social security benefits more fair, she, too, concludes that both the government and the public at large failed to "grasp the magnitude of Māori needs – needs which had to some extent been exacerbated by the war years."[82] Notably, Orange also argues that "the Maori Battalion's casualties represented a major loss of human potential to a community that had been struggling even before the war."[83]

---

[79] See "Impact – Māori and the Second World War."

[80] King, "Between Two Worlds," 302.

[81] "Between Two Worlds," 307.

[82] Orange, "The Price of Citizenship? The Māori War Effort," 248.

[83] "The Price of Citizenship? The Māori War Effort," 248.

In Tu's attempt to find the 'legacy' left by the war, it is significant that he should read voraciously, particularly history books; "survivors can make sense of their sufferings by creating a historical context."[84] After two decades of reading, Tu concludes that "I shouldn't have gone, we shouldn't have gone, that it wasn't our war, that there should never have been a Maori battalion" (260). That it should have taken him so long to reach this conclusion is understandable; it is not unusual for trauma victims' reactions to be delayed, because the traumatic event "is not assimilated or experienced fully at the time, but only belatedly, in its repeated *possession* of the one who experiences it."[85] Furthermore,

> in trauma the greatest confrontation with reality may also occur as an absolute numbing to it, that immediacy, paradoxically enough, may take the form of belatedness.[86]

Tal, for her part, explains this phenomenon as follows:

> as the years pass and the immediacy of the event fades into memory the process of revision begins to occur in the mind of each survivor. The dislocation of trauma, which removed meaning from the world, is gradually replaced by new stories about the past that can support a rewritten personal myth.[87]

The notebooks which Tu admits to having rewritten and revised reveal that, like Pita, he has been haunted by intrusive, vivid memories, but also that, unlike Pita, he realizes that their effects had been latent, that they are more powerful now than they had been at the time of combat, when he was "so busy concentrating on where [he] must go, what [he] must do to stay alive" that he was "immune" to the "noise" and the "racket" (125). He confesses that he cannot forget the sight of "men on fire [...] a tin hat rolling, spinning across the embankment with the head of a man inside" (125), and acknowledges that

> Sights and sounds wait inside me along with the stink of smoke, gunpowder, mud and rot and burning flesh. They invade my waking hours as well as my dreams. (125)

---

[84] Tal, *Worlds of Hurt*, 125.

[85] Cathy Caruth, "Introduction" to *Trauma: Explorations in Memory*, ed. Cathy Caruth (Baltimore MD & London: Johns Hopkins UP, 1995): 4.

[86] Caruth, "Introduction," 6.

[87] Tal, *Worlds of Hurt*, 125.

Like Pita, he laments there is nothing he can do to keep these "half-formed recollections from making their way into his head" (232), and these memories, like Pita's, interrupt his personal narrative and plunge him into a kind of liminal space, a "disjunctive social world" which does not become "postliminal" upon a soldier's return, but continues to remain "liminal."[88] One of the ways in which traumatized soldiers can move towards postliminality consists in "expression, in the form of narration," which can then "rewire the traumatic events that severed their connections to the rest of society."[89]

In his notebooks – his form of expression and narration – Tu confesses that his research has led him to several bitter conclusions, the first being that the Maori Battalion "took part in the most stupid and meaningless sector" of the Italian campaign (277). The battles around Cassino were, he writes, "ad hoc," "ill-conceived," as much to do with the "whim and fancy and desiderata of politicians" as with the "blundering, indecision, failure and ego of high command" (277). Moreover, the "laugh was on the Maori Battalion," who blamed so much "death and destruction" on "fates and misfortune" (278). The second bitter conclusion Tu reaches is that Māori believed that, "once the brown man had fought in the white man's war, maybe then he'd be deemed equal" (278). Different tribes

> offer[ed] their sons, encourage[d] them to list, even demand[ed] that their youth be part of this new Battalion which would show the world who we were and what we could do, what heights we could reach. (278)

Many said that

> war was part of our inheritance, part of our history, and that because of this we must have some kind of inborn aptitude. Here was an opportunity to show this special ability to the world. (278)

It was also said that "this was the opportunity to demonstrate pride of race. The price, the hopes of the people, were pinned on this Battalion of volunteers" (278). Only now, by re-telling his story, does Tu realize that Māori soldiers' desire to enlist had nothing to do with "God and King"; moreover, they were "too far away for it really to be about [their] country" (278). Rather, it was about being

> true citizens, being equal, proving worth, having a prideful place [...]. Freedom was what was being talked about [...] the freedom we meant

---

[88] Eric J. Leed, quoted in Tal, *Worlds of Hurt*, 117.

[89] *Worlds of Hurt*, 122.

was our own freedom, the freedom and status of the people. Our citizenship. (279)

The third and most bitter conclusion that Tu reaches is that the "price" was "too high," for it has left "the small nation beheaded, disabled, debilitated" (279).[90] The Maori Battalion took "full part in a war but haven't yet been able to take full part in peace" (279), for, once the war was over, and even though their Pakeha brothers had held them in high esteem on the battlefield, back on New Zealand soil, they told them to "Know your place Maori boy" (279). The war had not, then, as Sir Apirana Ngata had promised, gained the Māori "the respect of [their] Pakeha brothers," nor had it earned them "a higher profile in New Zealand life."[91]

With both his personal and his national myths now finally shattered, Tu signs himself out of the asylum, moves back to the base of Mount Taranaki, where he is (ironically) referred to as an "old man," even though he is only thirty-eight. He occasionally seeks out mates at a nearby pub and tends sheep and gardens on his uncles' land, but is still not ready to make his story public, as he steadfastly refuses to allow "stickybeak journalists" to read his notebooks (13). Only after spurning Rimini and Benedict, now young adults who attempt to visit him in the asylum, does Tu recognize that they have the right

---

[90] Māori women were also devastated by the war. As this novel shows, they were prevented from saying their 'final goodbyes' to men whom they might never see again, because the troop ships departed before the women and children got there (156). As Tu records in his notebook, the "days of waiting," often for news of death, were also tragic, particularly for a culture in which "Death in far-off lands, death without a body, was a death not fully believed. There was only a photograph as a reminder, only a photograph to touch, to stroke while the death ceremonies took place, and no burial to bring about conclusion" (95–96). Later on, he describes how his sisters and Ani Rose spent their days waiting for telegrams they hoped that they would never come (202), but Tu's mother nevertheless receives news that two of her sons have died. Moreover, "sadness was what emanated from the laughter and [...] eyes" of Tu's sisters (264). Sophie never marries or has children; Moana and her husband are childless; and Ani Rose, crushed by her belief that Pita had fathered Jess's child, born three weeks after their son Benedict, dies of tuberculosis without ever learning that Rangi was Rimini's father. Jess's story is equally heartbreaking: rejected by her father, with nowhere to live and no way of supporting herself, she deposits the nine-month-old Rimini with Pita's mother (270). Although she marries an American and moves to the USA, she has had no further contact with Rimini. Benedict is truly an orphan.

[91] See "Māori and the Second World War."

to know they are cousins, not siblings, and how he came to alter his feelings about the war. Tu's desire to bear witness – to be a "disturber of the peace [...] a man who undermines [...] the validity of existing norms"[92] – represents what many trauma critics consider to be the central theme of trauma literature. Telling the trauma story only to fellow survivors (as Tu did after the war) does not allow his whole community to be fully aware of what happened and its consequences, and it is only the community that can help individual victims to assimilate and work through their personal traumas, mainly by regarding them as a quintessential part of their collective/cultural traumatic legacy. When Tu describes his combat experience later on, he escapes the liminal space of the trauma cycle, since he carries "the tale of the horror back to the halls of normalcy and testif[ies] to the people the truth of their experience."[93] As he writes in his notebook, under the date 1 November 1944,

> I'll write because it'll help me sort out what took place and how it all happened. Now that I've begun to remember, there's nothing I can do to keep half-formed recollections from making their way into my head, and nothing to prevent these scraps from gathering themselves together and becoming whole memories. It's too late to forget. (232)

A few sentences later, Tu describes how he pushes "these fragments on to paper, piecing the puzzle together" (233). In assembling his stories, he adheres to a typical pattern: "the theme of drawing together fragments into a whole is found again and again in the literature of trauma; re-piecing a shattered self."[94]

Telling the trauma story, Herman observes, is a work of reconstruction that "actually transforms the traumatic memory," for the story "in its untransformed state [is] a prenarrative. It does not develop or progress in time, and it does not reveal the storyteller's feelings or interpretation of events."[95] Putting the story into words after some time has passed allows the storyteller to try and give these 'prenarrative' memories meaning an historical context. As Tal explains,

> the dislocation of trauma, which removed meaning from the world, is gradually replaced by new stories about the past that can support a

---

[92] Terence des Pres, quoted in Tal, *Worlds of Hurt*, 121.

[93] Tal, *Worlds of Hurt*, 125.

[94] *Worlds of Hurt*, 137–38.

[95] Herman, *Trauma and Recovery*, 175.

rewritten personal myth [...] survivors can make sense of their
sufferings by creating a historical context.

In one sense,

> all writing about atrocity represents a retrospective effort to give
> meaningless history a context of meaning, to furnish the mind with a
> framework for insight without diminishing the sorrow of the event
> itself.[96]

The trauma sufferers' desire to tell their stories is, according to Tal,

> an aggressive act. It is born out of a refusal to bow to outside pressure
> to revise or to repress experience, a decision to embrace conflict rather
> than conformity, to endure a lifetime of anger and pain rather than to
> submit to the seductive pull of revision and repression. Its goal is
> change.[97]

Tu's goals in writing his notebooks are similar. By sharing them with his
niece and nephew, Tu not only indicates that he needs to make his experience
real for future generations but also contributes to creating something useful
out of the destruction of the war. To that end, he seeks 'change' by pleading
with Rimini and Benedict "not to follow" in either their father's footsteps or
his (281), and expresses relief when he hears that neither are interested in
"soldiering" (281). In some small way, he feels that, by having told the stories
of their fathers to his niece and nephew, he may not be an "entirely useless
piece of rubbish taking up space on the planet" (281). Most significantly, he
makes it clear that he is willing to rejoin his family and his community; and
he offers to take Benedict, Rimini, his mother, and several aunts to Italy so
that they can visit the graves of their fathers, uncles, and cousins, see the "old
and eerie" beautiful country, meet the people, listen to their music, and learn
that the sacrifices of the Maori Battalion have not been forgotten in that
country (281). As Grace's fiction seems to suggest, however, this might be
the only legacy from the war for the Maori Battalion, for their attempt to forge
a national unity through violence and loss have been, on the whole, futile.[98]

---

[96] Tal, *Worlds of Hurt*, 125.

[97] *Worlds of Hurt*, 7.

[98] Phillips writes that fictional narratives (although not specifically those on the
Māori experience of war, like Grace's) that tackled the Second World War may "lack
the credibility of immediate reaction, and they lack a factual accuracy, but the fictional
disguise does allow the writer to capture the attitudes and the oral culture of the soldier

WORKS CITED

Ashton–Warner, Sylvia. *Spinster: a novel*, intro. Fleur Adcock (1958; Virago Modern Classics; London: Virago, 1980).

Broughton, Agnes et al. *The Silent Migration: Ngati Poneke Young Maori Club 1937–48: Stories Told to Patricia Grace, Irihapeti and Jonathan Dennis* (Wellington: Huia, 2001).

Caruth, Cathy. "Introduction" to *Trauma: Explorations in Memory*, ed. Cathy Caruth. (Baltimore MD & London: Johns Hopkins UP, 1995): 3–12.

Cowan, James. *The Maoris in the Great War: A History of the New Zealand Contingent and Pioneer Battalion Gallipoli 1915, France and Flanders 1916–18* (Auckland: Whitcombe & Tombs, 1926).

Gardiner, Wira. *Te mura o te ahi: The Story of the Maori Battalion* (Auckland: Reed, 1992).

Grace, Patricia. *Cousins* (Auckland: Penguin, 1992).

——. "Going For the Bread," in Grace, *Electric City and Other Stories* (Auckland: Penguin, 1987): 47–51.

——. *Tu* (Auckland: Penguin, 2004).

Heim, Otto. *Writing Along Broken Lines: Violence and Ethnicity in Contemporary Māori Fiction* (Auckland: Auckland UP, 1998).

Herman, Judith. *Trauma and Recovery: From Domestic Abuse to Political Terror* (New York: HarperCollins, 1992).

"Impact – Māori and the Second World War," Ministry for Culture and Heritage. http://www.nzhistory.net.nz/war/Maori-and-the-second-world-war/impact (accessed 20 October 2007).

Kedgley, Sue, ed. *Our Own Country: Leading New Zealand Women Writers Talk About Their Writing and Their Lives* (Auckland: Penguin, 1989).

King, Michael. "Between Two Worlds," in *The Oxford History of New Zealand*, ed. W.H. Oliver & B.R. Williams (Oxford: Clarendon, 1981): 285–307.

——. *Te Puea: A Biography* (Auckland: Hodder & Stoughton, 1977).

Laub, Dori. "Bearing Witness or the Vicissitudes of Listening," in *Testimony: Crisis of Witnessing in Literature, Psychoanalysis, and History*, ed. Shoshana Felman & Dori Laub (New York & London: Routledge, 1992): 57–74.

——. "Truth and Testimony: The Process and the Struggle," in *Trauma: Explorations in Memory*, ed. Cathy Caruth (Baltimore MD & London: Johns Hopkins UP, 1995): 61–75.

---

to a much greater extent. Despite their limitations [...] these sources suggest that in the culture of the ordinary soldier, war held a very different meaning from the public mythology" ("War and National Identity," 98).

McGibbon, Ian. *New Zealand and the Second World War: The People, the Battles and the Legacy* (Auckland: Hodder Moa Beckett, 2003).

"Māori and the Second World War," Ministry for Culture and Heritage. http://www .history.nzhistory.net.nz/Maori-in-second-world-war (accessed 21 August 2009).

Ngata, Apirana. *The Price of Citizenship* (Wellington: Whitcombe & Tombs, 1943).

O'Connor, P.S. "The Recruitment of Maori Soldiers, 1914–18," *Political Science* 19.2 (1967): 48–83.

Orange, Claudia. "The Price of Citizenship? The Maori War Effort," in *Kia Kaha: New Zealand in the Second World War*, ed. John Crawford (Auckland: Oxford UP, 2000): 236–51.

Panny, Judith Dell. "A Cultural-Historical Reading of Patricia Grace's *Cousins*," *Kotare* 6 http://www.nzetc.org/tm/scholarly/tei-Whi06Kota-t1-g1-t1.html (accessed 20 September 2010).

——. *Turning the Eye: Patricia Grace and the Short Story* (Christchurch: Lincoln UP, 1997).

Phillips, Jock. "War and National Identity," in *Culture and Identity in New Zealand*, ed. David Novitz & Bill Willmot (Wellington: GP Books, 1989): 91–109.

"Response to War – Maori and the Second World War: The Maori Response to the Declaration of War," http://www.nzhistory.net.nz/war/Maori-in-second-world-war /response (accessed 2 April 2008).

Tal, Kalí. *Worlds of Hurt* (New York: Cambridge UP, 1996).

Walker, R.J. "Maori Identity," in *Culture and Identity in New Zealand*, ed. David Novitz & Bill Willmott (Wellington: GP Books, 1989): 35–52.

◄❖►

Passion to *Pasyon*
Playing Militarism

MERLINDA BOBIS

"Ay, IRAYA!"[1] This lament is the wellspring of this essay. *Ay* is an everyday exclamation in Bikol, my home region in the Philippines. It is a spontaneous response of surprise or strong emotion, be it joy, grief, hope, or despair. *Iraya*, meanwhile, is a directional reference to place. In my native language Bikolano, it means 'from where the water flows, the wellspring in the hills' – as opposed to *Ilawod*, which means 'away from the water source'. Consider this framework: if water is the physical basis of survival, story is its psychic heart. Daily we move to *Iraya* or *Ilawod*, towards and away from the original source of water or story, but always our frame of reference is water and story.

"We tell ourselves stories in order to live," the writer Joan Didion observes, as quoted by the anthropologist Michael Jackson in his book *The Politics of Storytelling*. He writes about storytelling as

> a vital human strategy for sustaining a sense of agency in the face of disempowering circumstances. To reconstitute events in a story is no

---

[1] Merlinda Bobis sings this lament as a refrain in her play *River, River* (2009). View the video clip http://www.merlindabobis.com.au/dramatic.htm (accessed 21 July 2010).

longer to live those events in passivity, but to actively rework them, both in dialogue with others and within one's own imagination.[2]

This agency can literally save lives. In the 1987–89 total war against communist insurgency in the Philippines, storytelling was a strategic counter-deployment against armed conflict, as in this instance, when someone recounts: "The children are caught in between … They're very good at storytelling, at lying, in order to manipulate both sides [the military and the rebels] to prevent an encounter."[3]

Note how I start with a writer's take on 'story for survival' and slip into an anthropologist's point about the potency of storytelling – from print to oral medium – and conclude with this oral medium subversively at work in actual life, where story is literally a matter of life and death. Such is the case in the Philippines, not only in that total war waged in the countryside, but more so now and even in the very public sphere of the media. In May 2005, the Committee to Protect Journalists (CPJ) cited the Philippines as "the most murderous country of all" for journalists.[4] In January 2009, a blog in the *Straits Times* reported that, according to the National Union of Journalists of the Philippines, the latest victim was

> the 63rd journalist killed since [then current] President Gloria Arroyo came to power in 2001. That's just over half the total number of slain journalists since the fall of the Marcos regime in 1986 […]. Many of the [victims] were radio broadcasters from small provincial towns, who had fatally tangled with local politicians, corrupt officials or crime bosses.[5]

---

[2] Michael Jackson, *The Politics of Storytelling: Violence, Transgression, and Intersubjectivity* (Denmark: Museum Tusculanum Press, 2006): 15.

[3] Interview conducted by Merlinda Bobis (Bikol, 1997). See also the extensive discussion of the deployment of story relating to the writing of "Fish-Hair Woman" in Bobis's article "Storying: Dream and Deployment," *Social Identities: Journal for the Study of Race, Nation and Culture* 15.1 (2009): 85–94.

[4] "Marked for Death: The Five Most Murderous Countries for Journalists," *Special Report: CPJ New York* (2 May 2005), http://cpj.org/reports/2005/05/murderous-05 .php (accessed 3 March 2009).

[5] Alastair McIndoe, "Reporters at Risk," *The Straits Times Blogs* (24 January 2009), http://blogs.straitstimes.com/2009/1/24/reporters-at-risk (accessed 3 March 2009).

These disparate quotations and examples share a special feature: the oral rendition of story, whether it is on radio, in storytelling, and even in Didion's statement "We tell ourselves stories in order to live," where the verb *tell* is, for me, the operative word. Story is in the mouth, in the body. Immediate, urgent, in-your-face. When the story about a journalist's murder or a village massacre is told by the 'performing' body, it is as if the violated bodies were themselves put on display to be witnessed by the listener. One is instantly dragged back to *Iraya*, the wellspring of the story. But where is this wellspring? Is it in the initial witnessing of the violence? Or does it go further back, deeper? Could it be that bodily articulation casts up other bodies to the surface, even those that were never retrieved and laid out, like the histories that were buried or erased?

Disappearance and retrieval. These are at the heart of this essay and the two texts that I will be discussing: my yet unpublished novel *Fish-Hair Woman*, which is about the 1987–89 total war in my home region of Bikol, and its play version. In this story, *Iraya* is the name of the militarized village where the Fish-Hair Woman, Estrella Capili, uses her twelve-metre-long hair to fish out corpses from the river, the main water-source of the village. When a body is dumped in the water, it changes flavour: from river sweetness to brine, then, one day, to lemon grass. *Iraya* is based on my maternal grandmother's village, Estancia, which was a hotbed of insurgency; during the total war, a battalion of scout rangers, an elite military unit, was deployed in its elementary school. Other areas in my region tell stories about military atrocities, but Estancia's stories are also about the abuses committed by the communist insurgents, the New People's Army (NPA). Around the Philippines, the phenomenon of the *desaparecidos*, the disappeared, has always been a commonplace story since the more than twenty-year Marcos dictatorship. Added to *disappeared* is another word that is just as evocative, though perplexing to the outsider – *salvage*, which now means extra-judicial killing. Both the military and the NPA have been guilty of salvaging.

> They marched as if in a major offensive towards the river. Around us the fireflies kept guard, violence dressed as salvation. What hopeful word, the sibilants a gentle hush: *salvacion.* The soldiers and the rebels spoke of this same cause, even as they remained in opposite camps and our village festered in between. We were the narrow space that deepened into a groove between the right and the left ventricle.
> The left and the right, left, right, left, right: the cadence of politics in uniform, marching head on towards each other to redeem the tiny

village in between. Consider their intent: to salvage a village. Consider the word: *salvage*. From the Latin *salvare*: "rescue, retrieve, preserve from loss or destruction." But in Iraya, we whispered *salvage* with a weight in the tongue, sinking the word like a body thrown into the river. Liquidated, made liquid, made to disappear. Such was our new definition of the word.

Salvage: summarily execute.

Wooed by political *cariño* from the eye of a gun, our beloved village disappeared in the bid for salvation by the rebels and the military. Beloved: *Padaba. Pa-da-ba.* Three birds shot down in mid-flight. All salvaged ones, someone's father, son, sweetheart, wife. I found them in the water. Which hand did they serve or repudiate? The left or the right? Which hand pulled the trigger? Listen, I must tell stories about dying in mid-speech, mid-love, mid-air, so you can tell them back to me. Perhaps the shots would ring clearer, if not truer. And when death becomes certain, love might just be completed.[6]

In this excerpt from the novel, 'I' is Estrella, the Fish-Hair Woman picked up by the soldiers to retrieve a body from the river. Here violence-and-salvation, disappearance-and-retrieval are inextricably bound, in various ways and contexts of storying, of fabrication. Estrella is told a story: someone has been salvaged, made to disappear in the water. The body must be retrieved, not only to save it but to save the water, the life-source of the village. The village is told the same story by both sides in the conflict: that the war is meant to save it from the rebels or the military. But in the act of salvation, the village becomes collateral damage. It disappears, crushed by the opposing causes, their respective narratives. Also, the original meaning of words disappears, then are retrieved/refabricated as something else. Like *salvage*. Or the term of endearment *beloved, padaba*, the syllables now broken up. *Pa-da-ba*: like three birds shot down in mid-flight. It is not just bodies, but also language that is violated; and so *storying* inevitably becomes a site of violence. In the village, *story* is negotiated orally, and *storytelling* is supposed to retrieve some sense of agency. But story is in the mouth, in the violated body. Where do you find agency, then? Perhaps in the uttering, or in the sound produced, when the shots ring clearer, truer – when certainty is established (This really happened!), even if the words are somehow all wrong. A mother says, "*Na-salvage ang aki kong si Mario*" – My son Mario was salvaged; and as a listener conspires with her, saying, "I hear you, I know," the testimony is cer-

[6] Merlinda Bobis, "Fish-Hair Woman" (unpublished novel): 33.

tified, the story is completed. But what if the listener understands the mother's remark as: My son Mario was salvaged, saved? Because she does not share the mother's peculiar language? Then there is no story at all, if we take story to mean a completed negotiation-affirmation between teller and listener. So the mother's loss could disappear in the public discourse.

Consider another word: *militarization.* According to a military officer whom I interviewed for the novel, this word is propaganda, an 'untruth' coined by the left. He argues, "If you put a military detachment in an area, that's not militarization. It's like putting in a police detachment in an area for security."[7] But a community living under imposed curfew, constant surveillance, and ongoing violence will swear that the *militarization* of their village is 'true'. Jackson writes:

> the politics of storytelling concerns precisely these vexed and unstable contrasts between truth and untruth, articulated as an opposition between public and private domains. [...] As [the professor of anthropology] Michael Herzfeld has shown, stories involve disemia – a tension between the legitimate and the intimate: "a formal or coded tension between official self-representation and what goes on in the privacy of collective introspection."[8]

The word *terrorism* and, following on, the phrase *global war on terror* were 'officially coded' by the Bush administration and 'the coalition of the willing', seemingly only after 9/11, thus negating previous acts of terrorism and assigning the label *terrorists* only to specific 'Other' groups. What I find most disturbing is the attachment of the word 'global', which collectivizes the act of war and automatically assimilates me to it: we are in this together, we have a shared enemy. Now, take the phrase *the age of trauma* in reference to this and the previous century, which causes me some unease, because it could exclude the trauma caused by, say, nearly four hundred years of Spanish colonization of the Philippines, which began in 1521. But then the word and concept of *trauma* are not in the native Philippine vocabulary.

After reading theories and accounts of trauma to prepare for this essay, I realized that my other novels are about trauma, but I never thought of them as such, nor did I hear the word *trauma* used when I was researching formerly militarized communities. The Associate Professor of Psychology Rogelia Pe-

---

[7] Interview by Bobis (1997).

[8] Jackson, *The Politics of Storytelling,* 27.

Pua, a Filipino-Australian, argues that *trauma* is a Western concept and is medical in origin.

> [Trauma] has to do with diagnosis and naming a condition to pin down a phenomenon, which can be fixed by therapy. Labeling is an industry because it gives them a handle or tool to promote the profession, and earn a living from it. [...] When dealing with children of war, [the Director of the Children's Rehabilitation Centre] Elizabeth Protacio de Castro uses [the Pilipino word] *ligalig* [literally meaning, 'agitation' or 'trouble'] [...] so [those] in the militarized zones are *naligalig* [troubled], not *na-trauma* or *traumatized* as though they've lost their minds. We don't go for counselling or therapy. We simply confide in family or friends. They are our 'therapist,' and we don't have to pay! 'Therapy' again is part of that industry.[9]

This is not to say that this industry is invalid or any less than the native Philippine concepts, which thrive within a kinship system, or that therapy does not exist among contemporary middle- and upper-class Filipinos. Of course, they can pay. The Filipino psychologist Edwin Decenteno, who worked with casualties of conflict from the Marcos regime, writes:

> Working with [the organization] FIND (Families of Victims of Involuntary Disappearance), [...] we tried to make sense of the term *relief* and *rehabilitation*. [...] Our problem with the term was that most of the families of FIND were so poor that they were always in need of relief.[10]

Poverty is a violent phenomenon, and yet it is hard to say one is traumatized by this violence, because it seems the concept of trauma is something that happens suddenly, disrupting normal life. But for most of the militarized communities in my region, poverty was (and still is) normal life. Natural calamities like tropical cyclones and volcanic eruptions are part of this 'normalcy,' hence this local saying about resilience: *nabubuhay sa tagilid na daga* – surviving on tilted earth. Bikol is "the fourth-poorest region in the country" and "one of the most fertile grounds for Communist insurgency since the 1960s," writes literature Professor and activist Paz Verdades M. Santos.[11] In

---

[9] Rogelia Pe-Pua, email correspondence (1 March 2009).

[10] Edwin Decenteno, *Rehab: Psychological Rehabilitation for Social Transformation: Some Programs and Concepts* (Manila: Bukal, 1997): 8.

[11] Paz Verdades M. Santos, "Centre of Gravity: The New People's Army in Bikol (A Case Study)," in *Primed and Purposeful: Armed Groups and Human Security Ef-*

the research for the novel, my guide tells me about a soldier explaining why he joined the military:

> "I have not gone to school. I was invited to join the NPA, the rebel army, but I thought if I get killed, my parents will have no pension. But if I'm with the military, at least they'll have a pension, and I can come home in a box."[12]

So if you are from a poor, militarized village, how can you tell your story to the wider public or to the West, where the story/media machine is all-encompassing? To name something is to tell a story. How does your story gain legitimacy without the 'professional names' in the dominant global discourses promoted by the media or medical industry? Decenteno had to retrieve indigenous terms and concepts not so much to tell the story to the industry but to assist storytelling among the casualties of war, in order to facilitate their rehabilitation. Language is the site of disappearance and retrieval of lost and hidden stories, in order to cope with the present and hopefully move on, and, for those who have very little to start with, on a day-to-day basis.

Retrieving stories: back to *Iraya*, the wellspring. This return was for me paramount in creating the Fish-Hair Woman, a mythical figure that retrieves not only the dead but also history. For fifteen years, I researched and wrote and re-wrote the novel, constantly arguing with myself about the ethics of the process. In 1997, ten years after the total war, I returned to my grandmother's village of Estancia to find a river.

I found the river of Ugub, a neighbouring village. In an idyllic time long before the war, this river was a favourite landmark of my maternal family. My aunties used to tell stories about their encounters with this body of water, which has many tributaries or capillaries, among them a stream that ran all the way to where I used to bathe as a child when I spent summer holidays with my grandmother. This river was not used as the dumping-ground for corpses during the total war; that detail is my fiction. Nor did I visit this river until 1997, when my grandmother, once a respected matriarch of the village, was already living in Manila, and I in Australia. I left for Australia in 1991, a month after my writer friends found out about a new disappearance. I was giving them a writing workshop when the news came: that their friend, a

---

forts in the Philippines, ed. Soliman Santos, Jr., Paz Verdades M. Santos, et al. (Geneva & Manila: South-South Network for Non-State Armed Group Engagement and Small Arms Survey, 2010): 43.

[12] Interview by Bobis (1997).

social worker, was 'picked up' by the military. She was never found, most likely salvaged. Much later, it was confirmed that she was initially detained in the military camp in the city where my family lives and which is an hour's drive from Estancia, and this river.

So, in 1997 I returned to the village as a stranger, but my mother's high-school friend, my research guide, made sure I was introduced as the grand-daughter of Manay Tinding, the matriarch – thus I was welcomed with gene-rosity and stories. I had to 'know the landscape'; my body had to know this river, so it could come alive in the novel. On the day I went to the river, there was a washerwoman busy at the bank and another woman crossing, coconuts and firewood balanced on her head. The two women stared at me, then pro-ceeded with their domestic occupations. And the third woman, this writer, went into the water, so it can be made real on the page. The scene was ridicu-lous. The occupation of the writer was so out of place there, when there were more pressing occupations than 'researching the river', such as washing the family's clothes and bringing home firewood and food to cook a meal.

Maybe the washerwoman found me out. She stared and smiled, perplexed at this stranger immersed in the water – for what? She is not doing anything! Even if I believed I was doing something significant. Mine was immersion for story's sake; hers was immersion for survival. I came and went; she never had the chance to leave. I gathered my river flora and fauna and returned to Aus-tralia, where there are washing machines and electric hot-plates. I took with me not only the river but also the stories, faces, and bodies of the village. My own firewood, in my head.[13]

In writing, the 'kindling' for story that I take away and how I take away from actual lives is a point of ethical debate. I do not only gather stories but re-tell them as I interrogate the human condition. Do I also interrogate my own condition of privilege? From what and whose context, and for whom, am I storying? Have I fairly storied all sides of the conflict? Who wins, who loses out in this process? How are actual lives implicated in this fiction? There is the Fish-Hair Woman who embodies memory in her hair which grows a handspan each time she remembers a moment of anguish, and who uses this never-ending memory to retrieve the lost ones. There is her Australian lover, a journalist, who comes to *Iraya* to write about the total war, and disappears in

---

[13] This encounter is told and discussed by Bobis in *A Novel-in-Waiting: Creative Research: Towards Writing Fiction* (Manila: The Centre for Intercultural Studies, 2004): 13.

the process. There is the migrant writer who writes the Fish-Hair Woman story in her new home in America, and the journalist's son who visits the Philippines to reluctantly search for his father. Everyone is trying to return to the river, to retrieve something. At its heart, the novel is an ongoing argument about the retrieval and refabrication of stories, about writing.

> The river's womb is pitch-dark at night. So how to search the riverbed for my lemon grass lover. How to draw him out of the water with my memories, when they can only rise as dead fishes with scales that peel then float like a beautiful, silver alphabet. How to trust language that can only make the disappeared appear as lovely.[14]

This excerpt from the novel echoes an ongoing doubt about my own medium, even while I tell myself that

> Writing visits like grace. In an inspired moment we almost believe that anguish can be made bearable and injustice can be overturned, because they can be named. And if we're lucky, joy can even be multiplied, so we may have reserves in the cupboard for the lean times.[15]

My self-reassuring poetics allows me to navigate away from the original passions. From *Iraya*, the wellspring in the hills, to *Ilawod*, 'away from the water-source', and thus to the lowlands where the topography is level and safer, so to speak. This movement from the firsthand accounts of the war to writing the novel in Australia is fraught and ambivalent – here I am 'translating' the story of that war for a Western sensibility. The *Iraya*-to-*Ilawod* framework is contentious, though. To fixate on retrieving 'the original story' denies the fact that the ongoing storytelling in the village has refabricated its initial experience many times over. According to Jackson,

> one may no more recover the 'original' story than step into the same river twice. The fault is not with memory per se, but an effect of the transformations all experience undergoes as it is replayed, recited, reworked and reconstrued in the play of intersubjective life.[16]

Moreover, I found that, in retrieving stories of that total war, I was uncovering older wars. The wellspring kept shifting, going further back in time, but also coming closer to home.

---

[14] Bobis, "Fish-Hair Woman" (unpublished novel), 38.

[15] Bobis, *A Novel-in-Waiting*, 26.

[16] Jackson, *The Politics of Storytelling*, 23.

During my research, my grandmother told me a family story about the Second World War, when the Philippines was occupied by the Japanese for three years (incidentally, after the Spanish colonization, we were occupied by America for forty years; the USA has always been involved in Philippine counter-insurgency operations, which were prevalent during the Marcos dictatorship). Now, Grandmother's war story: 1945.[17] In the hills, the Japanese executed her seventy-five-year-old mother-in-law, my great-grandmother. The terror wrought by the retreating Japanese army was such that the menfolk, including the dead woman's own son, my grandfather, refused to go to the hills to retrieve the body. "You'll let Mother rot there?" Grandmother, who was pregnant then, protested, and organized the hammock for the dead, then forced the men to retrieve the body. When it arrived, she washed it with herbs. Bayonet, and a wound the size of a piggy bank's slit, she said. The story hit me like layers of epiphany: here was Grandmother echoing the task of the Fish-Hair Woman, and a war echoing other wars, and our intimate storytelling retrieving family and Philippine history. Personally implicated in my fiction, I decided to use both histories in the novel. But then, the wellspring of the fiction has always been personal.

It began with my grandmother – with her hair, or my memory of her stories about her hair that flowed to the back of her knees, and her hair-washing rituals in the river, how it took a full day to dry that thick, black mass. Storytelling sessions happened regularly when I spent summer holidays in the old house in Estancia, before there was electricity in the village. Night was lit by kerosene lamps and shadows loomed large with ghosts and magical beings, and outside the fireflies covered the trees like live tinsel. The magical has always been part of our imaginary and crucial to negotiating and explaining daily reality, long before 'magical realism' became a 'phenomenon' in literary theory. Always there were unseen creatures around me. The neighbours believed grandmother's house was haunted. Each night, my fear grew as the sun set and I cried non-stop, wanting to return to the city where there were electric lights. It was a little ritual of fearfulness that I played out nightly for the whole summer. Was it a portent of what was going to happen to the village? Or a harbinger of the horror in my fiction that 'just happened' in 1994, when I wrote the short story "Fish-Hair Woman" in Australia? Was I, in fact,

---

[17] This story is told as a basis for fictionalizing in Bobis, "Storying: Dream and Deployment," 87.

snagged by grandmother's hair, 'retrieved' by the strands of history and pulled back home to *Iraya*?

Perhaps one does not find story; one is found by story.

In 1997, when I was gathering stories from my home region to expand the short story into a novel, I interviewed a rebel commander who had lived in hiding in the hills for twenty-five years, and was back in the lowlands, in peace negotiations with the government. He told me not only about war but also his love story. When he and his wife, also a guerrilla, were apart on different missions, "*Ang suratan, nagbubulos iyan. Ang iriulusyonan poon, mantang, sagkod na magadan*"[18] (the love letter writing gushes and flows. The courtship begins from the beginning, until death). Note the water evocation. Like his protracted war, his love was as passionate and flowed until death, like a river. In his storytelling, he went into deeper waters, further back into history, into many stories. One of them was the most chilling of all, the *Lambat Bitag*, literally 'Fish-Net Trap'. I realized that my fiction about the hair as a net to save the dead was aligned with another net, an instrument of death. The human-rights advocate Arnel de Guzman writes:

> President Aquino and her U S military advisers mapped out a strategy dubbed *Lambat Bitag* (Operation Fish-Net Trap), a Filipino expression that suggests a noose tightening around a victim's neck. *Lambat Bitag* relies on traditional military offensives bolstered by political and psychological warfare that are supposed to pave the way for peace and development. The strategy is not new; it was used by the United States in the Philippine-American War, was used to crush the Huk [peasant] rebellion in the 1950s, and was the mainstay of Marcos-directed counter-insurgency warfare in the 1970s and 1980s.
>
> The victims of the tightening noose are of course meant to be the insurgents, especially the leaders, but since they are so elusive, a broad net with small openings is needed. Casting such a net risks catching innocent fish, but this, reasons the military, would be an acceptable byproduct of war. In regions where the net fails, the entire population (the water) may have to be removed in order to starve the fish.[19]

Life affirming art. This writer was snagged back to the source, which probably she has never left, because it is of the body, like hair, as much as it is in

---

[18] Interview by Bobis (1997).

[19] Arnel De Guzman & Tito Craige, "Counter-Insurgency War in the Philippines and the Role of the U S," *Bulletin of Concerned Asian Scholars* 23.1 (1991): 40.

the shared cultural psyche. In those writing years I had regular nightmares, one of them about trying to wash my hair in the middle of the ocean and discovering that my hair and the water were infested with maggots. My 'fish-net hair' of salvation is an accidental subversion of the deadly military strategy 'Fish-Net Trap', the *Lambat Bitag*.

> Lambat na itom na itom
> Pero sa dugo natumtom
> Samong babaying parasira
> Buhok pangsalbar-pangsira
> Kang samong mga padaba
> Hale sa salog … hale sa salog.
> Very black net
> But blood-soaked
> Our fisherwoman
> Hair to save-fish
> All our beloved
> From the river … from the river …[20]

This is the Fish-Hair Woman's hair ditty, which I first wrote as text in the original short story.[21] In the play *River, River*, I sing it both in my Bikol language, using the *Pasyon* tradition, and in English with composed music. The *Pasyon* is the popular epic narrative about 'The Passion of Christ' read, sung or performed on Holy Week celebrations in the Philippines. The *Pasyon* chanting style that I use is from the Bitabara family, Filipino-Australians originally from my region; they have not stopped singing the *Pasyon* every Holy Week for twenty-two years since they migrated to Australia. The music for the English text is by the Australian composer Sarah de Jong. I am now descending into different waters: from a Philippine to an Australian river.

I sang the *Ay, Iraya!* lament at Simmo's Beach, a river in Australia, as part of the creative development of the stage play, my adaptation of the short story, which also became the first chapter of the novel. Moving from the print medium to oral rendition in storytelling and the *Pasyon* is another story of disappearance and retrieval. Interestingly, however, with my obsession to write

---

[20] Merlinda Bobis, "Fish-Hair Woman," in *White Turtle* (North Melbourne: Spinifex, 1999): 13–14.

[21] I adapted the short story "Fish-Hair Woman" into the play *River, River* with minimal text added from other chapters of the novel. Then I re-invented the poetic prose of the story into verses, which became most of the songs of the play.

into the novel the voices of the village, I was, in fact, constantly working with a sense of the oral–aural. I wanted the reader to return with me to *Iraya*. I wanted their placid air assaulted, rippled with the inflections of my native tongue that is ornate and dense, the storytelling of daily life, and the spontaneous, in-your-face cry of grief of that total war.

> *Paghaya.* Deep weeping. *Pag-haaaa-ya.* The wail is in the middle syllable. For some, a stifled exhalation; for others, a near-scream, but always the breath travels the full distance from the groin to the gut, welling up to the throat. It is a weeping that is not about this or that moment. It has a history as long as the distance covered by that breath.
>
> [The gravedigger] Pay Inyo told me not to forget this lesson of weeping: "You have to weep not from the throat but from lower down, just as in singing, so you don't grow hoarse, because it takes forever to get to the last note. Remember, weeping is like singing and vice-versa, so everyone can sing, truly-truly, so let's hear you, [Estrella], take it from lower down, a lot of breath in there, and it doesn't run out, go on, sing!" he urged us in his strange logic.
>
> [...]
>
> If only the final tableau that our dead memorize and take to the other side is about trusting that infinite breath, then dying would be kinder. None of the agonizing finality, no *last* breath. Death would simply mean breathing at the other side, where the dead would be soothed by the thought that those who mourn them at home would not also expire, because there's a lot of breath down there, an inexhaustible well in the groin, and it does not run out. Weeping is like singing.[22]

In this excerpt from the novel, the gravedigger teaches the children how to sing, and, in fact, how to grieve. The breath must be retrieved a long way down from within the body, and the articulation of that breath must be sustained, so it can go further back into history. It might even reach the ears of the dead. Weeping, like singing, has both lightness and gravitas: it is irreverent and incantatory, individual and collective, spilling over and through borders, affirming life for both the living and the dead.

Introducing a book on 'the politics of mourning', David L. Eng and David Kazanjian write:

> Loss as a whole embraces this counterintuitive perspective. Instead of imputing to loss a purely negative quality, the essays in this collection

---

[22] Bobis, "Fish-Hair Woman" (unpublished novel), 107.

apprehend it as productive rather than pathological, abundant rather than lacking, social rather than solipsistic, militant rather than reactionary. [...] They insist that, if loss is known only by what remains of it, then the politics and ethics of mourning lie in the interpretation of what remains – how remains are produced and animated, how they are read and sustained.[23]

In *River, River*, I sing bodily remains.[24] There is the "Song of the Face" for the sixteen-year-old rebel and her mutilated body:

Here, here, my brow unkissed
Angog ... hadoka   (Brow ... kiss it
Mata ... piyunga   Eyes ... close them
Here, here, my eyes unclosing
Here, here, my cheeks too pale
Hear my lips bewail
Pisngi ... kolora   Cheeks...colour them
Ngabil ... kiputa   Lips ... close them)
Ay, Iraya!

The "Song of the Feet," while her grandmother rubs the dead feet with her hands, as if trying to remember something:

I am flat footed
I am honestly splayed
No airs about my toes
My nails are rimmed with earth
Packed in for sixteen years
My nails are black and broken
Long dead before I died

There is the "Song of Gems," when bones become precious stones. These songs are a 're-membering' of the dead. Body parts are animated, reconnected

---

[23] David L. Eng & David Kazanjian, "Introduction" to *Loss: The Politics of Mourning*, ed. Eng & Kazanjian (Los Angeles, London: U of California P, 2003): ix.

[24] The songs are from the stage script *River, River* (2009), but originally drawn from the novel: i.e. "Song of the Feet" was rephrased and reformatted by Bobis from her novel's prose into verse, then translated into Bikol. The Bikol verses became songs in the tradition of the *Pasyon*, and their English versions were later set to music in the Western tradition. Thus, in the creative production, loss and its remains are constantly in translation–transition between different languages and cultures; the storytelling and the story are never fixed, and the community of storytellers keeps growing.

by notes, restored by breath. Singing is, in fact, a return to the living body, also a rationale of the *Pasyon*, the story of Christ's death and resurrection. The suffering Christ, especially the Nazarene carrying the Cross, is much venerated by Filipinos because they identify with Him in their own suffering, in a country that has endured wars and militarism, poverty and political strife, until now. With this Christ, they hope for relief, for their own resurrection.

However, it is a fact that this foreign Christ has also made native Philippine gods disappear. They are the very early *desaparecidos*, in an era of colonial militarism (the Passion of Christ is itself a story of military brutality). In his book *Pasyon and Revolution*, Reynaldo Clemeña Ileto writes that, while Catholicism was imposed by the Spanish missionaries, the Philippines "creatively evolved its own brand of folk Christianity from which was drawn much of the language of anti-colonialism."[25] In the popular *Pasyon* text, Christ appears as

> a subversive figure [...] who attracts mainly the lowly, common people [the masses], draws them away from their families and their relations of subservience to the *maginoo* [the wealthy authority], and proclaims a brotherhood (*catipunan*) that will proclaim a new era of mankind.[26]

The *Katipunan* became the name of the anti-Spanish revolutionary movement.

As performance, the *Pasyon* evokes the traditional chanting of precolonial epics. While a *Pasyon* reading–singing session takes place around a Catholic altar in the house, the singing style employs indigenous rhythms. The Philippine composer Ramon Santos writes that its "musical structures used pre-Christian tunes embellished through the Christian communities, assuming a myriad of vernacular texts, tunes and styles of performance."[27] Clemeña Ileto cites a "particular style called *tagulaylay* [native dirge], in which a complete stanza is chanted in one breath with fancy curls and trills [that] hark back to pre-Spanish modes of singing."[28] So the Christ story, this tool of colonization, is made to flow back to the native vocal wellspring. The *Pasyon* that I used to

---

[25] Reynaldo Clemeña Ileto, *Pasyon and Revolution: Popular Movements in the Philippines, 1840–1910* (Quezon City, Manila: Ateneo de Manila U P, 1979): 16.

[26] Clemeña Ileto, *Pasyon and Revolution*, 16.

[27] Ramon Santos, "Constructing a National Identity Through Music," *Bulawan: Journal of Philippine Arts and Culture* 2 (2003), http://www.ncca.gov.ph/about-culture-and-arts/articles-on-c-n-a/article.php?i=60&subcat=13 (accessed 4 March 2009).

[28] Clemeña Ileto, *Pasyon and Revolution*, 21.

hear in our neighbourhood as a non-stop lament from Holy Thursday to Good Friday is at its heart a revolutionary cry. For these reasons, I use the *Pasyon* in the play *River, River*, which I consider as a militant dirge. In performance, I am *somehow* returned to my body and its native inscriptions, and I *somehow* recover my agency as a migrant writer in Australia. I qualify the statement with 'somehow' because I write in the West, and, to survive, I have to operate with the story-making rules and aesthetics recognizable by the West, thus re-fabricating my native sensibility. In a conference paper, I discuss the gate-keeping that happens in the literary industry, where the writer seemingly has to tell an Australian/'australianized' story in order to hurdle the gate.[29] Of course, the nation wants its literature to mirror the 'home experience' but, in multicultural Australia, home is not homogeneous. It is home for Aboriginal and migrant stories, and the mainstream literature, which is predominantly white. With migration, home keeps growing, shifting texture and shape. "*Pero yo ya no soy yo / ni mi casa es ya mi casa*" (But I am no longer I / nor is my house now my house). A fitting line, though re-contextualized, from Federico García Lorca's "Romance Sonámbulo" ("Somnambular Ballad"), from his well-known *Romancero Gitano / Gypsy Ballads* (1924–27).[30] All of us who are born in Australia, or who come from somewhere, or whose roots come from somewhere can no longer live in 'the original cultural home'; the concept of home and nation, and of story, are constantly renegotiated. But it seems that, for successful negotiation in the industry, 'the Australian story' must be aligned with the predominant white literature. As the Australian Broadcasting Corporation (ABC) Radio arts producer Jane Ulman remarked,

> It seems the source of a culture is not as interesting or as legitimate as the Australianization of that culture.[31]

---

[29] This argument, and the discussion in this paragraph and the one following, are key ideas in Bobis's keynote paper "'The Asian Conspiracy': Deploying Voice/Deploying Story" for the 2008 Conference of the Association of Australian Literature Studies, organized by the Asian-Australian Studies Research Network (AASRN). This paper will soon be published by *Australian Literary Studies*.

[30] Federico García Lorca, *Selected Poems*, tr. & intro. J.L. Gili (Harmondsworth: Penguin, 1960): 40.

[31] A remark made by Jane Ulman (producer of the radio version of the play *River, River* and sound director of the creative development of the stage version) when we were negotiating the artistic choices of the play with the arts centre.

"Getting into the literary gate is its own story of migration. When you migrate the body, you migrate its voice, its stories, its modes of story-making"[32] – that you might need to excise from the body or re-fashion and deploy as something like what the gate-keepers know, in order to complete a successful migration. I have been supported by generous Australians, who have listened not only to my stories but also to their context; thus, I have had some publication success. But story-making as a migrant writer in the West is a continuous struggle, a serenading / wooing of the guardians of the industry's gate. One has to keep fine-tuning one's literary voice to suit their ears. In *River, River*, a grandmother keeps rubbing the feet of the dead as if trying to remember something, then she offers these feet to the Australian journalist, saying, "Take them, take them." It is like the migrant writer trying to retrieve something – what is lost, 'dismembered' in migration that must be evoked by what remains, these feet, this story – hoping that both story and 'that something', that loss evoked, are accepted by Australia. This supplicant image is problematic. In a far-reaching parallel, I am reminded of Heidi Grunebaum and Yazir Henri's argument about South Africa's Truth and Reconciliation Commission (TRC): that it has co-opted testimonies of violence under apartheid and the recovery of bodies into the discourse of the nation:

> Requests to recover bodies in order to grieve, to begin to mourn, to ritualize death in a specific personal and socio-political context are reconfigured in media representations as a transcendental and symbolic expression of a shared common memory in the name of national reconciliation and nation-building. The body – whose dismembered materiality is evoked time and again – comes to function as an agent of its own elision.[33]

In performance, I retrieve bodies and a specific cultural experience with my own body, hoping to speak to our 'shared memory' of loss, our collective need to grieve. Bodily remains are visceral. It is harder to dismiss a body than a book. I find greater agency in orality. The storytelling theorists Norma Livo and Sandra Rietz write:

---

[32] "'The Asian Conspiracy': Deploying Voice / Deploying Story," *Australian Literary Studies* (forthcoming).

[33] Heidi Grunebaum & Yazir Henri, "Re-membering Bodies, Producing Histories: Holocaust Survivor Narrative and Truth and Reconciliation Commission Testimony," in *World Memory: Personal Trajectories in Global Time*, ed. Jill Bennett & Rosanne Kennedy (New York: Palgrave Macmillan, 2003): 112.

> Oral stories make noises, assume postures, and voice effects; they
> move, bend, and breathe. The oral story is soft and malleable. It yields
> to the pleasures and needs of the audience.[34]

Perhaps so, even with a culturally different audience like Australia. But in one
significant instance, I am proven wrong. It seems shared memory is possible
only if the body is re-inscribed by the nation's imaginary, which can erase the
body's original cultural markings. In 2008, I did a creative development of
River, River with a team of Australian and Filipino migrant artists, and a community choir of Filipino-Australian women. To familiarize the choir with the
play, we had storytelling sessions on its key images. We filmed these sessions. The cross-cultural and cross-genre work with the community was most
productive. Then the art centre hosting the creative development and possibly
producing the play began interrogating it at meetings that became perplexing
and quite distressing. The centre argued that the play was not contemporary
and cutting-edge, so we should use the film footage of the women telling
stories in Australia. These films in contemporary Australia would make the
play more cutting-edge and would avert the possible audience perception that
it is "simply folklore." I could not believe my ears. First, it is not folklore but
a metaphor, a mythopoeic creation. And what if, indeed, it is folklore? Is it
then a lesser narrative? I stressed the obvious: this story is not set in Australia
but in a militarized village in the Philippines, where shadow play (an old village game that I wanted to employ) is the more logical theatrical device
artistically than film – and, of course, we should use the filmed storytelling in
Australia, but in another art work, perhaps a multi-media installation (or a
documentary film) on the artistic process. I argued the case of the play, trying
very hard not to sound like the difficult, precious artist – these were my pat-
rons, I wanted a production. In one conciliatory discussion, I was likened to a
young horse that has to be reined in. When I did a double take, I was apo-
logetically reassured that the metaphor was not meant to offend, because, in
fact, a young horse is a beautiful thing. Finally, I had to give up on this colonizing framework of artistic production. I wrote to the arts centre, clarifying
their brief, whether, in fact, they want me to tell an Australian story, then I
raised this question: Does this mean, then, that the embodied stories from the
first home that migrants bring to Australia – the old stories that migrants use
to negotiate Australia, are *not* of Australia, and are thus not worthy of being

---

[34] Norma Livo & Sandra A. Rietz, *Storytelling Process and Practice* (Boulder:
Colorado Libraries, 1986): 15.

told on their own? And the only thing that can legitimize these stories is the obvious Australian landscape/experience?[35]

They have never answered me; until now, complete silence. In the midst of this stress I found out that the rebel commander whom I interviewed more than a decade ago, who told me his war and love stories, had been shot, assassinated by gunmen zipping past on a motorcycle. Absurd timing: a similar mode of assassination (of a journalist this time) is the opening of my novel *The Solemn Lantern Maker*, which is about the new and ongoing total war in Mindanao, the Philippines' Muslim south, waged within the framework of the global war on terror.[36] This book was launched so close to that stressful negotiation, and to my finding out about the shooting. Here were connected and conflicting stories that confounded me. I could not stop weeping. It seemed as if all the bodies that I had been story-told ten years ago were again laid out before me. As if to say: We cannot allow these to be co-opted, to disappear.

The current performance version of *River, River*[37] has been adjusted and abridged because of production constraints. I 'sing-shuttle' to and from my Bikol dialect and English, from the *Pasyon* to the music of the Australian composer Sarah de Jong. Her process of setting the English text to song was a far cry from the attitude of the arts centre. She and I visited the home of the Bitabaras, the Filipino-Australian family who sang my Bikol text in their *Pasyon* style, and the composer *listened*. She worked with the Bitabaras's notes and chanting style, and the emotional texture of the *Pasyon*. "This [process] made it possible for me to compose music which grows so easily out of the *Pasyon* and the text when performed."[38] Each time I sing, I marvel at how fluid the breath can be, a river between two musical traditions. In the play, the singing and storytelling happen around a Catholic altar and a music stand, another 'altar' for chamber performances. I negotiate between the private rituals from my first home and the demands of the wider public arena. *Namamangka sa dalawang ilog* (sailing-balancing in two rivers), as we say in

---

[35] The play's creative development is discussed extensively in "'The Asian Conspiracy': Deploying Voice/Deploying Story."

[36] For more stories/discourses on trauma, see also my novel *The Solemn Lantern Maker* (Sydney: Pier 9/Murdoch, 2008), and my essay "Hush, I know a story you don't know," *Wet Ink* 13 (2009), on the novel's research and writing.

[37] The performance is the Spain premiere of *River, River*, (Jaca: Palacio de Congresos, 27 March 2009).

[38] Sarah de Jong, email correspondence (28 February 2009).

Pilipino. I 'play militarism', and the audience plays with me – *play* in the sense that we conspire in momentarily 'living the story' while knowing that it is mediated by artifice. And hopefully in our bodies, we also *play against* fixed cultural borders, which are as much of a human artifice. Despite our continuous reinstating of difference, because we have to in this current climate, we must also keep affirming the resonances, our shared human experiences, which are as life-saving in these times. Understanding differences allows us to recognize the plurality of stories, while collectivity inspires kinship, perhaps compassion. However, differentiation and collectivization have also been used as tools of discrimination and violence against the 'Other', as anyone different from us is regarded as lesser and thus should be subsumed under our 'much better' narrative. There will always be tension between differentiation and collectivization, which for some are irreconcilable. A Chinese student from the testimony class of the trauma theorist Shoshana Felman reflects on this tension. What Felman's student arrived at, after hearing the testimony of a child survivor, is most reassuring:

> In an odd sort of way, I feel a strange sort of collectivity has been formed in the class. This, of course, is a most frightening thing [...] my mode of interaction with those whom I do not know, has always been one of radical differentiation, rather than of collectivization. My autonomy has been rendered precarious, even fragile. Somehow, though, I have managed to survive, whole and a bit fragmented at the same time; the same, but decidedly altered.[39]

The utterance of the Chinese student is her own story, as original and authentic (and valid) as, yet different from, the testimony of the child survivor. So, then – where is the wellspring? It is in the mouth, in the moment of articulation that resonates with and at the same time reconstrues other and multiple moments of articulation. But then, which mouth gets air-time and ear-time – the space to speak and be heard?

In *Four Corners*, an Australian television programme, the journalist Matthew Carney reported on the Taliban violence in Pakistan and the government response, which in one instance was to 'clean up' Bajaur, allegedly a Taliban refuge, thus displacing 300,000 people. Mohammed Zahir, a Bajaur resident, tells this story in a refugee camp:

---

[39] Shoshana Felman & Doris Laub, *Testimony: Crises of Witnessing in Literature, Psycholanalysis, and History* (New York: Routledge, 1992): 55.

"In our village, there was my neighbour Haji, a good man. He, his wife, daughter and grandchild were all killed by an airstrike. Two months later they found the ear of the grandchild in the rubble, the whole family, the entire village gathered to look at this ear. They were crying and grieving."[40]

Let us look at this ear and listen with it – and try to retrieve all the body parts in all the conflict zones of the world and through history. These are also about our own mortality. But, of course, the business of dying and getting violently killed are entirely different. I recall the dying man's wish in García Lorca's "Romance Sonámbulo" ("Somnambular Ballad"):

> Compadre, quiero morir
> *decentemente en mi cama.*
> *De acero, si puede ser,*
> *con las sábanas de holanda.*[41]

> (Friend, I want to die
> decently in my bed.
> Made of steel, if possible,
> with sheets of fine Holland.)

There is hardly any good or easy death, but when our time comes, we all hope for a decent passing with the comfort and particular rituals of home.

In March 2009, the attack against Sri Lankan cricketers by Pakistani terrorists dominated the Australian headlines. Cricket is prime in the nation's imaginary, so there was shock, outrage. Understandably, but I wonder if among the television viewers there was as much passion over that child's ear in the rubble, when, in a moment of storytelling, it was as if we were all enjoined to look at the ear with "the entire village." When we look at the daily conflicts and losses around us, what are we looking at? What are we looking for? What do we wish to retrieve? What do we take home with us? What do we venerate on our altars? The old gravedigger in the novel *Fish-Hair Woman* has seen too much violence, payback, and counter-violence, so he gives this radical advice:

> "*Magdara ki balde sa danaw nin sakit*
> *Siguraduhang ruloho ini*

---

[40] Matthey Carney, "Pakistan on the Brink," in *Four Corners*, Australian Broadcasting Corporation (23 February 2009) , http://www.abc.net.au/4corners/content/2008/s2499266.htm (accessed 3 March 2009).

[41] Federico García Lorca, *Selected Poems*, 40.

Magdara ki balde sa hararumon na danaw
Iwalat mo duman ini."
"Take a pail to the pool of grief
Make sure it has holes
Take a pale to the deepest pool
And leave it there."

This is the wake of the world: each of us standing around a pool
that we have collected for centuries. We are looking in with our little
pails. We try to fathom the depth of the pool until our eyes are sore.
We try to find only what is ours. We wring our hands. Ay, how to go
home with only my own undiluted pail of grief? To wash my rice with
or my babies, to drink? But the water is my dead kin, an enemy, a
beloved, a stranger, a friend, someone who loved me or broke my
heart. How to tell them apart? How to cleave water from water?

Don't query the water. Leave your pail and go home. The rice will
still boil, the baby will crawl and walk, and you will drink your thirst
dry, but without the burden of history.[42]

But the villageers protest: How dare you erase our stories, thus negating our
right to redress? The collectivization of loss can lead to further loss of justice
in specific lives. Perhaps loss is an almost impossible pool to negotiate in, so
the Fish-Hair Woman returns us to the individual heart, and leaves it to resolve this query in its own good time:

How much can the heart accommodate? … Only four chambers, but
with infinite space like memory, where there is room even for those
whom we do not love.[43]

WORKS CITED

Bobis, Merlinda. "'The Asian Conspiracy': Deploying Voice/Deploying Story," *Aus-
tralian Literary Studies* (forthcoming).
——. "Fish-Hair Woman," in *White Turtle* (North Melbourne: Spinifex, 1999): 10–23.
——. "Fish-Hair Woman" (unpublished novel, forthcoming with Spinifex).
——. "Hush, I know a story you don't know," *Wet Ink* 13 (2009): 10–15.
——. Interview transcripts on the Philippines' Total War 1987–89 (Bikol, 1997).

---

[42] "Fish-Hair Woman" (unpublished novel), 226.
[43] "Fish-Hair Woman" (unpublished novel), 111.

——. *A Novel-in-Waiting: Creative Research: Towards Writing Fiction* (Manila: The Centre for Intercultural Studies, 2004).

——. *River, River*, Spain premiere performance for the international Conference "Between the 'Urge to Know' and the 'Need to Deny': Ethics and Trauma in Contemporary Narrative in English," Universidad de Zaragoza (Jaca: Palacio de Congresos, 27 March 2009).

——. *The Solemn Lantern Maker* (Sydney: Pier 9/Murdoch, 2008).

——. "Storying: Dream and Deployment," *Social Identities: Journal for the Study of Race, Nation and Culture* 15.1 (2009): 85–94.

Carney, Matthew. "Pakistan on the Brink," in *Four Corners*, Australian Broadcasting Corporation (23 February 2009), http://www.abc.net.au/4corners/content/2008 /s2499266.htm (accessed 3 March 2009).

Clemeña Ileto, Reynaldo. *Pasyon and Revolution. Popular Movements in the Philippines, 1840–1910* (Quezon City, Manila: Ateneo de Manila U P, 1979).

Committee to Protect Journalists (C P J). "Marked for Death: Five Most Murderous Countries for Journalists," *Special Report: C P J New York* (2 May 2005), http://cpj .org/reports/2005/05/murderous-05.php (accessed 3 March 2009).

De Guzman, Arnel, & Tito Craige. "Counter-Insurgency War in the Philippines and the Role of the U S," *Bulletin of Concerned Asian Scholars* 23 (1991): 38–47.

De Jong, Sarah. Email correspondence (8 February 2009).

Decenteno, Edwin T. *Rehab: Psychological Rehabilitation for Social Transformation. Some Programs and Concepts* (Manila: Bukal, 1997).

Eng, David L., & David Kazanjian, ed. *Loss: The Politics of Mourning* (Berkeley: U of California P, 2003).

Felman, Shoshana, & Doris Laub. *Testimony: Crises of Witnessing in Literature, Psychoanalysis, and History* (New York: Routledge, 1992).

García Lorca, Federico. *Selected Poems*, tr. J.L. Gili (Harmondsworth: Penguin, 1960).

Grunebaum, Heidi, & Yazir Henri. "Re-membering Bodies, Producing Histories: Holocaust Survivor Narrative and Truth and Reconciliation Commission Testimony," in *World Memory: Personal Trajectories in Global Time*, ed. Jill Bennett & Rosanne Kennedy (New York: Palgrave Macmillan, 2003): 101–18.

Herzfeld, Michael. *Cultural Intimacy: Social Poetics in the Nation-State* (New York: Routledge, 1997).

Jackson, Michael. *The Politics of Storytelling: Violence, Transgression and Intersubjectivity* (Denmark: Museum Tusculanum Press, 2006).

Livo, Norma J., & Sandra A. Rietz. *Storytelling Process and Practice* (Boulder: Colorado Libraries, 1986).

McIndoe, Alastair. "Reporters at Risk," *The Straits Times Blogs* (24 January 2009), http://blogs.straitstimes.com/2009/1/24/reporters-at-risk (accessed 3 March 2009).

Pe-Pua, Rogelia. Email correspondence (1 March 2009).

Santos, Paz Verdades M. "Centre of Gravity: The New People's Army in Bikol (A Case Study)," in *Primed and Purposeful: Armed Groups and Human Security Efforts in the Philippines*, ed. Soliman Santos, Jr., Paz Verdades M. Santos et al. (Geneva & Manila: South-South Network for Non-State Armed Group Engagement and the Small Arms Survey, 2010): 43–57.

Santos, Ramon. "Constructing a National Identity Through Music," *Bulawan: Journal of Philippine Arts and Culture* 2 (2003), http://www.ncca.gov.ph/about-culture-and-arts/articles-on-c-n-a/article.php?i=60&subcat=13 (accessed 4 March 2009).

Poetics of Dislocation

Trauma, Language, Memory

MEENA ALEXANDER

I. Migrations of Sense

I WOULD LIKE TO THINK about poetry, migration, and trauma, about memory and how it flashes up for us in the face of danger, about the work of the imagination and how it allows us to dwell in the world. What does it mean to belong in a violent world? It is a question that keeps coming back to me. I ask myself how forgetfulness is linked to the condition of migration, and how traumatic knowledge marks the transitional life that migrants often make up for themselves. Contemporary writing exists in a vital mesh of filiation. The international movements of migration and settlement, as well as the existence of internal exiles, those who feel displaced as minorities within their own land, have created a pulsing, throbbing net of meanings within which the poet can exist, within which she tries to make sense. What becomes of the past, in such an existence, and what of traumatic awareness with its abrupt flashing up of sense?

In *The Art of Memory*, the Renaissance scholar Frances Yates begins with a reflection on Cicero's *De Oratore*.[1] She tells us how the poet Simonides of Ceos was able to remember the precise places at which guests at a banquet

---

[1] Frances A. Yates, *The Art of Memory* (1966; Chicago: U of Chicago P, 2001): 1–2.

were seated. The banquet hall suddenly collapsed, but the poet, who was miraculously called out, was able to return and identify the missing, naming the dead so their relatives could claim them for burial. Poetry in place as a powerful elegiac force, a functional force in our shared world, and memory as aftermath. The tale of Simonides makes us think of this. For Cicero, the art of memory was essential and stood as a guiding force both for life and for rhetoric. And for memory to work, clear arrangement was essential: the arrangement of place.

> He inferred that persons desiring to train this faculty (of memory) must select places and form mental images of the things they wish to remember and store those images in the places, so that the order of the places will preserve the order of the things.[2]

What happens, we might ask, when we confront loss so that, rather than following through to the order of things preserved in memory, the rupture of place forces us to confront the radical dislocation of things, images, even sensations? When the internal map of place is torn, we are faced not with fixed settlements but pinhole scatterings, dismemberments, a "line of flight," several lines of flight? I draw the potent phrase from the reflections of Deleuze and Guattari,[3] that mad, utterly brilliant philosopher-couple, the two speaking here, as it were, in one breath. I think of cyberspace. How to make sense of Cicero's mnemonic – the order of places securing the order of things – in a world that faces the plethora of postings in cyberspace? In order to enter that zone we must finally let go of the embodied distances that place grants. But what does this do to what we commonly think of as the past? I think of cyberspace, which is no place at all, as akin to the dark imaginary out of which poems come, their rhythms, their discrete music punctuating the inner life. And perhaps even more persistent for me is the way in which the flashing up of disembodied messages provides a curious fit with my migratory life. The life I have lived is lost to me when I travel to another town or city. I have to learn a new way of dressing, of figuring out buses and cabs and trains, of fronting the world. The table where I once sat to write, the window out of which I gazed, the tea or the glass of wine I enjoyed, all this is cast aside in a

---

[2] Quoted by Frances A. Yates, *The Art of Memory*, 2.

[3] Gilles Deleuze & Félix Guattari, *A Thousand Plateaus: Capitalism and Schizophrenia*, tr. & intro. Brian Massumi (*Mille plateaux: Capitalisme et schizophrénie*, 1980; Minneapolis: U of Minnesota P, 1987): 24–25.

newness without hold, and all that I am seems poised precariously on the rim of a future which has come into being quite precisely by undercutting the past. So memory becomes virtuality: other lives, other places lived in, a shimmering back-story to a radically unstable present. We are faced with at least two ways of touching the past. One ties us with silken bonds to the densities of ordinary life. The other chops and scatters our identity in the air, bits and pieces capable of ceaseless rearrangement. In our lives, as in our poems, we need to play both rhythms, stitch ourselves into history through two kinds of music, one and the other coming together to reveal the ordinary densities of our lives as well as the curving lines of our poems, lines that live in a space underwritten by the imagination, *cire perdu* to the sensorium of our days. But how is this sensorium ruptured or, indeed, constituted by violent events?

II. Dark September

I have poems that were composed in the aftermath of two Septembers, one and the other making a figure of eight, time torqued into a loop, space severs – September 11, 2001, in New York City and September 11, 2002 when I was in Ahmedabad, visiting relief camps for the survivors of ethnic violence. In many ways, the book *Raw Silk* that I published in 2004 was torn out of me; the poems scratched themselves into the palimpsest of my days and nights, needing to be written out. Later, in arranging the manuscript, I was troubled by what it might mean for a book of poems to draw so deeply on narratives of violence, yet there was no way out if I was going to be true to myself, by which I mean true to that inchoate, utterly voiceless subjectivity that lies buried within, too deep for tears. Yet it is with this part of ourselves that we reach out to others, and in this bodily reaching, lit by the power of the senses, we are allowed to remember. In Manhattan, after 9/11, I wrote in my journal:

> The devastation is enormous, mounds of rubble and metal and glass and innocent lives blown to tiny bits. It rains and the leaves are very green. Elsewhere by Ground Zero rain mixes with ash and makes the rescue work very difficult. This is our floating life, this peril, this sweet island with its southern tip burning. When I was a child I saw the sea burn ...

I then wrote a narrative, all in the present tense. It was what I needed to do.

After the planes hit the towers and they burst into flames and fell, rock started to burn in all its crevices, too, a slow burn through the veins of the

earth where gases leaked out and caught fire, and wires and fuselage and plas-
tics and metal and bone and hair started to mass and fuse in a sortilege that
this island of Manhattan had never seen before. Two days after September 11
there were clouds massed in the sky in New York City and then it started to
rain. The leaves are very green outside my window. Leaves of linden and
birch and, in the distance, across a stone wall, the Hudson river. The garden in
between the two apartment blocks is still sweet, at the edge of autumn, over-
grown, plants gone to seed. At night I dreamt of a flash of fire, a plane with
fire from its wings, bursting apart the bricks, then vanishing in a puff of
smoke. This keeps repeating. The plane is not coming through our building
yet, but, rather, through the one next to ours, a building, exactly like this, with
which we share a garden. In the dream I am floating, above my own body. I
wake up, sit bolt upright in shock as I start to remember. I know I cannot keep
up prose any more. I put aside the prose piece I was working on, a piece about
childhood I did not want to be swallowed up in the past, with so much molten
and flowing all around, the world I love in turmoil. I needed to bear witness to
what is now and the poem will allow me to do what I can. I make tiny notes
on scraps of paper. The lyric poem will allow me to catch the edginess of
things, the sharp nervosity, the flaming, falling buildings. I must work back
from the pressure of the present into the past, for that is the only way I will
reach into the real. And when someone questions me about this I say: In all
my work place is layered on place to make a palimpsest of sense. That is the
kind of art I make.

But the very indices of place have been altered by traumatic awareness. It
seems to me that the lyric poem is a place of extreme silence, which is protected from the world. To make a lyric poem you have to enter into a dream
state. Yet, at the same time, almost by virtue of that disconnect, it becomes a
very intense place to reflect on the world. The day I went into the university
to teach my class I started a cycle of three elegies for the dead. I called them
"Aftermath," "Invisible City," and the last "Pitfire." I used couplets, making
twelve lines for each poem, and somehow the form helped me to crystallize
and think through without fear. Here are the first two poems; they need to
stand side by side.

AFTERMATH	INVISIBLE CITY
There is an uncommon light in the sky	Sweet and bitter smoke stains the air
Pale petals are scored into stone.	The verb stains has a thread torn out

I want to write of the linden tree
That stoops at the edge of the river

But its leaves are filled with insects
With wings the color of dry blood.

At the far side of the river Hudson
By the southern tip of our island

A mountain soars, a torrent of sentences
Syllables of flame stitch the rubble

An eye, a lip, a cut hand blooms
Sweet and bitter smoke stains the sky.

(New York City,
13–18 September 2001)

I step out to the linden grove
Bruised trees are the color of sand.

Something uncoils and blows at my feet
Sliver of mist? Bolt of beatitude?

A scrap of what was once called sky?
I murmur words that come to me

Tall towers, twin towers I used to see.
A bloody seam of sense drops free.

By Liberty Street, on a knot of rubble
In altered light, I see a bird cry.

(New York City,
17 October–3 November 2001)

While making my poems, I kept walking down to Ground Zero, as close as I could get, making returns, a pilgrimage, the site a graveyard for thousands, the stench of burning flesh and wires. On one trip down there, as I walked past Liberty Street I was struck by the extreme youth of the soldier guarding the perimeter, a young lad, freckled, fresh-faced. Behind him the shell of Tower 2, against which an ancient patriarch was getting photographed. Small children screaming in delight at pigeons, a rescue worker, hands on his own throat, face sunk with tiredness, his gas-mask at his hip. I made a third poem as part of this cycle and called it "Pitfire."

PITFIRE

In altered light I hear a bird cry.
By the pit, tor of metal, strut of death.

Bird song yet. *Liturgie de cristal.*
Flesh in fiery pieces, mute sediments of love.

Shall a soul visit her mutilated parts?
How much shall a body be home?

Under these burnt balconies of air,
Autumnal duty that greets us.

At night, a clarinet solo I put on:
Bird song pitched to a gorge, a net of cries.

Later a voice caught on a line:
'See we've touched the bird's throat.'

(New York City, 20 November–5 December 2001)

The clarity of the poem needs to be sharp, facetted as broken glass. It must pick up the multitudinous cries of the world that we are.

There was a meeting of a newly established Asian/Asian-American Research Institute. I had been asked to serve on the governing board and there was a meeting at the Graduate Centre. As I recall, it was barely a week after September 11. But now that I think of it again, surely that meeting was postponed and we met in October. It was the sort of occasion to which I would wear a sari without thinking twice. But now something nagged at me. Two of my South Asian students had encountered trouble wearing non-Western dress, men yelling, one throwing a paperback. A friend of mine who had gone out one evening in Boston told me on the phone how a man had yelled and spat at her. There was a zone of suspicion that was extending over Asians, South Asians, brown people who looked like they could be Arabs. I wanted to pick my battles. In all the grief and torment of a city under siege, I wanted some control over the small things of life. If it could be dangerous to look different, it made no sense to deliberately stick out. My daughter had told me how the cousin of an Iranian friend of hers, a young woman with long black hair, had had to face a man in the subway who brandished scissors and cut off some of her hair. Immigrants were being swept up and put in detention with no charges lodged against them. I needed to save my energies for writing, and I was writing a great deal of poetry. I rolled up my sari in a manner that would not crease it, set it carefully in a plastic bag that I lodged in the centre of my book-bag. In the fourth floor Ladies Room, I slipped out of my slacks and put on my sari. I watched the silk on the tiled floor and stared at my face in the mirror. How dark I looked, unmistakably Indian. I needed to think through my fear. Later, as I made my poem, I heard Kabir, the medieval poet–saint, singing to me, giving me the courage to live my life. This is the poem I made.

KABIR SINGS IN A CITY OF BURNING TOWERS

What a shame
they scared you so
you plucked your sari off,
crushed it into a ball

then spread it
on the toilet floor.
Sparks from the towers
fled through the weave of silk.

With your black hair
and sun dark skin
you're just a child of earth.
Kabir the weaver sings:

O men and dogs
in times of grief
our rolling earth
grows small.

I had written my poems quickly, in order to survive. But after writing there came a time of fragmentation, being torn apart in so many directions: the fear here on this island, the condition of our lives, not knowing what could strike next, fire, pestilence – that bitty white powder filled with anthrax spores (a floor of the building where I teach, right next to the Empire State building, was shut down for a while); and on the other side of the globe in Afghanistan, the terrible bombardment, stones ground down, children starving, women in burkhas fleeing. Both are real, disjoined in space, they coexist in time, in a molten time.

As a child I had lived on the borders of war, moving back and forth across the Indian Ocean between Kerala and Khartoum in the Sudan. In Sudan there was a civil war raging. On the way to India we often stopped in Aden, in what is now Yemen. There were British Tommies on the rocks, and Yemeni fighters hidden by the broken walls. More recently, in India, in the last few years there has been the rise of a fascist Hindu movement and ethnic violence and now, with Pakistan, the fear of war. This has been part of my personal history and has left a mark on my poetry and my prose. How can these violent versions of the real that cut into memory be translated into art? Art in a time of trauma, a necessary translation, "Fragments of a vessel that are to be glued together," Walter Benjamin said in his luminous essay "The Task of the Translator."[4] But what if the paste shows, the seams, the fractures? It seemed

---

[4] Walter Benjamin, "The Task of the Translator" (1923), in *Selected Writings 1913–26*, vol. 1, ed. Marcus P. Bullock & Michael W. Jennings (Cambridge MA: Harvard UP): 260.

to me then, at the edge of a city blown up at its southern tip, that the work of art must use the frame of the real, translating a script almost illegible, a code of traumatic recovery.

There is a zone of radical illiteracy out of which we translate our selves in order to appear, in order to be in place. A zone to which words do not attach, a realm syntax flees. A zone that cannot recognize the moorings of place, sensuous densities of location, coordinates of compass and map. Sometimes, in the act of composition, I have felt that I was translating from a place of no words – 'translate' in the early sense of the word, meaning to transport across a border. An art of negativity, translation seems to me akin to the labour of poetic composition in precisely this: it reaches beneath the hold of a given syntax, beneath the rocks and stones and trees of discernible place in order to make sense.

III. Notebooks

I have kept notebooks ever since I was a teenager growing up both in India and in the Sudan. I bought two new black notebooks with spiral bindings. In one, I pasted in the 9/11 poems. In the other I pasted out the pages I was printing of the cycle of Gujarat poems I had started writing after a 2002 visit to the relief camps there, camps that housed the survivors of ethnic carnage. All of the poems, including the cycle "Letters to Gandhi," had come in an overflow of emotion that kept me from sleep. I needed the security of a boundary, covers within which I could turn pages and take flight from poem to poem. I had to move back and forth between the poems to make a deeply personal sense out of that chaos. A week or two later, I started a third notebook, which I labelled "Raw Silk," and in that book I set drafts of three poems which also came to me at great speed, a wind-smashed bouquet, pain and grief at the destruction of war, joy in the face of beauty that can sustain us. Some of the images that came to me echoed those that had blossomed in my head in the days and nights of a Delhi winter when I sat in quiet in a patch of sunlight brooding on what I had seen and heard in the relief camps in Gujarat. So, into my second notebook I pressed the images that came to me, through layer after layer of sense. Running my fingers through this notebook, I see lines I have written in my squiggly hand. They are lines that tell of how I had tried to make a pure lyric out of the title poem of my new book *Raw Silk*; but, without my knowing it, a border was crossed.

What happens in my poetic production is that, almost without knowing it, the violence of history enters in. Creeps in through the back door, as it were, enters my consciousness, so that in the poem "Raw Silk," which will be the title poem of the new book, I started off by wanting to write a simple poem about a scrap of raw silk that my mother gave me from her mother's sari (and about the mulberry patch my grandmother planted after her return from China) and, instead, into that entered the soldiers, the tear gas, the grenades of a childhood in Sudan, just as no doubt in my daughter's consciousness the war (now), the bomb drills in school, all enter in.

So it was that, in writing the poem once again, I used lines that I emailed back to myself from my office. I would then retrieve them at home and work with them. The department printer was not working and I needed typed hard copy, not the edgy scrawl that passes for my handwriting. At home, opening the email with the half-finished lines, I sensed that I was in search of an answer to the oldest of questions – Who are you? The lyric is a response. The American bombardment of Iraq had just started and I searched on the internet for lines by Enheduanna, the great poet of Mesopotamia, the first poet in recorded history. Afterwards, I could not bear the windowless office I had been given, and so I walked up to the eighth floor atrium and opened my eyes and on a high wall saw the Dove of Tanna, Frank Stella's piece filled with light. As I sat in my office and wrote, I thought of bombs that burst roofs and walls, a woman poet who did not have the luxury of sitting at her desk and writing, a poet flung out of her home, forced to cross the shattered street. This is some part of the email I sent myself. There is in it, I think, some impatience with myself and also some real awareness of the limits of the poem.

> Friday March 07, 2003, 4:26 pm
> Dear Meena,
> You are not so far today. Why must you email these messages, as if pen and paper were hard to find, or a printer. On the Dove of Tanna the artist cut up bits of aluminum and painted them over into the dove's tail, the arrow's flight, the green bough that signifies the lifting of the waters... While you're at it why not think of the door you have opened, perhaps portal would be a better word, onto the layering of fragile places whose petals spurt scents from Paris and Istanbul and Rome. Or blood spurting from the cut aorta. Wrapping it in raw silk will do no good …

And yet, what if it is not wrapping in raw silk but, rather, laying the silk out so that, in tatters and tears, the eyes of a weaver stare out at you. I am thinking now of Kabir and the poem I had written in 2001 – "Kabir Sings in the City of Burning Towers." In making a poem, I work back from the pressure of the present into the past, for that is the only way I will reach into the real. And when someone questions me about this I say: in all my work, place is layered on place to make a palimpsest of sense. That is the kind of art I make. Yet the very indices of place have been altered by traumatic awareness. It seems to me that the lyric poem is a form of extreme silence, which is protected from the world.To make a lyric poem, I have to enter into a dream-state. But at the same time, almost by virtue of that disconnect, it becomes a very intense location in which to reflect on the world.

IV. Gujarat 2002

On 11 September 2002, exactly a year after that very difficult time in Manhattan, I found myself in Ahmedabad in Gujarat, India. The city of Ahmedabad lies on the banks of the river Sabarmati. It is where Gandhi, the father of Indian independence, the creator of non-violent action, had chosen to set his ashram. In the clear morning light, in the company of a dear friend, I crossed the river over the main bridge. My friend and I found a decrepit three-wheeler that dropped us off in Shahpur, a poor neighbourhood. With the help of a Dalit activist – 'Dalit' is a term of resistance used by those who were previously called 'Untouchable' – we made our way to a large relief camp, Quraish Hall, that in better times had been used for weddings. Bare bones telling of the back-story. In February 2002, a Muslim mob had allegedly torched a train carrying Hindu activists and fifty-nine people lost their lives. The aftermath of Godhra – a single word suffices to summon up that tragedy – was carefully orchestrated by right-wing Hindu groups. The plundering and burning of Muslim properties, the killing and mutilation of men, and the mass rape of women all showed signs of meticulous planning. As we sat, two women in our cotton kurtas on the low wooden stools in the courtyard, the people pressed around us. They were the survivors of the killings in Naroda Patiya, a neighborhood of Ahmedabad. Svati explained that she was collecting information for the PUDR, the People's Union for Democratic Rights, as part of their project of documenting human rights violations. "I don't have anything material to give you," Svati said, "but please tell us what happened." People pressed forward. There was a terrible hunger to tell their stories. Afterwards, I could not sleep, hearing those voices. A thin, elderly woman in an orange sari told us how her daughter-in-law Kausar Banu, nine months pregnant, was set upon by armed Hindu men, her belly ripped open, the unborn child pierced by a sword, thrown into the fire. A small dark man, Bashir Yusuf, had survived by hiding under dead bodies. He showed us the marks on his back from knife blades where the Hindutva men had attacked him. He had to run for his life from the Civil Hospital – "You are a Muslim," a doctor said to him, "I won't help you live." Then a tiny child, barely two, was raised up in the arms of a thin woman. The child's name was Yunus. He was dressed in a torn green shirt, and the woman who was carrying him and said she was his mother turned him around and lifted his shirt and we saw the burn marks on his bottom, where the skin had scarred, the marks stretching over his tiny back, making it look like a raw fruit, terribly disfigured. He had been thrown into a fire and someone had pulled him out and rescued him. The child had enormous eyes and kept staring at me. Even now, back in this wintry city, I see his eyes staring into mine.

I cannot forget that, when people desperate for help approached the Sabarmati Ashram, those who were in charge of the ashram told them they could not keep them safe, closed the doors on them. Now, in this season of difficulty, I felt the peace inside Gandhi's dwelling. I stopped, touched the walls of the small whitewashed kitchen I have always held in memory. Low shelves, windows, small receptacles for food. There was peace here, but at what cost was it maintained? At the threshold I shut my eyes. I saw the Mahatma, in his pale loin-cloth. He tore open the doors of the house, he strode down the path under the neem trees. He cried out in words that were hard to understand. He leapt into the river, a flash of flesh and cloth. In bold, unhurried strokes he swam across the Sabarmati. Then, just as he was, Gandhi walked into the burning city. That afternoon, as always, there were green parrots. I saw them as I walked down the steps of Gandhi's house. They flitted through the trees, into the holes in the outer wall of the ashram. The walls went down all the way to the river. On the other side of the river, innocent human beings had been killed and raped, watched the parrots disappear into their hiding holes. Slowly it grew dark, then darker. The river, with the smoke-stacks on the other side, kept flowing on.

Later I travelled to Delhi, where I was to give a reading at the Sahitya Akademi, the National Academy of Letters. On my first day in the city, I went to Bengali Market to buy fruit. I had a great longing to taste pomegranate, and this was the right season for them. I felt that before I read my poems I had to eat this fruit with its hard skin, its brilliant red seeds. Although pomegranates are available in many parts of India, somehow I associated them with Delhi, with its red sandstone buildings and brilliant winter skies. Entering the market, I thought I heard the voice I had heard in my head in the days and nights after my return from Gujarat. It was the voice of the great Russian poet Anna Akhmatova, who, in her "Instead of a Preface" to the poem "Requiem," describes how she stands in a winter street in Leningrad, in a long line of people in front of a prison, and a woman recognizes her, a woman with blue lips who comes over to the poet and whimpers "Can you describe this?" and Akhmatova replies "I can."[5] One draws strength from the great ones who have gone before, and as I stood in that Delhi street, Gujarat already another place, far away, I heard Akhmatova's words. And I saw in front of me, wrapped up in a khadi shawl and wools, a dear friend. He was leaning forward in an autorickshaw, a three-wheeler that was about to start. The autorickshaw was parked in front of a tiny storefront clinic, one of many in Delhi that dispense medicines and basic health-care to urban dwellers. This clinic had a sign in it in big red letters that caught my eye: Dr. Gandhi's Clinic. I went forward and embraced my friend, whom I had not seen for many years. I wanted to tell him about my visit to Gujarat, but just then there was no time. That had to wait for later. He was Ramu, Gandhiji's grandson. Many months later, back in New York, when I wrote my poems, his voice and figure entered in, restoring time, restoring me to place.

The present is not another country. It is where we live. When I started to write the Gujarat poems, I knew I had to rely on beauty. Otherwise the rawness of what had happened, the bloody bitter mess, would be too much to take. The poem can take a tiny jot of the horror but evoke grief, restore tenderness, so that we are not thrust back into an abject silence. As if we have heard and seen nothing. After the poems were completed, I sent them to a friend at *The Times of India* and he in turn sent them on to a friend at *The Hindu* with the thought that they might publish them on the Sunday literary page. The editor at *The Hindu*, who is also a poet, wrote back to me. First he spoke of how, for many years, he had followed my work, then he wrote a few lines about my poems that made me stop in my tracks:

> Dear Meena, I am frankly amazed by the poems provoked by the pogrom and its aftermath in Gujarat, by the way they weave terror and disturbance with beauty and elegance of form in the way that sometimes

---

[5] Anna Akhmatova, "Requiem," in *The Complete Poems of Anna Akhmatova* (Boston MA: Zephyr, 2000): 384.

makes people who are distrustful of the claims of art suspicious of
poetry and its intentions.

He was a poet himself and I valued his words, but what did he mean by the
distrust of beauty? He had touched a nerve, and I wrote back the same day, 18
March 2003, by email:

> Dear,
> Beauty and terror – we must speak of all that sometime. I needed beau-
> ty there to work so that the pity of it would strike the reader. Too much
> horror, raw, the mind cannot take – and here beauty can work for us,
> for the good, so I dare to believe as a poet.

I will close with some poems from the cycle "Letters to Gandhi."

IN NARODA PATIYA

Dark eyes
the color of burnt
almonds, face
slashed, lower
down where her belly
shone
a wet gash.
Three armed men.
Out they plucked
a tiny heart
beating with her own.
No cries
were heard
in the city.
Even the sparrows
by the temple gate
swallowed their song.

LYRIC WITH DOVES

I set doves on
my writing fingers
feel them fly.
The page is hushed.
From way beyond
hyenas howl.

There is too much
riveted into death,
what they bruised
and broke
– thighs arms
lips throat
precious inner organs –
is brushed
with brilliant ink
cavalcades of pain.
It rains in your city,
the heart's
flung back.
Torn bodies
clattering
in an ox drawn cart.

SLOW DANCING

Dear Mr Gandhi
please say something
about the carnage in your home state.

How did you feel when they shut
the gates of Sabermati Ashram
that February night

and the wounded clung outside?
What has happened to ahimsa?
Is it just for the birds and the bees?

What lips, what soles
swarmed across the river?
Is it hot on the other side?

O so many questions sir,
I cannot help myself
I cannot shut my mouth.

It's hard to hear you,
birds peck at sounds
maggots gnaw since

even syllables have skin.
The kingdom of heaven
is tiny as a mustard seed

and you have crawled therein.
Mist pours from mango trees,
the moon soars in a sea of blood.

I see you at the rim of heaven
grown older still, bewildered, stooped
dhoti flecked with drops of mud,

face seared by a moon
that has nothing
except its own inhuman glow,

the archipelago of light
afloat in monsoon air
where souls frail as pin pricks go.

Dear Mr. Gandhi
please talk to me now.
I am slow dancing

in the dark
with the untimely dead
and that is all I know.

BENGALI MARKET

Dear Mr Gandhi
It was cold the day the masjid
was torn down stone by stone,
colder still at the heart of Delhi.

Ten years later entering Bengali market
I saw a street filled with bicycles
girls with rushing hair, boys in bright caps.
I heard a voice cry

Can you describe this?
It sounded like a voice
from a city crusted with snow
to the far north of the Asian continent.

I saw him then, your grandson
in a rusty three wheeler
wrapped up in what wools he could muster.
Behind him in red letters

a sign: Dr Gandhi's Clinic.
So he said, embracing me, you've come back.
Then pointing to the clinic –
It's not that I'm sick

that gentleman gets my mail and I his.
That is why I am perched in this contraption.
I cannot stay long, it is Id ul Fitr.
I must greet friends in Old Delhi, wish them well.

Later he sought me out in dreams,
in a high kitchen in sharp sunlight
dressed in a khadi kurta, baggy jeans.
He touched my throat in greeting.

Listen my sweet, for half of each year,
after the carriage was set on fire
after the Gujarat killings,
I disappear into darkness.

In our country there are two million dead
and more for whom no rites were said.
No land on earth can bear this.
Rivers are criss-crossed with blood.

All day I hear the scissor bird cry
cut cut cut cut cut
It is the bird Kalidasa heard
as he stood singing of buried love.

Now our boys and girls take
flight on rusty bicycles.
Will we be cured? I cried
And he: We have no tryst with destiny.

My hands like yours are stained
with the juice of the pomegranate.
Please don't ask for my address.
I am in and out of Bengali market.

All of the poems quoted in this essay are published in Meena Alexander's *Raw Silk* (Evanston IL: TriQuarterly Books/Northwestern UP, 2004).

WORKS CITED

Akhmatova, Anna. "Requiem," in *The Complete Poems of Anna Akhmatova*, ed. Roberta Reeder, tr. Judith Hemschemeyer (Boston MA: Zephyr, 2000): 384–94.

Alexander, Meena. *Raw Silk* (Evanston IL: TriQuarterly Books/Northwestern UP, 2004).

Benjamin, Walter. "The Task of the Translator" (1923), in *Selected Writings 1913–26*, ed. Marcus P. Bullock & Michael W. Jennings (Cambridge MA: Harvard UP, 2003): 253–63.

Deleuze, Gilles, & Félix Guattari. *A Thousand Plateaus: Capitalism and Schizophrenia*, tr. & intro. Brian Massumi (*Mille plateaux: Capitalisme et schizophrénie*, 1980; Minneapolis: U of Minnesota P, 1987).

Yates, Frances A. *The Art of Memory* (1966; Chicago: U of Chicago P, 2001).

◄❖►

Women and Cultural/Colonial Trauma

Trauma, Madness, and the Ethics of Narration in J.M. Coetzee's *In the Heart of the Country*

SUSANA ONEGA

Coetzee's Apartheid Novels in the Context of Trauma Studies

I N THE LAST THREE DECADES OR SO, a number of critics have
started to respond to an increasing number of fictions dealing with
trauma by attempting to identify their basic characteristics and to provide an overall explanation for their appearance. According to Anne Whitehead, the rise of trauma fiction is "inextricable from three interrelated back-
grounds or contexts: postmodernism, postcolonialism and a postwar legacy or
consciousness."[1] Concurring with Roger Luckhurst, Pierre Nora, and Andreas
Huyssen,[2] Whitehead contends, first, that postmodernist and trauma fiction
share the same critical attitude to history as grand narrative and the same tendency to take conventional narrative techniques to their limit as a way of
calling attention to the complexity of memory. Secondly, that

---

[1] Anne Whitehead, *Trauma Fiction* (Edinburgh: Edinburgh U P, 2004): 81.

[2] Roger Luckhurst, "Memory Recovered/Recovered Memory," in *Literature and the Contemporary: Fiction and Theories of the Present*, ed. Roger Luckhurst & Peter Marks (Harlow: Longman, 1999): 80–93; Pierre Nora, "Between Memory and History: *Les Lieux de Mémoire*," tr. Mark Rondebush, *Representations* 26 (Spring 1989): 7–25; Andreas Huyssen, *Twilight Memories: Marking Time in a Culture of Amnesia* (London & New York: Routledge, 1995).

> Trauma fiction overlaps with postcolonial fiction in its concern with
> the recovery of memory and the acknowledgement of the denied, the
> repressed and the forgotten.[3]

And, thirdly, that trauma fiction shares with novels about the two World Wars
or the Vietnam War an obsession with the representation of war and its
effects.

This commonly accepted outlook on trauma fiction singles out as its defining characteristic the presentation of the protagonist against an historical
background of collective trauma, what Ronald Granofsky describes as the
"'collective' disasters of the contemporary world – Nazi camps, nuclear wea-
pons, the dehumanizing Soviet Gulag, catastrophic environmental pollution,
and others" – like apartheid, we might add.[4] Clearly, the definition excludes
from the category of trauma fiction those works dealing with individual
traumas caused by punctual events lacking a socio-cultural or historical component, like traffic accidents, sexual abuse, or the loss of a beloved one. It also
implicitly endorses the view, popularized by trauma critics such as Cathy
Caruth or Shoshana Felman and Dori Laub,[5] that trauma is an extraordinary
external event affecting collectivities and leaving its traces on individuals regardless of differences in each victim's psychological capacity to assimilate
the traumatic events.

In contrast to other trauma critics, who are interested both in the non-fic-
tional narratives of survivors and in trauma fiction, Granofsky's aim is to
establish the defining characteristics of the 'trauma novel' by opposition to,
on the one hand, testimony and, on the other, the more general category of
'literature of trauma', which, unlike the trauma novel, does not have recourse
to linguistic symbolism to provide a fictional depiction of imagined trauma.[6]

---

[3] Whitehead, *Trauma Fiction*, 82.

[4] Ronald Granofsky, *The Trauma Novel: Contemporary Symbolic Depiction of Collective Disaster* (Bern: Peter Lang, 1995): 3.

[5] *Trauma: Explorations in Memory*, ed. Cathy Caruth (Baltimore MD & London:
Johns Hopkins UP, 1995); Shoshana Felman & Dori Laub, *Testimony: Crises of Witnessing in Literature, Psychoanalysis, and History* (New York & London: Routledge,
1992).

[6] In Granofsky's own words: "I reserve the 'trauma novel' for those contemporary
novels which deal symbolically with a collective disaster. (I use the more general term
'literature of trauma' for works of any genre and any period which deal centrally with
trauma.) The collective disaster will, of course, leave its traces on the individual, and

According to Granofsky, the use of symbolic language in the trauma novel allows for the transformation of a given collective trauma and its effects on the individual into an allegory of human nature at large: "the individual trauma at the centre of the fictional world is linked to a general *angst* related in turn to the horrors seen to reside at the heart of human nature."[7]

In keeping with this definition, Granofsky argues that the trauma novel shares key defining traits with modernism, rather than with postmodernism, and he characterizes the trauma novel as, basically, a quest fiction, like the modernist *Bildungsroman*, with the difference that the protagonist's quest for self-unification and cosmic integration is set against a specifically traumatic historical background, itself requiring drastic transformation, so that "the individual search itself will represent a cultural effort at realignment."[8] Drawing on Jean Piaget's distinction between psychic assimilation – or incorporation of an alien experience within the existing categories of one's operating model of the world – and accommodation – or the requirement of a shift in world view itself to take account of the new experience – Granofsky defines the psychological trauma affecting the trauma-novel hero as "*a painful experience which defies assimilation and demands accommodation.*"[9] Thus, where the modernist hero would progress from self-fragmentation to the eventual achievement of an integrated, stable identity, in the trauma novel the protagonist's incapacity to assimilate reality strongly jeopardizes his or her individuation process, threatening the perpetuation of self-fragmentation and even regression to a pre-symbolic stage. Granofsky's contention is that the overcoming of this danger necessarily involves the transformation of the worldview that had allowed the traumatic events to take place by naturalizing them. As he explains, by placing its protagonists against a traumatic historical background and choosing to fictionalize the effects of collective trauma on a single individual, the trauma novel suggests both that "the collective must be understood in individual terms,"[10] and that "the trauma novelist is one who deals

---

the nature of fiction is such that the collective will be played in individual terms. That is precisely why the symbolic technique is crucial. The linguistic symbol, in pointing beyond itself, is an ideal vehicle to link individual and communal experience." *The Trauma Novel*, 5–6.

[7] Granofsky, *The Trauma Novel*, 2.

[8] *The Trauma Novel*, 8.

[9] *The Trauma Novel*, 8, 9; emphasis in the original.

[10] *The Trauma Novel*, 152.

with extreme and threatening change on a scale where the survival of a world view […], an identifiable group […], or the entire human race is called into question."[11]

Although Granofsky considers the search by the trauma-novel's hero for an integrated, stable identity to be a modernist feature, the critic is eventually led to concede that, often, the contemporary trauma novel situates itself in an intermediate position between modernism and postmodernism, with its more fluid and polymorphous sense of self.[12] Interestingly, the two writers he signals as representatives of this mid-way position are Thomas Pynchon and J.M. Coetzee, whom he places at the centre of "the vogue after World War Two of rewriting classic texts [in order to] make clearly discernible subtexts that were previously invisible […] in that they reflected the dominant ideology of their culture."[13] The Coetzee novel Granofsky chooses to exemplify this assertion is *Foe* (1986), which he describes, as "a rich pastiche of the varying conventions of the English novel over time"; "a post-colonial work of some power"; "a parody of *Robinson Crusoe*"; and "a postmodern work that is concerned with the collective trauma of slavery."[14] These descriptions point to self-reflexivity as the most salient feature of the novel, and thus to the fact that, in *Foe,* Coetzee paradoxically chooses to give voice to the unspeakable collective trauma of slavery – personified by a tongueless Friday – in overtly literary terms, through the parodic reworking of the novelistic conventions employed by Daniel Defoe in his canonical work.

Foe meets all the requirements of Granofsky's own definition of trauma novel. However, Granofsky is reluctant to see Coetzee as a trauma-novel writer, precisely because of the self-reflexivity of his work in general, which he interprets as an endorsement of relativism. This fact, together with his insistence that the trauma novel ultimately seeks to provide an allegorical picture of the evil residing in human nature at large through the symbolic use of language, is good proof of Granofsky's realism-biased, mimetic position. However, as Nelson Goodman contends in the first chapter of *Languages of Art*, entitled "Reality Remade,"[15] it should not be forgotten that symbolic sys-

[11] Granofsky, *The Trauma Novel*, 153–54.

[12] *The Trauma Novel*, 151.

[13] *The Trauma Novel*, 156.

[14] *The Trauma Novel*, 157.

[15] Nelson Goodman, *Languages of Art: An Approach to a Theory of Symbols* (1968; Indianapolis IN: Hackett, 1976): 3–40.

tems do not copy but, rather, 'make' and 'remake' the world, and that, as Paul Ricoeur has put it, "our aesthetical grasping of the world is a militant under-standing that 'reorganizes the world in terms of works and works in term of world'."[16] Rejecting the classical definition of art as mimesis that is implicitly endorsed by Granofsky, Ricoeur establishes a basic difference between the portrait image, which necessarily refers back to a pre-existing original, even if it is *in absentia*, and the fictional image, whose model, in the sense of an original already there, exists nowhere. The unreality of fiction is, then, based on its referential nothingness.[17] And herein lies its essential paradox: because it has no previous referent, fiction may refer to reality in a productive way, and even *increase* reality.[18]

Ricoeur's contention that the unreal images created by the writer's imagination are not less but *more* real than the most realistic photograph or portrait image, because they can re-describe reality, points to fictional language as the most efficient medium less to convey a moral lesson or abstract reflection on human nature, as Granofsky argues, than to (in Jean Piaget's terms) offer the traumatized subject and collectivity the imaginative means they need to assimilate the alien experience and foster the necessary shift in world-view that would accommodate the traumatic events and refashion the world.

Indeed, as Anne Whitehead points out, the sustained tendency of trauma narratives to defamiliarize and take to the limit their own thematic and formal features by means of intertextuality, repetition, self-reflexivity, the fragmen-tation and dispersal of narrative voice, and the disturbance of the willing sus-

---

[16] Paul Ricoeur, "The Function of Fiction in Shaping Reality," *Man and World* 12.2 (1979): 123.

[17] Ricoeur, "The Function of Fiction in Shaping Reality," 125–26.

[18] In Ricoeur's own words:

> The ultimate role of the [fictional] image is not only to diffuse meaning across diverse sensorial fields, to *hallucinate* thought in some way, but on the con-trary to effect a sort of *epoche* of the real, to suspend our attention to the real, to place us in a state of non-engagement with regard to perception or action, in short, to suspend meaning in the neutralized atmosphere to which one could give the name of the dimension of fiction. In this state of non-engagement we try new ideas, new values, new ways of being-in-the world. Imagination is this free play of possibilities. In this state, fiction can […] create a *redescription* of reality.

— "The Function of Fiction in Shaping Reality," 134; emphasis in the original.

pension of disbelief of the reader "with coincidences and fantastic elements which just lurk beneath the surface,"[19] are all techniques and devices meant "to make us believe the unbelievable," prompted by the intractability of the subject-matter and the need "to suggest that traumatic knowledge cannot be fully communicated or retrieved without distortion."[20] In this sense, it might be said that linguistic experimentation, far from being an expression of relativism, is in fact an ethical imperative for the trauma-novel writer. As Derek Attridge puts it,

> The distinctive ethical force of literature inheres not in the fictional world portrayed but in the handling of language whereby that fictional world is brought into being. Literary works that resist the immediacy and transparency of language – as is the case in modernist writing – thus engage the reader ethically.[21]

Implicitly contradicting Granofsky, Attridge ascribes Coetzee's experimentalism to the influence of modernism, rather than postmodernism, and insists that the defamiliarization brought about by "modernist techniques can be especially powerful as a means of involving the reader ethically [...w]hen the fiction itself concerns the ethics of otherness, as in J.M. Coetzee's two earliest fictions, *Dusklands* and *In the Heart of the Country*."[22] According to Attridge, Coetzee's experimentalism stems from the ethical impulse to give voice to "figures of otherness, individuals or groups who, because they belong to a different, and always subordinate, class, cannot be fathomed by the dominant consciousness of the novel." As he explains, in order to convey that resistance to a reader, the novelist must challenge "the Enlightenment discourses of moral rationality and moral judgment" endorsed by "the tradition of the realist novel (still scarcely questioned in South African writing in English in the 1970s)":[23] i.e. the decade when *Dusklands* (1974) and *In the Heart of the Country* (1977) were published.

◁❖▷

---

[19] Whitehead, *Trauma Fiction*, 84.

[20] *Trauma Fiction*, 84.

[21] Derek Attridge, "Ethical Modernism: Servants and Others in J.M. Coetzee's Early Fiction," *Poetics Today* 25.4 (2004): 653.

[22] Attridge, "Ethical Modernism," 653.

[23] "Ethical Modernism," 655.

Reception of *In the Heart of the Country*

Of the five narrative fictions written by J.M. Coetzee between 1974 and 1990 that are situated in South Africa[24] the second, *In the Heart of the Country*, is probably the one that has received least critical attention, even though it provides the reader with one of the most radical examples of a figure of otherness in the South African apartheid period: the white woman farmer. As Attridge explains, "the novel exists in two forms, the 1977 British and American version (differing only in the title – the American publisher preferred *From the Heart of the Country*) and the 1978 South African version," which combines English and Afrikaans.[25] As Attridge notes, the novel was virtually ignored in South Africa at the time of publication because it failed to meet the requirements of realism and political engagement expected of white South African writers in the 1970s. Chiara Briganti similarly describes its reception as one of "neglect and careless dismissal" and she remarks that the main concern of early critics such as Josephine Dodd, Teresa Dovey, and David Attwell[26] was to establish the ideological and textual assumptions made by the novel, with the result that, "for most of her critics, Magda [the protagonist], is simply mad, and she is mad because she is a spinster."[27] Even a critic like Paul A. Cantor, basically concerned with demonstrating the extent of Samuel Beckett's influence on *In the Heart of the Country*, ends his analysis of the novel's formal experimentalism on an embarrassingly apologetic note that reveals his mimetic bias:

---

[24] *Dusklands* (1974), *In the Heart of the Country* (1976), *Waiting for the Barbarians* (1980), *Life & Times of Michael K.* (1983), and *Age of Iron* (1990).

[25] Derek Attridge, *J.M. Coetzee and the Ethics of Reading* (Chicago: U of Chicago P, 2004), 22.

[26] Josephine Dodd, "Naming and Framing: Naturalization and Colonization in J.M. Coetzee's *In the Heart of the Country*," *World Literature Written in English* 27.2 (1987): 153–61; Theresa Dovey, *The Novels of J.M. Coetzee: Lacanian Allegories* (Craighall: Ad. Donker, 1988); David Attwell, *J.M. Coetzee: South Africa and the Politics of Writing* (1992; Berkeley: U of California P, 1993).

[27] Chiara Briganti, "A Bored Spinster with a Locked Diary: The Politics of Hysteria in *In the Heart of the Country*," *Research in African Literatures* 25.4 (Winter 1994): 33–49; Academic OneFile (Gale: Florida International U, Gale Document Number: A16026665): 1–17, http://find.galegroup.com.ezproxy.fiu.edu/itx/start.do?prodld=AONE (accessed 19 January 2009).

> Although I have been guilty of deflecting attention from the story that
> the novel tells in order to explore the complexities of how it tells it, in
> the end I fully sympathize with those readers and critics who find
> themselves in the grip of Magda's tale.[28]

This type of humanist approach to the novel is still very much at work. Thus,
for example, in an article published in 2007, Charlotte Truman dismisses *In
the Heart of the Country* with the characteristic realism-biased argument that
Magda is an unreliable narrator and that her unreliability stems from the fact
that she "does not actually recount what has occurred, but rather what she
wishes to occur, or perhaps fantasizes such situations." Truman's conclusion
is that the narration is "a blur of reckless accounts" asking "the reader to interpret the text by defining the line between sanity and reality" and "to put together the pieces and create a whole picture."[29]

A far more accurate and nuanced interpretation is that of David Attwell,
who describes *In the Heart of the Country* as "an act of consciousness and an
act of language [...] that is deeply transgressive."[30] For Attwell, the transgression does not lie in the unreliability or incoherence of Magda's narration, but
in the supposed requirement the novel makes of the reader to interpret her
troubled narration allegorically, as a symptom of the pathological nature of
South African society. Endorsing Mary Douglas' contention that taboos define the boundaries of legitimate social behaviour,[31] Attwell argues that
"Magda's is a transgressive consciousness that reveals the structures of relationship and authority – with their accompanying pathologies – of the settler-
colonial context."[32] Thus, he interprets Magda's disjointed family situation,
with its Oedipal implications, and the fact that she calls herself one of the
"melancholy spinsters" who are "lost to history," as evidence that "she does
not have access to a subject-position that is *inside* the history-making self-

---

[28] Paul A. Cantor, "Happy Days in the Veld: Beckett and Coetzee's *In the Heart of
the Country*," *South Atlantic Quarterly* 93.1 (Winter 1994): 105.

[29] Charlotte Truman, "Magda is an Unreliable Narrator in J.M. Coetzee's *In the
Heart of the Country*," *Associated Content* (28 February 2007), http://www.associated
content.com/article/155766/magda_as_an_unreliable_narrator_in.html?page=2&cat=3
8 (accessed 3 January 2009).

[30] Attwell, *J.M. Coetzee*, 60.

[31] Mary Douglas, *Purity and Danger: An Analysis of the Concepts of Pollution and
Taboo* (1966; New York & London: Routledge, 1985).

[32] Attwell, *J.M. Coetzee*, 60.

representations offered by the father."[33] His main argument is that Magda's production of fictions and her attempt to create a story with "a beginning, a middle and an end" are to be read as self-affirming gestures aimed at finding the place in time and history secularly denied the white woman in the deeply authoritative, patriarchal structure of the South African colonial family.

Although there is ample textual evidence to justify this reading, and although there is no denying that 'the personal is political' and that the consciousness of a human subject is inseparable from the determinations of gender and history,[34] there is a basic flaw in Attwell's approach, in that it equates literary characters with human beings and fictional worlds with the real world. Derek Attridge points to this when he warns the reader against the widespread tendency to read Coetzee's novels and novellas as representing "the truths – often the dark truths – of the human condition."[35] As he explains, allegorical meanings are often based on the "assumption that any responsible and principled South African writer, especially during the apartheid years, will have had as a primary concern the historical situation of the country and the suffering of the majority of people," and this assumption leads critics "to treat fictional characters as representatives of South African types or even particular individuals."[36]

Rejecting this kind of *a-priori* imposition of allegorical meanings on fictional works, Attridge contends that Coetzee's are "novels which, to a greater degree than most, concern themselves with the acts of writing and reading, including allegorical writing and reading," and that, "therefore, we need to ask how allegory is *thematized* in the fiction, and whether this staging of allegory as an issue provides any guidance in talking about Coetzee's use of allegory (and about allegory) more generally."[37] In keeping with this, he approaches *In the Heart of the Country* as a self-conscious literary text, making specific ethical demands on the reader. Thus, he assumes the common view that Magda is an unreliable narrator, not so much, as Truman argues, because she refuses to "recount what has occurred" (see above) as because of her "disquieting" tendency to foreground the fictionality of her narration by offering

---

[33] Attwell, *J.M. Coetzee*, 61; emphasis in the original.

[34] Sandra Lee Bertky, *Femininity and Domination: Studies in the Phenomenology of Oppression* (New York & London: Routledge, 1990): 1.

[35] Attridge, *J.M. Coetzee and the Ethics of Reading*, 32.

[36] *J.M. Coetzee and the Ethics of Reading*, 33.

[37] *J.M. Coetzee and the Ethics of Reading*, 34; my emphasis.

the reader various, often incompatible versions of the same events, so that "the question 'What really happened?' becomes unanswerable, and, in a sense, unaskable, since we have been made conscious of what we usually keep out of our minds as we read: that novels, unlike histories, do not tell of what happened."[38] However, in the light of Anne Whitehead's contention that linguistic experimentation is an ethical imperative for the trauma-novel writer, we should refrain from taking Magda's unreliability and madness at face value, and look instead at the way in which the text *thematizes* these features in order to create its own linguistic universe.

In *The Rhetoric of Fiction*, Wayne Booth calls "a narrator *reliable* when he speaks for or acts in accordance with the norms of the work (which is to say, the implied author's norms), *unreliable* when he does not." On the whole,

> difficult irony is not sufficient to make a narrator unreliable. Nor is un-reliability ordinarily a matter of lying, although deliberately deceptive narrators have been a major resource of some modern novelists [...]. It is most often a matter of what James calls *inconscience*, the narrator is mistaken, or he believes himself to have qualities which the author denies him.[39]

If irony and lying are not enough to make a narrator unreliable, we will have to decide whether Magda is unreliable because she does not abide by the implied author's norms, or – the most common case – because of her *inconscience*. The first option would be ruled out by those critics who see Magda as the mouthpiece of Coetzee's anti-apartheid ideology as well as by those who attribute her unreliability to madness, since mental derangement is an extreme form of 'inconscience'. But we cannot say that Magda is mad either because she does not know who she is or because she believes herself to have qualities the author denies her, for she is perfectly aware that she is a literary character living in a textual world of her own making. If she does not fit into any of these categories, what kind of a madwoman is she, then?

◄❖►

---

[38] Attridge, *J.M. Coetzee and the Ethics of Reading*, 23–24.

[39] Wayne C. Booth, "Types of Narration," in *The Rhetoric of Fiction* (1961), in *Narratology: An Introduction,* ed. & intro. Susana Onega & José Angel García Landa (London & New York: Longman, 1996): 152. (Emphasis in the original.)

Trauma, Madness and the Ethics of Narration in *In the Heart of the Country*

The narrative often referred to as a diary is described by Magda as "the mono- logue of my life."[40] This phrase brings to mind both the monologues of female characters like Beckett's Winnie (*Happy Days*) or Joyce's Molly Bloom (*Ulysses*), and Shelley's 'poetry of life'. In *A Defence of Poetry*, Shel- ley defines poetry as the product of the creative imagination and insists on its capacity to provide insights into the moral problems facing human beings in a way that neither reason and logic nor the natural sciences can provide. As he explains, since love and sympathy can be awakened only by the active imagi- nation, it follows that poetry, in the broad sense of the word, is the *sine qua non* of the *Good Life*.[41] In other words, Magda's description of her narration as the monologue of her life points to it as, essentially, an exercise in creative imagination prompted by love, sympathy and the desire to live the Good Life, and aimed at counteracting the life-denying effects of logic and reason – what Blake called "Single vision & Newton's sleep"[42] – that lie at the heart of the modernity project in general and the racist and imperialist Boer culture of apartheid South Africa in particular.

In *Happy Days*, Winnie organizes her monologue sequentially, "between the bell for waking and the bell for sleep," so as to prolong her exis-

---

[40] J.M. Coetzee, *In the Heart of the Country* (1976; London: Vintage, 2004): 13. Further page references are in the main text.

[41] In Shelley's own words:

> We have more moral, political and historical wisdom than we know how to reduce into practice: we have more scientific and economical knowledge than can be accommodated to the just distribution of the produce which it multiplies [...]. We want the creative faculty to imagine that which we know; we want the generous impulse to act that which we imagine; we want the poetry of life: our calculations have outrun conception; we have eaten more than we can digest [...]. Man having enslaved the elements remains himself a slave.

— Percy Bysshe Shelley, "A Defence of Poetry," in *English Essays: Sidney to Macaulay* vol. XXVII (1840; Harvard Classics; New York: P.F. Collier & Son, 1909–14), Bartleby.com (2001): para. 37. http://www.bartleby.com/27/23.html (acces- sed 2 February 2009).

[42] William Blake, "Letter to Butts" (22 November 1802), in *The Complete Writings of William Blake*, ed. Geoffrey Keynes (London: Nonesuch & New York: Random House, 1957): 818.

tence/assuage her boredom and pain for yet one more day. Although she rarely gets an answer from Willie, she always has him in mind as an interlocutor, for her greatest fear is to find herself one day "merely talking to [her]self," alone "in the wilderness."[43] Magda's monologue, triggered off by a similar fear, is also presented sequentially, in her case in the form of numbered paragraphs, and aimed at a potential reader. Paul A. Cantor interprets the division of the novel "into 266 numbered sections separated by spaces" as a Beckettian technique meant to "emphasize the elliptical quality of the novel" and to disrupt "the illusion of a seamless web of narrative."[44] But Attridge unintentionally calls this interpretation into question when, after conceding that the numbering of paragraphs is a "device announcing from the outset that we are not to suspend disbelief as we read," he admits to its disruptive inefficiency: "It is testimony to the power of fictional narration that it is not difficult to forget the numbering as we read."[45]

At the beginning of the novel, Magda's narration is rendered in the well-constructed syntax associated with autobiographical writing. However, the realism effect is simultaneously undermined by the literary allusiveness of the prose and the juxtaposition of various, often incompatible versions of the same events, introduced by "Perhaps," "Or perhaps," or simply "Or." Cantor interprets this feature of the narration in overtly pejorative terms as "Magda's tendency to make false starts and abrupt reversals in her narrative reinforc[ing] our sense of a story that does not cohere."[46] However, as a careful reading of the novel shows, the proliferation of alternative versions and the numbering of paragraphs is not primarily meant to baffle the reader. Rather, it responds to Magda's strenuous effort to *imagine* and record sequentially every *possible* alternative to the drab future allotted to her by her race, family, and culture: "I pick up and sniff and describe and drop, moving from one item to the next, numbering the universe steadily with my words" (29).

Right in the very first paragraph of the novel, Magda offers two different versions of her father bringing home his new bride. She writes: "Today my father brought home his new bride. They came in a dog-cart drawn by a horse with an ostrich-plume [...]" (1), and then adds: "*Or perhaps* they were drawn

---

[43] Samuel Beckett, *Happy Days* (1961; London & Boston MA: Faber & Faber, 1966): 8.

[44] Cantor, "Happy Days in the Veld," 90.

[45] Attridge, *J.M. Coetzee and the Ethics of Reading*, 21.

[46] Cantor, "Happy Days in the Veld," 90–91.

by two plumed donkeys, *that is also possible*" (1, emphasis added). She goes on to describe the two figures' clothes – "My father wore his black swallow-tail coat and stovepipe hat, his bride a wide-brimmed sunhat and a white dress tight at waist and throat" (1) – and then interrupts herself:

> More detail I cannot give unless I begin to embroider, for I was not watching. I was in my room, in the emerald semi-dark of the shuttered late afternoon, reading a book or, more likely, supine with a damp towel over my eyes fighting a migraine. I am the one who stays in her room reading or writing or fighting migraines. The colonies are full of girls like that, but none, I think, so extreme as I. My father is the one who paces the floorboards back and forth, back and forth, in his slow black boots. And then, for a third, there is the new wife, who lies late abed. Those are the antagonists. (1)

Derek Attridge reads Magda's remark that she cannot give further details un-less she "begins to embroider" as an ironic metacomment, enhancing the nar-rator's unreliability.[47] However, her concern is not so much with recording "what happened," as with *imagining* various *possible* versions of the moment that triggers off the traumatic event: the arrival of her widowed father with a much younger bride who will compete with her for his love.

The facts that, in both versions, the horse and donkeys wear ostrich plumes and that the couple are dressed in puzzling old-fashioned ceremonial clothes enhance the traumatic symbolism of the scene through its association with Victorian children's funerals,[48] and its suggestion of belatedness: i.e. the exis-tence of a chronological gap between the event itself and Magda's rendering of it.[49] This reading would explain the multiplicity of versions, since the trau-matized subject feels the compulsion to repeat the traumatic event over and over again and, given their belatedness, traumatic memories are subject to

---

[47] Attridge, *J.M. Coetzee and the Ethics of Reading*, 13.

[48] In Victorian funerals, the horses that carried the coffins of children usually wore ostrich plumes and the children themselves were dressed in white.

[49] In the Introduction to *Trauma: Explorations in Memory*, Cathy Caruth, drawing on Freud, asserts that the defining characteristic of post-traumatic stress disorder is its structural belatedness: "The pathology consists [...] solely in the *structure of its experience* or reception: the event is not assimilated or experienced fully at the time, but only belatedly, in its *possession* of the one who experiences it. To be traumatized is precisely to be possessed by an image or event" (4–5).

endless retrospective transformation and reinterpretation by the subject,[50] aimed in principle at achieving retrospective mastery over the shocking or unexpected event.[51]

Echoing this, Magda gives this primeval traumatic scene a significant turn of the screw when she offers yet another version of it in which her father and bride metamorphose into Hendrik, the black servant, and Anna, his pubescent new wife (18). The arrival of the doe-eyed, beautiful child triggers off a frenzy of desire in the powerful *pater familias* that neither Magda nor Hendrik can control, for it combines the requirements of sexual gratification with a pattern of racial empowerment and submission that is recurrently exerted by the white farmer as the prerogative of the Law-giver, as is suggested by the fact that she is called Anna, like an older female servant on the farm. Although Magda tries to differentiate the two women by calling the younger one Klein-Anna and the older one Ou-Anna (32), it is clear that her father does not see them (and their husbands) as subjects. He dismisses Ou-Anna and Jakob as soon as he becomes obsessed with having sex with Klein-Anna, and he prefers to bribe her husband rather than trick him (66). Further, Magda points to a pattern of repetition that enhances the absolute and infinite alterity of the servants, in Levinas' sense of the term,[52] when she refers to "Anna and Jakob, or to the Anna and Jakob who came before them" (50).[53]

At the same time, in keeping with the hallucinatory and fantastic nature of traumatic memories, the scene is overtly presented as a pastiche of literary styles and genres: Magda employs a parodic women's novelette style to describe her confinement in her room in "the emerald semi-dark of the shuttered late afternoon," and a fairy-tale style to characterize her ogre-like father, pacing "the floorboards back and forth, back and forth with his slow black

---

[50] Roger Luckhurst, "Mixing Memory and Desire: Psychoanalysis, Psychology, and Trauma Theory," in *Literary Theory and Criticism*, ed. Patricia Waugh (Oxford & New York: Oxford UP, 2006): 501.

[51] Whitehead, *Trauma Fiction*, 119.

[52] Emmanuel Levinas, *Otherwise than Being: or, Beyond Essence*, tr. Alphonso Lingis (*Autrement qu'être ou au-delà de l'essence*, 1974; The Hague: Martinus Nijhoff, 1981).

[53] Magda suggests a similarly undifferentiated treatment by her father of his own wives and children when she suggests that she might be the daughter of "the mousy unloved second wife who died in childbirth" (52), and is incapable of telling exactly how many "brothers and sisters, or stepbrothers and stepsisters" she had (51–52).

boots." In this description, the Freudian association of "boots" with male sexual power points to patriarchy as the triggering force behind the antagonists' conflict, with the awe-inspiring colonial farmer playing the role of fierce upholder of the Law/the phallus, and Magda, with her romance-heroine's migraines and boredom, that of jealous "wifely daughter" competing with her "sisterly (foster)mother"[54] for the fruits of forbidden desire.

In "About Chinese Women," Julia Kristeva explains the psycho-sexual development of a little girl in monotheistic capitalist society as a preparation for access to the social order (to symbolism, power, knowledge), that necessarily requires the sacrifice of sexual desire or *jouissance*.[55] As she explains,

> The symbolic order functions in our monotheistic West by means of a *system of kinship* that involves transmission of the name of the father and a rigorous prohibition of incest, and a *system of speech* that involves an increasingly logical, simple, positive and 'scientific' form of communication, that is stripped of all stylistic, rhythmic and 'poetic' ambiguities.[56]

Therefore, if Magda is to mature and enter the Boer social order, she must repress her incestuous desire for her father and renounce the use of the ambiguous, nonsensical, and highly metaphoric 'semiotic' language associated with motherly love, poetry, and laughter, in favour of the logical, unambiguous, and denotative 'symbolic' language associated with the Law of the father.

In the light of this, the fact that Magda's monologue progressively deteriorates from fully-fledged English to the point of near mutism, when she is barely able to communicate with "the sky Gods" (150) by writing to them inchoate and barely intelligible messages with stones, has been interpreted by Chiara Briganti as evidence that Magda is an hysterical woman "like Dora, who refused to be a character in the story that Freud was composing for her and wanted to finish for herself."[57] Thus focused, Magda's monologue

---

[54] Or "daughterly wife," as John A Stotesbury would call the young woman "who has taken an older man away from his daughter, who throughout her adolescence has played the role of a 'wifely daughter' to her widowed father," in the traditional South African romance. Stotesbury, *Apartheid, Liberalism and Romance: A Critical Investigation of the Writing of Joy Packer* (Uppsala: Swedish Science Press, 1996): 178.

[55] Julia Kristeva, "About Chinese Women" ("Des Chinoises," 1974), tr. Leon S. Roudiez, in *The Kristeva Reader*, ed. Toril Moi (Oxford: Basil Blackwell, 1989): 148.

[56] Kristeva, "About Chinese Women," 151, emphasis in the original.

[57] Briganti, "A Bored Spinster with a Locked Diary," 6.

becomes a parody of Freud's "talking cure," in which, Brigati argues, Magda herself has little faith:

> The discontinuities of her [Magda's] narrative reflect not only the nature of woman's process of "writing the self," (10) but also, more specifically, her struggle not to give in to aphasia – the destiny that attends the hysterical daughters – and to continue to talk, even though it is only a "father-tongue" (97) that is available to her.[58]

From Brigati's perspective, Magda's madness would be the madness awaiting every rebellious daughter in patriarchy, trapped between the desire to enter the Symbolic order and the fear of losing her *jouissance* and, with it, the capacity to laugh associated with the poetic rhythms of the maternal language and the Dionysiac forces of sex and love.

With characteristic awareness, Magda, echoing Beckett's Winnie as well as Breuer's Anna O. and Freud's Dora, confides to the reader that, for a time, she had faith that "the talking cure" would help her understand her social position on the Boer farm: "There was a time when I imagined that if I talked long enough it would be revealed to me what it means to be an angry spinster in the heart of nowhere" (5). However, she soon realizes that telling the "story of my rage and its dire sequel" (5) is not enough, that in order to give meaning to her life she would have to discover "the point of my story" (5). As she reflects,

> But what other tale is there for me? Marriage to the neighbour's second son? I am not a happy peasant. I am a miserable black virgin, and my story is my story, even if it is a dull black blind stupid miserable story, ignorant of its meaning and of all its many possible untapped happy variants. I am I. Character is fate. History is God. (5)

The comprehension that she is not a happy peasant and that her destiny has been forged by history (rather than by a flesh-and-blood author) evinces a yearning for *jouissance* and a refusal to accept her allotted role as the lonely spinster left behind by her luckier "brothers and sisters or half-brothers and half sisters" (90) "to watch over [her] father's last years" (52). At this stage, the rebellious daughter is full of optimistic reliance on character to correct the course of her destiny and live her own story, with "all its many possible untapped happy variants" (5), for she is convinced that her existence depends on her own creative capacity: "I create myself in the words that create me. [...]

---

[58] "A Bored Spinster with a Locked Diary," 9.

While I am free to be I nothing is impossible" (8). Carried along by this optimism and yearning for love and significant action, Magda embarks on the formidable task of imagining/impersonating in succession every possible variation on the role of jealous daughter in the triangular family structure within which she has gained access to the social order. Thus, she presents herself as "among other things a farmgirl living in the midst of the hurly-burly of nature" (45); as "a black widow in mourning for the uses I was never put to" (44); as "a thin black beetle with dummy wings who lays no eggs and blinks in the sun" (20); as "a straw woman, a scarecrow, not too tightly stuffed" (45); and as "a hole with a body draped around it [...] a hole crying to be whole" (44). These bizarre descriptions are ironically charged meta-comments pointing to Magda's awareness that she is a fictional character with a double literary ancestry: she is the ever-compliant and charming daughter of a masterful father characteristic of the South African pastoral, whose origins go back to Richardson's Pamela and the Victorian 'angel in the house'; and also its 'demonic contrary', to put it in Blake's terms: a black beetle, like Kafka's Gregor Samsa, a straw woman, like Eliot's hollow men, and, most chillingly, an unloved, lonely figure of otherness struggling for wholeness and recognition by the gaze of her father.

With characteristic prescience, Magda envisions her life, in words that echo Virginia Woolf's snails in *The Waves*, as that of "the hermit crab [...] that as it grows migrates from one empty shell to another," temporarily exposing her "anxious softbodied self" (47). Implicitly rebuking critics who interpret the proliferation of alternative versions of the events narrated as proof of her unreliability and madness, she insists that, for all her rage at her father, she must not get stuck in the role of avenger, but move on to other roles:

> Let me at all costs not immure myself in a version of myself as avenger. [...] The grim moralist with the fiery sword is only a stopping-place, a little less more temporary than the haggard wife knitting on the stoep, a little more temporary than the wild woman of the veld who talks to her friends the insects and walks in the midday sun, but temporary all the same. Whose shell I presently skulk in does not matter, it is the shell of a dead creature. What matters is that my anxious softbodied self should have a refuge from the predators of the deep [...]. (47)

Unlike Elektra, who wholeheartedly embraced the role of avenger and, renouncing *jouissance*, condemned herself to madness, and also unlike Chrysothemis, who arrested her individuation process by passively clinging to her mother, Magda's course of action is to use her creative imagination to liberate

her "anxious softbodied self" from the structures of power.[59] Thus, after imagining in farcical terms her prescribed marriage to a neighbouring farmer, her
falling pregnant, and her living closeted in the farm for a decade, breeding "a
litter of ratlike, runty girls, all the spit image of myself" (46), she reflects:
"Perhaps that is all that election means to me: not to have to figure in a buco-
lic comedy like the above, not to be explained away by poverty, degeneracy,
torpor, or sloth" (46).

But no sooner has she made the decision to write the monologue of her life
than she becomes aware that English, her father's tongue and the language of
colonial domination, is inimical to the fruition of desire: "Words are coin.
Words alienate. Language is no medium for desire. Desire is rapture, not ex-
change" (28). Thus, she wonders: "Is it possible that I am a prisoner not of the
lonely farmhouse and the stone desert but of my stony monologue?" (13). She
concludes that if she is to lead a fulfilling life she must oppose her father's
sexual advances on Hendrik's wife, since "there is a level, we both know, at
which Klein-Anna is a pawn and the real game lies between the two of us"
(37). As she reflects,

> I want my story to have a beginning, a middle, and an end, not the
> yawning middle without end which threatens no less if I connive at my
> father's philandering and live to guard his dotage than if I am led to
> the altar by a swain and die full of years, a wizened granny in a rock-
> ing chair. I must not fall asleep in the middle of my life (46).[60]

---

[59] Julia Kristeva's prototype of the girl who opts to sacrifice her *jouissance* in order
to enter the Symbolic order is Elektra, instigator of her mother's murder by her brother
Orestes, "not because Clytemnestra is a mother who kills the father, but because she is
a mistress (of Aegisthus). Let j*ouissance* be forbidden to the mother: this is the demand of the father's daughter, fascinated by the mother's *jouissance*." After the
death of her father, Elektra's life becomes a vendetta and the source of her madness,
but, as Kristeva acutely notes, "her own madness, contrary to Chrysothemis' passive
clinging to her mother, is what the leader of the chorus will call, at the end, an 'effort that crowns history,' for without it, there would be no 'freedom,' and no 'history' for the city from which, as a woman, she is none the less alienated." This is the
fundamental paradox of the patriarchal order: that its perpetuation and freedom depend on the alienation of the father's daughter. ("About Chinese Women," 152).

[60] Besides being an allusion to Winnie, who is prevented from falling asleep in the
middle of the day by the bell, Magda's words allude to the protagonist of Beckett's
"The Rockaby" (1982), a middle-aged woman dressed in black, who has spent her
whole life trying to see and be seen by another, and who ends up comforting herself

What is more, Magda knows that her plea is shared by numberless women, living, like her, on Boer farms in the heart of the country: "All over this land there must be patient middle-aged children waiting for their parent's grip on the keys to slacken" (42). And she dreams of the day when her father will die and she "will unlock the rolltop desk and uncover all the secrets he has kept from me," including "the point on the line from youth to man to husband to father to master [when] the heart must have turned to stone" (42).

Commenting on the South African version of the novel, Derek Attridge notes that the alternation of English and Afrikaans is a self-conscious device meant to make the reader "aware of the main narrative's mediation via English and via the European fictional tradition."[61] But even in the English-only version of the novel, Magda carefully distinguishes between English, her father's tongue, and Afrikaans, which she nostalgically associates with a long-lost time of multiracial and classless harmony, when she "grew up with the servants' children" and "spoke like one of them before I learned to speak like this" (7). Although she relates this fact to the premature death of her mother and her father's subsequent neglect, Magda has fond memories of her childhood, when, ignorant of colour and class barriers, she sat with the other children "at the feet of their blind old grandfather while he [...] told stories of bygone days" (7). Magda describes that period in mythic terms as a prelapsarian time "when beast and man and master lived a common life as innocent as the stars in the sky" (7). Hoarded in her memory as "a dream of a pristine age [...] in a language I have not unlearned" (7), this utopian description of harmony and communion with nature and with other human beings that she enjoyed during her pre-Oedipal stage provides Magda with the pattern of significance she needs to interpret "the ache of whatever it is that [has been] lost" ever since as an Edenic "myth of expulsion" (7). Her entry into the Symbolic thus becomes a traumatic fall into time and history, bringing alienation and an insatiable desire to recuperate the lost unity of self and other and of self and world.

In sharp contrast to this idyllic description, in the next two sections (17–18) Magda uses the cliché-ridden language of British imperialism to describe the

---

between the arms of a motherly rocking chair facing the window, while the public hear her thoughts through a recorded voice, until she pulls down the blinds of the window she had always kept up, hoping to see and be seen by another human being.

[61] Attridge, *J.M. Coetzee and the Ethics of Reading*, 22.

servants at the farm as lazy, quarrelsome and childish, malingering aliens (7–8), only, however, to subsequently disavow her words:

> ' What I say does not come from me.' Across valleys of space and time
> we strain ourselves to catch the pale smoke of each other's signals.
> That is why my words are not words such as men use to men. (8)

As this disavowal suggests, the multiple versions and contradictions in Magda's narration, rather than being signs of unreliability, are proof of her conscientious, trial-and-error probing of the adaptability of English, the received white masters' language of domination and bondage, to her own, fully creative *écriture féminine*:[62]

> Alone in my room with my duties behind me and the lamp steadily
> burning I creak into rhythms that are my own, I stumble over the rocks
> of words that I have never heard on another tongue. I create myself in
> the words that create me, I who living among the downcast have *never*
> beheld myself in the equal regard of mine. While I am free to be I,
> nothing is impossible. (8, emphasis in the original)

This description of herself as a solitary woman locked in her room and attempting to find a sense of self by forcing the language of patriarchy and empire into her own feminine rhythms is clogged with intertextual echoes not so much of Dora, Anna O., and other hysterical women treated by Freud and Breuer, but of these women's *fictional representations*: the mad women locked in the attics of Western romance, from Charlotte Brontë's Bertha Mason (*Jane Eyre*) to Jean Rhys' Antoinette Bertha Cosway (*Wide Sargasso Sea*), a character that shares striking traits and circumstances with Magda. It is important to draw this distinction between real women and their cultural representations, since, as Elaine Showalter argues in *The Female Malady*,

> the representations of the madwoman in legal, medical, and literary
> texts, and in painting, photography, and film [... are] not simply the

---

[62] In "The Laugh of the Medusa," Hélène Cixous contends that the way out of patriarchal oppression lies in an alternative, feminine practice of writing, capable of discursively creating subjectivities that would be plural and shifting (bisexual), and of breaking up the set of hierarchical oppositions which, she argues, structure Western thought and govern its political practice, such as 'culture/nature', 'head/heart', 'form/matter', 'speaking/writing', derived from the basic opposition 'man/woman'. Hélène Cixous, "The Laugh of the Medusa" ("Le Rire de la Meduse," 1975), tr. K. & P. Cohen, in *New French Feminists*, ed. Elaine Marks & Isabelle de Courtivron (Brighton: Harvester, 1980): 254–64.

reflections of medical and scientific knowledge, but part of the fundamental cultural framework in which ideas about femininity and insanity [are] structured.[63]

In other words, if Magda's struggle to re-describe her patriarchal and imperialist world is to be effective, it must be fought in the realm of its cultural framework.

In this connection, Caroline Rody offers significant insights into Magda's role as 'madwoman in the attic' when she suggests that *In the Heart of the Country* comes at the tail-end of the novelistic trend inaugurated by E.M. Forster's *A Passage to India* (1924), which fictionalizes the plea of the white female character in colonial contexts, "designed to enact the psychosexual fantasy of her race and thus to embody the failure of English liberal humanism." As she explains, in the hands of more recent anticolonial writers, such as Jean Rhys, Nadine Gordimer, Doris Lessing, and Caryl Churchill, the original essentially passive figure "rebels against her own passive construction."[64] Rody argues that *In the Heart of the Country* belongs in this generic tradition, with specific indebtedness to Olive Schreiner's *The Story of an African Farm* (1883), a novel discussed by Coetzee in *White Writing*.[65] Thus, she concludes that Magda is

a woman whose furious rebellion, in words and violent action, against the patriarchal, imperialist structure of her world reinflects the conventional 'madness' of her literary kind.[66]

Magda is not, then, just another madwoman in the attic, but a rebellious madwoman deconstructing the conventional madness of her literary type.

But Magda's rage is also directed against the madwoman's 'contrary': the 'angel in the house'. This essentially passive and all-complying Victorian character was incorporated into South African literature through the popular historical romances written by white women such as Helga Moray, Christina Laffeaty, Joy Packer, and many other lesser writers in the 'Mills and Boon'

---

[63] Elaine Showalter, *The Female Malady: Women, Madness and English Culture, 1830–1980* (1987; Virago: London, 2001): 5.

[64] Caroline Rody, "The Mad Colonial Daughter's Revolt in J.M. Coetzee's *In the Heart of the Country*," *South Atlantic Quarterly* 93.1 (Winter 1994): 159.

[65] Rody, "The Mad Colonial Daughter's Revolt in J.M. Coetzee's *In the Heart of the Country*," 166.

[66] "The Mad Colonial Daughter's Revolt in J.M. Coetzee's *In the Heart of the Country*," 159.

tradition, including Kathleen Mary Linsay, "credited with more than 400 novels under ten different names."[67] Drawing on Janice A. Radway,[68] John Stotesbury describes the type of female identity constructed by these highly stereotyped popular romances as a "limited version of female identity [...] linked with the formal closure of the romance" that prescribes marriage and a permanent loving relationship as the ideal and idealized expression of wo-man's desire.[69] This is the family role Magda is predestined to incarnate, as she herself suggests in the very first paragraph of the novel, when she presents herself both as a sickly and closeted romance heroine fighting boredom and migraine and as a jealous daughter competing with her father's new bride for his love and recognition.[70]

Magda's endeavour is, then, to escape both of these prescribed roles and define herself as a subject. Although the family romance fantasy can take various forms,

> it differs from children's sexual theories in that it does not address general questions about the origins of life but rather the question, 'Who am I?' – where 'I' denotes not an agency of the mind (or ego) but the result of an effort to place oneself in a history, and hence the at-tempt to form the basis of a knowledge.[71]

Her words perfectly fit Magda's description of herself as one of the "melan-choly spinsters [...] lost to history" (3), with no equal to love and look her in

---

[67] Stotesbury, *Apartheid, Liberalism and Romance*, 5n17.

[68] Janice A. Radway, *Reading the Romance: Women, Patriarchy and Popular Lite-rature* (Chapel Hill: U of North Carolina P, 1984).

[69] Stotesbury, *Apartheid, Liberalism and Romance*, 15.

[70] The antagonistic relationship ruling this 'eternal triangle' brings to mind the plot of Joy Packer's sixth novel, *The Blind Spot* (1967), summarized by John A. Stotesbury as the fictionalization of the rivalries between "the 'daughterly wife [...] who has taken an older man away from his daughter, who throughout her adolescence has played the role of a 'wifely daughter' to her widowed father." Needless to say, in Packer's stereo-typed and reactionary account, the rivalries are eventually overcome, the women re-conciled, and the triangle broken by the inclusion of a fourth element, a younger and virile man the daughter can marry, thus fulfilling "her husbandly father's dreams of family continuity and stability." *Apartheid, Liberalism and Romance*, 178, 179.

[71] Sophie de Mijolla–Mellor, "Family Romance," in *International Dictionary of Psychoanalysis,* ed. Alain de Mijolla (2005; Gale Cengage: eNotes.com, 2006), http://www.enotes.com/psychoanalysis-encyclopedia/family-romance (accessed 31 January 2009).

the face, to put it in Levinasian terms:[72] "I who living among the downcast have never beheld myself in the equal regard of another's eye, have never had another in the equal regard of mine" (8). Her rebelliousness stems, then, from her enforced arrested development and the fear of remaining trapped in the pre-Oedipal stage: "I live neither alone nor in society but as it were among children" (8). In keeping with this, her earliest signs of rebelliousness take the form of childish bouts of violence: knocking at the door of her father's bedroom while he is with Klein-Anna (59–60), or ringing the dinner-bell (61–62), while she assumes the form and voice of a despondent child (59), in a process of regression that ends in an awful climax of shapelessness strongly reminiscent of Beckett's the Unnamable:

> He is turning me into a child again! [...] I am a child again, an infant, a grub, a white shapeless life with no arms, no legs, nothing even to grip the earth with, a sucker, a claw; I squirm, again the boot is raised over me [...]. (55).

In this sense, Magda's description of the embrace of her father's and her own *faeces* "looped in each other's coils, the father's red snake and the daughter's black embrace and sleep and dissolve" (35), may be said to provide an accurate image of the symbolic nature of her struggle for self-definition, since it combines her yearning for love with an Oedipal-stage daughter's fantasy of competition over the paternal phallus. When all her attempts to move his "heart [of] stone" fail (42), Magda embarks on the only course of action left to her, which is to imagine herself attacking her father – with an axe (12) in one version; with a rifle (66–67) in another – and condemning him to a

---

[72] In *Otherwise than Being*, Levinas contends that the essential ethical moment is manifested to the I in its encounter 'beyond being' with the face of the Other. This encounter is a singular and unpredictable event of an epiphanic nature that inaugurates an unconditional and pre-rational responsibility of the I for the Other. In this encounter, the Other, conceived of as an absolute and infinite alterity, calls our ego into question and confronts it with that which escapes our cognitive powers, that which we will neither be able to reduce to our categories of thought nor to ignore or suppress. Accordingly, in *Totality and Infinity*, Levinas critiques totalitarian thought with the argument that, in Western culture, Otherness is neutralized by the attempt of the I to transform "the Other into the Same." Emmanuel Levinas, *Totality and Infinity: An Essay on Exteriority*, tr. Alphonso Lingis (*Totalité et Infini: essai sur l'extériorité*, 1961; London: Kluwer Academic, 1991). This threat of neutralization is what confers an ethical character on Magda's rebelliousness.

lingering death that literally transforms the grim Law-giver into an abject object,[73] oozing blood, faeces, and other bodily fluids with nauseating smells.[74] Echoing Thomas de Quincey's conception of murder as one of the fine arts, Magda describes her task as "the art of butchery" (16) and, after imagining various ways of getting rid of the corpse, including sawing off the sealed bedroom and shoving it off "into empty space" (89), she concentrates all her efforts on establishing a relationship of equality and love with Hendrik and Klein-Anna, in a utopian attempt to recover the harmony and wholeness of her remembered childhood. However, even in the absence of the awe-inspiring Law-giver, Magda's received language of patriarchy makes communication with the servants impossible:

> The lips [...] are tired of all the articulating they have had to do since they were babies, since it was revealed to them that there was a law, that they could no longer simply part themselves to make way for the long *aaaa* which has, if truth be told, always been enough for them [...]. How can I say, I say, that the law does not stand fullgrown inside my shell, its feet in my feet, its hand in my hands, its sex drooping through my hole, or that when I have had my chance to make this utterance, the lips and teeth of the law will not begin to gnaw their way out of this shell, until there it stands before you, the law grinning and triumphant again, its soft skin hardening in the air while I lie sloughed, crumpled, abandoned on the floor? (91–92)

Panic-stricken by this imagined invasion of her body by the Law, Magda asks the two servants to sleep in the house with her. But Klein-Anna is simply terrorized by her inconceivable familiarity and Hendrik vents his ancestral servant's rage on the inefficient and unprotected white mistress by abusing, hitting, and raping her. Again, Magda offers various versions of this rape, including one in which she positions herself in the role of submissive and humble "second wife" to the black servant, in a move of expiation and atone-

---

[73] On the male abject, see Keith Reader, *The Abject Object: Avatars of the Phallus in Contemporary French Theory, Literature and Film* (Amsterdam & New York: Rodopi, 2006; Chiasma 17).

[74] "I raise the bedclothes and look. He is lying in a sea of blood and shit that has already begun to cake. I tuck the bedclothes back under his armpits [...]. Under the bedclothes there is a liquid convulsion. He releases his breath with a gasp. [...] the afternoon heat and the stench together will be too much for anyone" (84–85).

ment for the wrongs of imperialism and apartheid that anticipates Lucy's decision to "marry" Petrus, in *Disgrace*.[75]

As the reader eventually learns, her father is still alive at the end of the novel and threatening to outlive Magda, who has in fact wasted her life dutifully taking care of him:

> I feed my father his broth and weak tea. Then I press my lips to his forehead and fold him away for the night. Once upon a time I used to think that I would be the last one to die. But now I think that for some days after my death he will still lie here breathing, waiting for his nourishment. (149)

By this stage the erstwhile powerful Law-giver has truly become the nauseating abject object of Magda's imaginings, struck dumb and blind and incapable of controlling his sphincters,[76] while Magda considers in succession the possibilities open to her: to set fire to the farm (129), as a madwoman in the attic is expected to do; to build patterns with stones, as Beckett's Molloy did with his sucking pebbles, "keeping count of them as I go, until I run dry" (130); or, like Winnie, make the best of her loneliness, boredom, and bondage "in the middle of nowhere, buried to my waist and commanded to live a life" (130). But Magda rejects them all since, as she reflects,

> I need people to talk to, brothers and sisters, or fathers and mothers, I need a history and a culture. I need hopes and aspirations. I need a moral sense and a teleology before I will be happy, not to mention food and drink. (130–31).

Like Molloy's birds,[77] the animals in the farm have run wild or are dead, and Magda, like the eponymous hero of *Life & Times of Michael K*,[78] is living on little more than "pumpkin" (131). Giving an ironic turn to Vladimir and Estragon's hopeful reception of the messenger with news from Godot, Magda scares away the twelve-year-old boy carrying a message from the Tax Office

---

[75] J.M. Coetzee, *Disgrace* (1999; London: Vintage, 2000): 202–05.

[76] The condition of Magda's father echoes that of Pozzo and Lucky in the second Act of *Waiting for Godot* (1956), as well as the terrifying, abject figure of the mummified corpse of Norman Bates's mother sitting upstairs in her rocking chair in Alfred Hitchcock's film *Psycho* (1960).

[77] Samuel Beckett, *The Beckett Trilogy: Molloy, Malone Dies, The Unnamable* (1959; London: Picador, 1979): 162.

[78] J.M. Coetzee, *Life & Times of Michael K.* (1973; London: Vintage, 1998): 101.

(135–36) – that is, from the invisible but powerful economic heart of the apartheid government – and she makes hers Beckett's radical insight that her existential emptiness and absence will never be fulfilled: "because it is the first condition of life forever to desire, otherwise life would cease" (125). She also realizes at this point that "only stones desire nothing" (125) and that she cannot communicate with Klein-Anna because

> That is what she gets from me, colonial philosophy, words with no his-
> tory behind them, homespun, when she wants stories [...] tales from a
> past that really happened, how grandfather ran away from the bees and
> lost his hat and never found it again, why the moon waxes and wanes,
> how the hare tricked the jackal. (125)

Her distinction between the barren and impenetrable "words with no history" of "colonial philosophy" and the fully significant "homespun" stories orally transmitted from generation to generation are proof of Magda's faith in the superiority of literary language to re-describe the world. Avowedly, she admits defeat in her attempt to communicate with Klein-Anna, but does so using Blake's own words: "Energy is eternal delight. [...] I could have burned my way out of this prison, my tongue is forked with fire [...] but all has been turned uselessly inward, what sounds to you like rage is only the cracking of the fire within" (110).

The novel ends with Magda becoming the mad hag she had imagined her-self to be: "time has flowed ceaselessly and I am now truly a mad old bad old woman with a stooped back and a hooked nose and knobbly fingers" (134). After Hendrik and Klein-Anna go away on their Beckettian bicycle, followed by the dog, Magda starts hearing voices and decides to respond to them, for she believes with Hobbes as well as Winnie that the way to "avoid becoming a beast" (136) is to speak to others, as "the sailor" – surely Robinson Crusoe – did "on the desert island speak[ing] to his pets" (137). The voices she hears speak "a Spanish of pure meaning such as might be dreamed of by the philo-sophers" (137), so that, although she knows no Spanish, she can understand everything. As Magda makes clear, the voices have nothing to do with her: "I could not make up such words as are spoken to me. They come from gods; or, if not, then from another world" (138).

The critic Dominic Head associates their appearance "with a utopian future [...] evoking the unifying ideal of Esperanto."[79] However, the flying gods

---

[79] Dominic Head, *J.M. Coetzee* (Cambridge Studies in African and Caribbean Lite-rature; Cambridge: Cambridge UP, 1997): 63.

have nothing utopian about them. On the contrary, they are transcendental gods, like the gods created by the dogmatic 'priests' in Blake's "The Marriage of Heaven and Hell" (c.1790), and they speak the Kantian language of pure reason on which the Enlightenment project is based. This is why Magda understands their messages, for they convey the same ideas that have been transmitted to her by her father in the Symbolic language of power that has spoiled all her attempts at communication with the servants. The fact that the messages are phrased in Spanish, rather than English, adds a specifically imperialist touch to them, since, for a Boer woman of Dutch origin, Spanish is the Ur-language of imperialism; while the fact that the transcendental gods hover over the farm in flying machines "which look like narrow silver pencils with two pairs of rigid wings" (138) associates them both with the readers who find fault with Coetzee's experimentalism and with the flying island or rock in *Gulliver's Travels*, fittingly named Laputa (Spanish, 'the whore'). Finally, the fact that the hovering entities appear after the teen-age boy has failed to deliver the message from the Tax Office to Magda's father, together with her description of them as "gods," further enhances the parallelisms and differences between the positions of Magda and of Vladimir and Estragon in *Waiting for Godot*. While, for the tramps, Godot embodies a vague, ever-postponed hope for meaning and salvation, Magda hotly disagrees with the messages sent her by the sky gods, who accuse her of being lost in futile dreams (138–39), of having turned her "life into a fiction out of boredom" (139), and of having made an enemy of herself (140). Magda's response to these accusations is the answer both of a self-conscious author–narrator and of a visionary poet–prophet, as the reference to blindness suggests:

> Are they gods and yet do not see, I ask myself, or is it I who am will-fully blind? Which is the more implausible, the story of my life as lived by me or the story of the good daughter humming the psalms as she bastes the Sunday roast in a Dutch kitchen in the dead centre of the stone desert? (140)

In a last titanic effort, Magda makes at this point the Sisyphus-like decision of carrying wheelbarrows full of pumpkin-sized whitewashed stones across the veld to write with them her answers to the gods (144). What she writes are inchoate phrases she calls "poems," written in "the true language of the heart" (145), and expressing her yearning for freedom and love and her desire to be the "medium, the median […]. Neither master nor slave, neither parent nor child, but the bridge between, so that in me the contraries should be reconciled!" (145).

The allusions to Blake's "contraries"[80] and to the Romantic definition of poet–prophets as Hermetic mediators between the two worlds[81] bring to mind Ross Woodman's contention that the madness of the Romantic poet–prophet and the ritual dimension of the language of metaphor and myth associated with it, with its patterns of repetition and recurrence, and its capacity for excess, has a potentially creative role, in that it has the power to deconstruct rationalism from within, allowing for "the release of consciousness from the Symbolic orders in which it inevitably becomes fixed and dead."[82] Thus, in order to address "a psychotic world, which for the Old Testament prophets is what history largely is, a poet–prophet like Blake himself must enter it as the demonic form of himself in order to redeem it." [83]

Woodman's words offer crucial insight into the true nature of Magda's madness: the monologue of her life is an act of imaginative creation prompted by the ethical obligation to deconstruct from within the oppositional, equally traumatic roles of madwoman in the attic / angel in the house prescribed to

---

[80] To the concept of negation Blake opposes the concept of 'contrary', the principle that makes artistic activity possible: "Without Contraries is no progression. Attraction and Repulsion, Reason and Energy, Love and Hate, are necessary to Human existence. / From these contraries spring what the religious call Good and Evil. Good is the passive that obeys Reason. Evil is the active springing from Energy. / Good is Heaven. Evil is Hell." William Blake, *The Marriage of Heaven and Hell*, in *The Poetical Works of William Blake*, ed. John Sampson (c.1790; New York & Toronto: Oxford UP, 1956): 248.

[81] According to this definition, poet–prophets are Hermetic magi or shamans with the ability to transform the particular into the archetypal and so bridge the gulf between the material and the spiritual worlds. As I have pointed out elsewhere, "in this light, their striving for unity and wholeness expresses a fundamental human need to reconcile time and eternity, matter and spirit, the Dionysian forces of wild nature expressed in emotion and sensation, and the Apollonian forces of reason and ideation associated with culture and art, what E.M. Forster described in *Howards End* as the need to 'connect' the prose in us with the passion, the beast and the monk in us." Susana Onega, *Jeanette Winterson* (Contemporary British Novelists Series; Manchester: Manchester UP, 2006): 230–31.

[82] Ross Woodman, *Sanity, Madness, Transformation: The Psyche in Romanticism*, afterword by Joel Faflak (Toronto: U of Toronto P, 2005): 4.

[83] Woodman, *Sanity, Madness, Transformation*, 58.

women in patriarchy in general and to the South African Boer woman in particular. Her narration is, then, an astonishing *tour de force* in imaginative self-
re-creation, with Magda in the position of the poet–prophet Los at the climac-
tic moment when he tells his weeping Spectre: "I must Create a System or be
enslav'd by another Man's / I will not Reason & Compare; my business is to
Create."[84]

The task of Los is to strive "with Systems to deliver Individuals from those
Systems."[85] In order for Magda to achieve a similar goal, she must enter the
psychotic world of South African apartheid culture in the demonic form of
herself: i.e. as the haggish and murderous spinster with the "divine madness"
of the poet–prophet, as Plato called it in *Ion*. For only by assuming madness
can the madness of the Logos be exposed. Magda is not, then, an unreliable,
'inconscious' narrator, intent on baffling the reader, but, rather, a preter-
naturally lucid and ethically committed author–character with the self-appoin-
ted, titanic task of deconstructing the Enlightenment project in the linguistic
terms available to her, knowing all the while that the task is impossible unless
she finds a flying god/critic willing to read the vital message of equality and
love hidden behind the feminine rhythms of her inchoate and mad stony
poems.

In this sense, the romantic note on which the novel ends, with Magda confessing her love of the veld and her ancestral allegiance to it – "It takes generations of life in the cities to drive that nostalgia for country ways from the
heart. [...] I am corrupted with the beauty of this forsaken world" (151) – may
be read not so much as "a gesture of ambivalent lyricism," as Dominic Head
suggests,[86] as an – avowedly utopian and romantic – affirmation of faith in the
possibility of refashioning the world through the transformative power of the
creative imagination and the poetic, feminine rhythms of the inchoate language of love:

> My hope was always that they [the flying gods] would descend and
> live with me here in paradise, making up with their ambrosial breath
> for all that I lost when the ghostly brown figures of the last people I
> knew crept away from me in the night. (151)

---

[84] William Blake, *Jerusalem: The Emanation of the Giant Albion*: 10.20–21, in *William Blake: The Complete and Illuminated Books*, intro. James Bindman (c.1804–20;
Thames & Hudson in association with the William Blake Trust: London, 2000): 307.

[85] Blake, *Jerusalem*, 11.5.

[86] Head, *J.M. Coetzee*, 64.

Arguably, therefore, the most relevant feature of Magda's narrative is not so much its self-consciousness and lack of coherence as its excessive literariness, the fact that the narration is overtly presented as a chaotic tissue of intertextual allusions and quotations from preexisting literary texts in what may be described as an attempt to materialize Shelley's magma-like, chaotic language of poetry, the mad "ghost within the machine of culture [...] with the power to deconstruct rationalism from within": i.e. to overturn culture's madness through sheer madness.[87]

In conclusion, in the light of Paul Ricoeur's definition of literary language and of Kristevan psychoanalysis, it is no longer possible to take Magda's madness and struggle for freedom at face value.[88] Rather, as argued above, we must learn to interpret it in figurative terms as the way in which the novel thematizes the cultural representations of female madness as a way to subvert the dominant discourse of South African Boer culture and bring to the fore its utterly traumatic and unspeakable socio-political contradictions, unconscious drives, and repressed desires. In this sense, the fact that Coetzee trusted Magda to achieve this ethical aim echoes Julia Kristeva's contention that the kind of truth he wishes to express "can be imagined only as a *woman*": "A curious truth: outside time, with neither a before nor an after, neither true nor false; subterranean, it neither judges nor postulates, but refuses, displaces and breaks the Symbolic order before it can re-establish itself."[89] As I have tried to show, this formidable task requires not only the imagination of a woman, but the *furor poeticus* of a lucid madwoman at that.

---

[87] Woodman, *Sanity, Madness, Transformation*, 231.

[88] Many a critic has interpreted the overt literariness of the novel as evidence that Magda is a self-conscious and unfree literary character unrealistically struggling to liberate herself from the prison-house of language. Thus, in an otherwise excellent reading of the novel, Caroline Rody interprets Magda's desire to live "a life unmediated by words" simply as the expression of "a striking desire to be a real person in a world outside of a book" (Rody, "The Mad Colonial Daughter's Revolt in J.M. Coetzee's *In the Heart of the Country*," 164), while Paul A. Cantor, after describing Magda as a crazy and unfree "postmodernist" flat character, dismisses her struggle for individuation and freedom with the curious reflection that, "as a character in a novel, she acts the way she does not because she has her own reasons or motives, but because that is the way her story is written" (Cantor, "Happy Days in the Veld," 2).

[89] Kristeva, "About Chinese Women", 153. (Emphasis in the original.)

WORKS CITED

Arizti Martín, Bárbara, & Silvia Martínez Falquina, ed. *"On the Turn": The Ethics of Fiction in Contemporary Narrative in English* (Newcastle upon Tyne: Cambridge Scholars, 2007).

Attridge, Derek. "Ethical Modernism: Servants and Others in J.M. Coetzee's Early Fiction," *Poetics Today* 25.4 (2004): 653–71.

——. *J.M. Coetzee and the Ethics of Reading* (Chicago: U of Chicago P, 2004).

Attwell, David. *J.M. Coetzee: South Africa and the Politics of Writing* (1992; Berkeley: U of California P, 1993).

Beckett, Samuel. *The Beckett Trilogy: Molloy, Malone Dies, The Unnamable* (1959; London: Picador, 1979).

——. *Happy Days* (1961; London & Boston MA: Faber & Faber, 1966).

Bertky, Sandra Lee. *Femininity and Domination: Studies in the Phenomenology of Oppression* (New York & London: Routledge, 1990).

Blake, William. "Letter to Butts" (22 November 1802), in *The Complete Writings of William Blake*, ed. Geoffrey Keynes (London: Nonesuch & New York: Random House, 1957): 818.

——. *Jerusalem: The Emanation of the Giant Albion*, in *William Blake: The Complete and Illuminated Books*, intro. James Bindman (c.1804–20; Thames & Hudson in association with the William Blake Trust: London, 2000): 297–397.

——. *The Marriage of Heaven and Hell*, in *The Poetical Works of William Blake*, ed. John Sampson (c.1790; New York & Toronto: Oxford UP, 1956): 247–60.

Booth, Wayne C. "Types of Narration," in *The Rhetoric of Fiction* (1961), in *Narratology: An Introduction*, ed. & intro. Susana Onega & José Angel García Landa (London & New York: Longman, 1996): 145–54.

Briganti, Chiara. "A Bored Spinster with a Locked Diary: The Politics of Hysteria in *In the Heart of the Country*," *Research in African Literatures* 25.4 (Winter 1994): 33–49; Academic OneFile (Gale: Florida International U, Gale Document Number A16026665): 1–17, http://find.galegroup.com.ezproxy.fiu.edu/itx/start.do?prodld =AONE (accessed 19 January 2009).

Cantor, Paul A. "Happy Days in the Veld: Beckett and Coetzee's *In the Heart of the Country*," *South Atlantic Quarterly* 93.1 (Winter 1994): 83–110.

Caruth, Cathy, ed. *Trauma: Explorations in Memory* (Baltimore MD & London: Johns Hopkins UP, 1995).

Cixous, Hélène. "The Laugh of the Medusa" ("Le Rire de la Meduse," 1975), tr. K. and P. Cohen, in *New French Feminists*, ed. Elaine Marks & Isabelle de Courtivron (Brighton: Harvester, 1980): 254–64.

Coetzee, J.M. *Disgrace* (1999; London: Vintage, 2000).

——. *In the Heart of the Country* (1976; London: Vintage, 2004).

——. *Life & Times of Michael K* (1973; London: Vintage, 1998).

de Mijolla–Mellor, Sophie. "Family Romance," in *International Dictionary of Psycho-analysis,* ed. Alain de Mijolla (2005; Gale Cengage: eNotes.com, 2006), http://www.enotes.com/psychoanalysis-encyclopedia/family-romance (accessed 31 January 2009).

Dodd, Josephine. "Naming and Framing: Naturalization and Colonization in J.M. Coetzee's *In the Heart of the Country*," *World Literature Written in English* 27.2 (1987): 153–61.

Douglas, Mary. *Purity and Danger: An Analysis of the Concepts of Pollution and Taboo* (1966; New York & London: Routledge, 1985).

Dovey, Theresa. *The Novels of J.M. Coetzee: Lacanian Allegories* (Craighall: Ad. Donker, 1988).

Felman, Shoshana, & Dori Laub. *Testimony: Crises of Witnessing in Literature, Psychoanalysis, and History* (New York & London: Routledge, 1992).

Goodman, Nelson. *Languages of Art: An Approach to a Theory of Symbols* (1968; Indianapolis IN: Hackett, 1976).

Granofsky, Ronald. *The Trauma Novel: Contemporary Symbolic Depiction of Collective Disaster* (Bern: Peter Lang, 1995).

Head, Dominic. *J.M. Coetzee* (Cambridge Studies in African and Caribbean Literature; Cambridge: Cambridge UP, 1997).

Huyssen, Andreas. *Twilight Memories: Marking Time in a Culture of Amnesia* (London & New York: Routledge, 1995).

Kristeva, Julia. "About Chinese Women" ("Des Chinoises," 1974), tr. Leon S. Roudiez, in *The Kristeva Reader*, ed. Toril Moi (Oxford: Basil Blackwell, 1989): 138–59.

Levinas, Emmanuel. *Otherwise than Being: or, Beyond Essence*, tr. Alphonso Lingis (*Autrement qu'être ou au-delà de l'essence*, 1974; The Hague: Martinus Nijhoff, 1981).

——. *Totality and Infinity: An Essay on Exteriority,* tr. Alphonso Lingis (*Totalité et Infini: essai sur l'extériorité*, 1961; London: Kluwer Academic, 1991).

Luckhurst, Roger. "Memory Recovered/Recovered Memory," in *Literature and the Contemporary: Fiction and Theories of the Present*, ed. Roger Luckhurst & Peter Marks (Harlow: Longman, 1999): 80–93.

——. "Mixing Memory and Desire: Psychoanalysis, Psychology, and Trauma Theory," in *Literary Theory and Criticism*, ed. Patricia Waugh (Oxford & New York: Oxford UP, 2006): 497–507.

Nora, Pierre. "Between Memory and History: *Les Lieux de Mémoire*," tr. Mark Rondebush, *Representations* 26 (Spring 1989): 7–25.

Onega, Susana. *Jeanette Winterson* (Contemporary British Novelists Series; Manchester: Manchester UP, 2006).

Radway, Janice A. *Reading the Romance: Women, Patriarchy and Popular Literature* (Chapel Hill: U of North Carolina P, 1984).

Reader, Keith. *The Abject Object: Avatars of the Phallus in Contemporary French Theory, Literature and Film* (Chiasma 17; Amsterdam & New York: Rodopi, 2006).

Ricoeur, Paul. "The Function of Fiction in Shaping Reality," *Man and World* 12.2 (1979): 123–41.

Rody, Caroline. "The Mad Colonial Daughter's Revolt in J.M. Coetzee's *In the Heart of the Country*," *South Atlantic Quarterly* 93.1 (Winter 1994): 157–80.

Shelley, Percy Bysshe. "A Defence of Poetry," in *English Essays: Sidney to Macaulay* vol. 27 (1840; Harvard Classics; New York: P.F. Collier & Son, 1909–14); Bartleby.com (2001), http:www.bartleby.com/27/23.html (accessed 2 February 2009).

Showalter, Elaine. *The Female Malady: Women, Madness and English Culture, 1830–1980* (1987; Virago: London, 2001).

Stotesbury, John A. *Apartheid, Liberalism and Romance: A Critical Investigation of the Writing of Joy Packer* (Uppsala: Swedish Science Press, 1996).

Truman, Charlotte. "Magda is an Unreliable Narrator in J.M. Coetzee's *In the Heart of the Country*," *Associated Content* (28 February 2007), http://www.associated content.com/article/155766/magda_as_an_unreliable_narrator_in.html?page=2&cat =38 (accessed 3 January 2009).

Whitehead, Anne. *Trauma Fiction* (Edinburgh: Edinburgh U P, 2004).

Woodman, Ross. *Sanity, Madness, Transformation: The Psyche in Romanticism*, afterword by Joel Faflak (Toronto: U of Toronto P, 2005).

◄❖►

"Softer than Cotton, Stronger than Steel"

Metaphor and Trauma in Shani
Mootoo's *Cereus Blooms at Night*

MAITE ESCUDERO

HE ARTICULATION of both collective and personal trauma often raises questions about whose stories, voices, and histories have been documented and whose have been marginalized or ignored. The debate between remembering versus forgetting a traumatic experience has been essential to trauma studies and the ways those accounts of suffering are – or are not – told. Not coincidentally, the remembering/forgetting binary remains central to feminist, postcolonial, gay and lesbian, and queer scholarship, particularly in that they all seek to fill in the gaps that dominant history and literature have left throughout decades. By focusing on whose legacies of resistance are remembered and whose are not, minority groups or individuals have sought to transform and to intervene in the concept of hegemonic memory. Written by an Indo-Caribbean-Canadian lesbian woman, Shani Mootoo's first novel *Cereus Blooms at Night* (1996) belongs to a cluster of works aimed at examining a politics of memory that acknowledges the ways in which subjugated groups have sought to shift or transform memory. *Cereus* deliberately addresses poignant questions related to the representation of trauma as an archive of racial, gendered, and sexualized violence.

Through the story of its female protagonist, Mala Ramchandin, this novel unravels hidden stories rooted both in colonization and in the violent heteronormative power exerted and imposed by diasporic communities. Moreover, it is engaged in what Joseph Roach has defined as "clandestine counter-memories" to name "those pasts that are deliberately forgotten within conventional nationalist or diasporic scripts,"[1] while also witnessing the traumas resulting from colonialism and the racial and sexual violence in them. In an attempt to imagine the term 'diaspora' differently, then, *Cereus* becomes an archive for storing "clandestine countermemories" that are violently erased from dominant diasporic subjectivities. Thus, Mootoo interweaves an intricate web of family and human relationships that can be defined as queer, if only because all of them trouble the 'perverse/natural' dichotomy. Through a spiralling narrative structure going forwards and backwards in a span of over sixty years, the homodiegetic narrator of the story – the effeminate male nurse Tyler – tells us the story of the Ramchandin family, descendants of Indian indentured labourers who set up in Lancatamara, the fictitious name for the Caribbean isle in which the events take place. Chandin Ramchandin was an Indian man adopted by the white Reverend Thoroughly, a missionary who "helped to convert Indians to Christianity."[2] Chandin soon fell in love with his step sister Lavinia, but since this was a forbidden relationship because of the threat of incest and the stigma of miscegenation – as the Reverend tells Chandin, "you cannot, you must not have desire for your sister Lavinia. That is surely against God's will" (37) – Chandin was forced to marry Sarah, an Indian "woman of his background" (45). Chandin and Sarah had two daughters, Asha and Mala, and eventually Sarah and Lavinia fell in love and eloped to the Shivering Northern Wetlands, an imaginary place standing in for Canada and the epitome of Western colonial values such as freedom, equality, and progress. The departure of Sarah and Lavinia constitutes the scene of Mala and Asha's original trauma, for Chandin begins to rape his daughters, particularly Mala, who tries to protect her younger sister. Asha finally runs away in her late teens; Mala thus suffers from the trauma of being doubly abandoned – by her mother and by her sister – and then from that of her father's sexual abuse. Although the depictions of psychological and physical violence are extreme in the novel, Mootoo shows the struggles and alienation of the Indian

---

[1] Quoted in Gayatri Gopinath, *Impossible Desires: Queer Diasporas and South Asian Public Cultures* (Durham NC: Duke UP, 2005): 4.

[2] Shani Mootoo, *Cereus Blooms at Night* (London: Granta, 1996): 29. Further page references are in the main text.

diasporic community in the Caribbean with an aura of healing and hope for all creatures, queer or traumatized.

With a few notable exceptions, most analyses of this novel have concentrated on the symbol of the Caribbean garden as an "alternative spatial imaginary"[3] that suggests hybridity in both cultural and racial terms. On the other hand, this garden also recalls the historical burden of colonialism, owing to the relevant role of botany in creating racist, sexist, and homophobic taxonomies to define reality. While the exploration of the garden and nature-related metaphors provides this novel with a richer spatial conception from which to re-image questions of place and belonging, it may also reinforce "the silence and discomfort surrounding disclosures of incestuous abuse."[4] Nevertheless, this essay will explore the issues of sexual abuse and the potential of nature as the source for a feminist ethics that "helps uncover and eradicate the devaluation and mistreatment of women."[5] In seeking to create alternative options that challenge the manichaean and hierarchical dualism 'human/ nature', *Cereus* goes a step further, claiming a space in which interwoven histories of oppression give rise to a queer understanding of the relationship between human and non-human entities. Far from enacting the essentialist notion that women are closer to nature than men, the present essay brings together the discourses of trauma and queer scholarship because they can serve as complementary epistemological tools with which to tackle both the incestuous sexual violation and abuse that lie at the core of the novel and a new paradigm of 'human/nature' through which to overcome the traumatic effects of rape and incest. Drawing on trauma theorists such as Cathy Caruth (1996), Judith Herman (1997), Dominick LaCapra (2001), and Laurie Vickroy (2002), my point of departure is that the melancholic condition of trauma can be overcome by means of an ethics of love and restorative care, not only among human beings, but also through nature and other types of attachments.

---

[3] Sarah Phillips Casteel, "New World Pastoral: The Caribbean Garden and Emplacement in Gisèle Pineau and Shani Mootoo," *Interventions: International Journal of Postcolonial Studies* 5.1 (2003): 14.

[4] Jeanie Warnock, "'Soul Murder' and Rebirth: Trauma, Narrative, and Imagination in Shani Mootoo's *Cereus Blooms at Night*," in *Adventures of the Spirit: The Older Woman in the Works of Doris Lessing, Margaret Atwood, and Other Contemporary Women Writers*, ed. Phyllis Sternberg Perrakis (Columbus: Ohio UP, 2007): 271.

[5] Chris Cuomo, *Feminism and the Ecological Communities: An Ethic of Flourishing* (London & New York: Routledge, 1998): 39.

Whereas psychoanalytical approaches to trauma have emphasized the important role of the therapeutic setting for the recovery of the victim because s/he
"can be listened to sympathetically,"[6] I would also point out the epistemological limitations of such a perspective, especially when the traumatic experience and its aftermath are characterized by silence/muteness, absence/loss,
and numbness. For, if the victim loses the ability to convey a word and is dis-
connected from both herself and her community, how can healing be
possible?

There is in the field of queer studies a growing interest in what Sara
Ahmed has called a "cultural politics of emotion,"[7] based on the affective
lives of non-human, natural, animal or object intimacies. What this means is
that, owing to their implication in sociability, emotions entail a structural freedom to adhere to different affects because "emotions are not only about
movement, they are also about attachments, or about what connects us to this
or that."[8] In *Cereus*, Mootoo crafts a narrative of trauma in which recovery is
possible not only through an ethics of human affects but, most remarkably,
also through other "queer attachments"[9] in which emotions ascribed to animals, nature, and objects can be included. This archaeology of emotions can
serve as a mechanism to disavow pathological melancholic attachments to
loss that cannot be resolved. Removed from Freud's melancholia or mourning
without end, Mala Ramchandin can be said to inhabit a hopeful politics towards "the inability to resolve the grief and ambivalence precipitated by the
loss of the loved object, place or ideal."[10] Along these lines, I would suggest
that while *Cereus* showcases a set of attachments to loss – the reiterated loss
of whiteness, heterosexuality, and Western middle-class values – it also establishes a difference between those who are able to transcend these conditions
(i.e. Mala, Sarah, Tyler, and Otoh) and those who remain trapped in the remains of a shameful past and fail to resolve those losses (i.e. Chandin, Ambrose Mohanty, and Asha). In both cases, however, there is a negotiation

---

[6] Cathy Caruth, "Introduction" to Caruth, *Unclaimed Experience: Trauma, Narrative, and History* (Baltimore MD & London: Johns Hopkins UP, 1996): 3.

[7] Sarah Amed, *The Cultural Politics of Emotion* (Edinburgh: Edinburgh UP, 2004).

[8] Amed, *The Cultural Politics of Emotion*, 11.

[9] Sally Munt, *Queer Attachments: The Cultural Politics of Shame* (Aldershot & Burlington VT: Ashgate, 2008).

[10] David L. Eng & David Kazanjian, "Introduction" to *Loss*, ed. Eng & Kazanjian
(Berkeley: U of California P, 2003): 3.

between mourning and melancholia which underlines the process of assimilation from a dominant culture and sexuality to other minority ones. This racial and gendered melancholia is neither pathological nor permanent but, rather, a "structure of feeling,"[11] an everyday feeling that is compelled to become a dynamic force of rebirth and renewal.

Not coincidentally, many critical trends in queer studies have pointed out that the affect of shame is the foundational structure of minority groups. Shame is conceived of as a powerful spatial emotion, "effecting displacement and effacement in its subjects,"[12] but also as a "structure of feeling" which may incorporate a productive account of personal, communal, and national identities. There is in *Cereus* an oscillation between understanding shame as a stigmatized affect that can produce aberrant practices of violence (Chandin's rape of his daughters), and as a malleable emotion that can be turned into a psychic act of survival. The potentiality of shame to be transformed into positive effects has been thoroughly theorized by Silvan Tomkins in his work *Affect Imagery Consciousness*.[13] In his study, Tomkins elaborates a theory of affects which is based on a distinction between drives and affects. Unlike the instrumentality of drives, affects, for Tomkins, are endowed with a greater structural freedom, both in intensity and in time. That is to say, while drives have a restricted temporal freedom because they depend on the biological urge to satisfy them, the affect system is provided with inhibitors and activators of other affects which may change their initial response: "affects may also be invested in other affects, combine with other affects, intensify or modulate them, and suppress or reduce them."[14] Such a contingency makes affects autotelic: i.e. self-reinforcing rather than self-fulfilling, thus challenging the teleological relationship between an affect and its object.

> Any affect may have any 'object.' This is the basic source of complexity of human motivation and behaviour. [...] Affects can be, and are, attached to things, people, ideas, sensations, activities, ambitions,

---

[11] Raymond Williams, *The Long Revolution* (Toronto: Broadview, 1961): 64.

[12] Munt, *Queer Attachments*, 80.

[13] Silvan Tomkins, *Affect Imagery Consciousness*, 4 vols. (New York: Springer, 1962–92). All quotations from this source are taken from the revised edition of Tomkins's work brought out in 1995 by Eve Kosofsky Sedgwick and Adam Frank under the title *Shame and Its Sisters: A Silvan Tomkins Reader*.

[14] Quoted in *Shame and Its Sisters: A Silvan Tomkins Reader*, ed. Eve Kosofsky Sedgwick & Frank Adam (Durham NC: Duke UP, 1995): 56.

> institutions, and any number of other things, including other affects.
> Thus, one can be excited by anger, disgusted by shame or surprised by
> joy.[15]

Interestingly, Tomkins focuses on shame as one of the most alienating and self-destructive of affects, "embedded" as it is "in the central assembly of components of the nervous system."[16] Moreover, shame regulates feelings of the Tomkinsian dyads "Interest–Excitement" and "Enjoyment–Joy,"[17] which are the essential affects connected with our desires, hopes, dreams, and loves. In short, these are indispensable activators for positive effects linked to joy and life; "joy and excitement provide rewards which enable human beings to counteract fear, distress, and shame."[18]

More specifically, Eve Kosofsky Sedgwick builds on Tomkins's premises to explore the relationship between identity, emotions, and affects. Sedgwick argues that, as an affect, shame is a component of all attachments that form identity and that, as such, it is

> not a discrete intrapsychic structure, but a kind of free radical that (in
> different people and also in different cultures) attaches to and perma-
> nently intensifies or alters the meaning of – of almost anything.[19]

The predominant role of shame over other affects[20] in the formation of identity and its potential to alter pathological accounts of minority identities based on their race, sexuality, class, or nationality must be seen as meaningful clues to a contingent drive towards the healing and flourishing of traumatized individuals and communities. Likewise, Sally Munt theorizes on the notion of 'shame' as produced by the circulation of different emotions that can be easily attached to "envy, hate, contempt, apathy, painful self-absorption, humiliation, rage, mortification, and disgust."[21] Furthermore, she considers shame as

---

[15] Quoted in *Shame and Its Sisters*, ed. Sedgwick & Adam, 54.

[16] Quoted in *Shame and Its Sisters*, 133.

[17] Quoted in *Shame and Its Sisters*, 153.

[18] Quoted in *Shame and Its Sisters*, 57.

[19] Eve Kosofsky Sedgwick, *Touching Feeling: Affect, Pedagogy, Performativity* (Durham NC: Duke UP, 2003): 62.

[20] Following Silvan Tomkins's theory of affects and emotions, Sedgwick distinguishes between shame and other emotions such as startle, fear, anger, guilt or distress. *Touching Feeling*, 116.

[21] Munt, *Queer Attachments*, 2.

a mobilizing agent of the self and communities that "can also produce a reactive, new self that has a liberatory energy."[22]

What interests me here is the possibility of approaching this transformative condition of shame, as experienced by Mala, via other powerful affects that can suggest a different paradigm of understanding the trauma of sexual and incestuous abuse. Unlike the most common forms taken by shame – anger, guilt, resentment – the protagonist of *Cereus* embodies familiar negative and painful symptoms of trauma that include "dysphoria, psychic numbing, traumatic flashbacks and emotional anesthesia."[23] In contrast to her father's shame about his Indian roots,[24] Mala's symptoms are resignified and transformed into hope and love, if only because she is able to endow these emotions and affects with a performative force. As Sedgwick notes, the forms taken by shame "are available for the work of metamorphosis, reframing, refiguration, transfiguration";[25] thus, Mala seizes such performative opportunities in order to disrupt, rather than reinforce, the pathological condition of shame. A distinction can be drawn, then, between shame as a monolithic entity that prevents any productive effect of trauma (i.e. Chandin's shame) and as a malleable affect which can be turned back against itself to re-create a new narrative of recovery. In *Cereus*, such a reparative reading stems from Mala's connection and fusion with the plants and animals that have lived with her in the garden for over forty years. Furthermore, Mala's use of sheer imagination to transform her traumatic emotions into beauty and excitement towards nature becomes an essential vehicle of endurance, as it also reveals the powerful role of imagination in the transfiguration of the victim's world. By con-

---

[22] *Queer Attachments*, 80.

[23] Judith Herman, *Trauma and Recovery: From Domestic Abuse to Political Terror* (New York: HarperCollins, 1992): 12.

[24] A cruel perpetrator of rape and violence, Chandin Ramchandin is also portrayed as the victimized target of oppressive colonial regimes. Furthermore, his internalized racism and shame can be seen as one of the repercussions of colonial violence against the lives of the natives. So, as a victim of his own failure to embrace the values, education, and physical appearance of the colonizers – embodied by the Reverend Thoroughly and his religion – Chandin began "to hate his looks, the colour of his skin, the texture of his hair, his accent, the barracks, his real parents and at times even the Reverend and his god. [...] His children's skin seemed suddenly too dark and their manner of talking crude. He wanted to remove himself from his wife and his children but knew it was impossible" (33, 51).

[25] Sedgwick, *Touching Feeling*, 63.

trast, Chandin's lack of imagination leads him to live a life of depravity and moral decadence. If Chandin does not connect his rape of his daughters to their awful consequences, it is because he never realized what he was doing.

It may be useful to borrow here the notion of the 'banality of evil' that Hannah Arendt developed in *Eichmann in Jerusalem* with regard to the trial of a Nazi mastermind of the Jewish Holocaust.[26] Arendt argues that the expression 'banality of evil' is not meant to define any inherent wicked or evil quality of men but refers, rather, to the perpetrators' lack of commonsense, which prevents them from realizing the gigantic significance of the aberrant acts they commit. Like Eichmann, Chandin fails to become aware, not even for a moment in the course of the novel, of the awful consequences of his abominable acts. His "sheer thoughtlessness"[27] is linked, then, to a lack of imagination and empathy, to a "curious, quite authentic inability to think."[28] From this standpoint, and as will be seen in the following pages, *Cereus* does indeed challenge those epistemological methods of thinking and feeling that have prevailed in colonial and diasporic frameworks of citizenship, reminding us that for a "woman who had not had a human visitor in at least a decade" (150), other ways of life connection are possible.

Dragged to the Paradise Alms House asylum, the elderly Mala Ramchandin is first described as being paralyzed by her fear and inhabited only by the violence and pain of her memories – as Tyler puts it,

> flesh and bones with a skeletal structure, full of fear even as she slept under sedation, she was uncommunicative and made no sounds besides crying, moaning, wailing, and sighing. (23)

Traumatic memories are wordless and static; eluding temporal order, they are "not encoded like the ordinary memories of adults in a verbal, linear narrative."[29] Mala embodies the pathological configuration of these memories, for they appear as repetitive and painful emotions, impossible to forget. Unlike some trauma victims who do not remember, Mala's speechless condition does

---

[26] Hannah Arendt, *Eichmann in Jerusalem: A Report on the Banality of Evil* (1963; Harmondsworth: Penguin, 1977).

[27] Margaret Canovan, "Arendt's Theory of Totalitarianism: A Reassessment," in *The Cambridge Companion to Hannah Arendt*, ed. Dana Villa (Cambridge: Cambridge UP, 2000): 41.

[28] Canovan, "Arendt's Theory of Totalitarianism," 41.

[29] Herman, *Trauma and Recovery*, 37.

not prevent her from feeling the sexual violence onto her body. Indeed, Mala's body becomes the somatic site where trauma is inscribed:

> she began to feel what was normally oblivious to: her face and neck, wet with sweat and tears, bruises on her legs, skin that felt as it had been torn off her back in thick chunks. Her lower stomach ached. Fear was breaking her. [...] She was reminded of what she usually ignored or commanded herself to forget: her legs being ripped apart, something entering her from down there, entering and then scooping her insides out. Her body remembered. Mala remembered. (174–75)

The suffering and harshness pervading the novel are so extreme that Mootoo raises complex questions of ethical and moral positioning for both herself and her readers. Herself a survivor of childhood sexual assault,[30] Mootoo's position as a self-conscious writer is relevant to making the readers become aware of the ways in which trauma is represented. The relevance of bearing witness to trauma in order to make the reader reflect on violence resulting from gender, racial, and sexual oppression has been thoroughly examined by Proma Tagore.[31] According to Tagore, the narrativization of extreme acts of violence illustrates, not only the ethics of telling and the difficulties that arise from such an act, but also the political engagement of rendering disenfranchised identities visible. Thus, apart from depicting Mala's disturbing cycle of pain and personal devastation with high doses of unsettlement for the reader, Mootoo is also concerned with "the development of formal techniques for conveying characters' traumatic experience."[32] Like other trauma theorists such as Herman, Jacobs, and LaCapra, Laurie Vickroy also highlights the ethical and healing functions of trauma literature by means of a variety of narrative techniques. For instance, the adaptation of a 'double self' in response to childhood sexual abuse has been remarked by Janet Jacobs as a common psychic defence. Unable to protect herself from the sexual assaults of her father, the child Mala splits herself and constructs an imaginary identity under the

---

[30] Candice Dias, "Shani Mootoo" (1998), http://www.english.emory.edu/Bahri/Mootoo.html (accessed 9 June 2009).

[31] Proma Tagore, "Witnessing as Testimony: Toni Morrison's *The Bluest Eye* and Shani Mootoo's *Cereus Blooms at Night*," in *The Shapes of Silence: Writing by Women of Colour and the Politics of Testimony* (Montreal & Kingston, Ontario: McGill–Queen's UP, 2009): 24–65.

[32] Laurie Vickroy, *Trauma and Survival in Contemporary Fiction* (Charlottesville: UP of Virginia, 2002): x.

name of Pohpoh. Pohpoh becomes Mala's refuge to create an alternative personality or "divided consciousness wherein the victimized daughter internalizes both the identity of the powerful father [and] a representation of self as powerless victim."[33] Mala and her name have been altered to protect her emotionally fragmented subject. As she states, "no one will ever touch you again like that. I will never let anyone put their terrible hands on you again. I, Mala Ramchandin, will set you, Pohpoh Ramchandin, free, free, free, like a bird!" (173).

The use of a homodiegetic narrator to unravel the story of incest is another meaningful strategy for offering a narrative that reinstates the possibility of healing, hence the important role of empathic listeners or readers to work through trauma. Thus, Tyler encapsulates "an ethical relation to the real testimony";[34] i.e. the responsibility of telling the truth but the ethics of avoiding appropriating the story as one's own. Further, LaCapra's notion of 'empathic unsettlement' can be applied to the way in which this novel highlights the narrator's "combination of affect and critical affect."[35] This duality of emotions is explicitly found in Tyler's "shared queerness" (48) with Mala. Tyler, the male nurse "who was neither properly a man or a woman but some in-between, unnamed thing" (71), can identify with Mala because, as he says, "Miss Ramchandin and I both had secrets [...] we had found our own ways and fortified ourselves against the rest of the world" (48). On the other hand, the reader soon realizes that he reveals himself to be an unreliable and self-conscious narrator, for he must remain faithful in order to tell Mala's story:

> the temptation is strong, I must admit, to be the romantic victim. There
> is in me a performer dying for the part, but I must be strict with myself
> and stay with my intention to relate Mala Ramchandin's story. (15)

The narrator's obtrusive incursions with his own laments and love affairs imbues the narrative with humorous and/or sentimental twists, thus offering the reader a critical distance. As he says on another occasion,

> the temptation to digress from my mission and to relate every scintil-
> lating detail of the romantic blossoming of my knowledge of Otoh

---

[33] Janet L. Jacobs, *Victimized Daughters: Incest and Development of the Female Self* (London & New York: Routledge, 1994): 12.

[34] Cathy Caruth, *Unclaimed Experience*, 92.

[35] Dominick LaCapra, *Writing History, Writing Trauma* (Baltimore MD & London: Johns Hopkins UP, 2001): 41.

> Mohanty is overwhelming. I must remind myself, however, that Mala
> Ramchandin's story is my prime purpose here. (105)

Funnily enough, and later in his narrative, Tyler will end up telling the reader
every detail of his falling in love with Otoh. Furthermore, and as part of his
digressions, we know through Tyler that Asha, Mala's sister, has written
letters to Mala which, very much like Nettie's letters to Celie in Alice Walker's *The Color Purple*, are never delivered to her. Yet Tyler also calls the
reader's attention by insisting that perhaps the narrative of *Cereus* itself will
help to locate Asha, who might have gone to the Shivering Northern Wetlands
in search of her mother Sarah and Lavinia:

> Asha, if these words have already found your eyes, for the sake of
> your sister who worships your memory please return and pay her a
> visit […]. You are, to her, the promise of a cereus-scented breeze on a
> Paradise night. (249)

Despite Tyler's interruptions, there is throughout *Cereus* an insistence on
the 'queerness' Tyler shares with Mala. In fact, this 'shared queerness' becomes a metaphoric vehicle to express the unspeakability and unrepresen-
tability of both queer sexuality and the traumatic effects of sexual abuse. The
link between incest and homosexuality is not coincidental; both share a
structure of secrecy that needs to be disclosed through coming-out narratives.
The silence around which homosexuality and incest are constructed embodies
the "epistemology of the closet,"[36] with sexually transgressive behaviours
being paradoxically defined through their secrecy. Furthermore, when Mala/
Pohpoh discovers the forbidden relationship between her mother and Lavinia,
she is preoccupied solely with keeping the women's secret, not so much out
of sympathy as to avoid the shame of exposure:

> Pohpoh's heart leapt when she saw the tips of Aunt Lavinia's fingers
> grasping Mama's waist. She understood something in that instant
> but, save for a flash of an image of her father's face in her mind, she
> had no words to describe what she suddenly realized was their secret
> […]. She imagined them kissing. She imagined Papa finding them
> kissing. (56–57)

Pohpoh's feeling that "something was being concealed" (54) resembles the
secret structures of incest and rape. Indeed, Pohpoh's inability to name the

---

[36] Eve Kosofsky Sedgwick, *Epistemology of the Closet* (1990; Harmondsworth:
Penguin, 1991).

forbidden lesbian relationship is replaced by the image in a photograph of
"Lavinia's hands resting tenderly on Mama's waist" (58). The image of the
two women in the photograph is engraved in Mala's memory forever and, as
if it were an intermittent flash of her traumatic experience, it becomes the
concealed language through which Mala's trauma is manifest. The departure
of her mother and Lavinia, even though they never intended to abandon
Sarah's children, marks the origin of Chandin's sexual assault on his daughters. According to Ann Cvetkovick, a theorist of queer culture, this maternal
abandonment intertwined with lesbian love "makes for an especially complex
source of trauma in the novel, preventing any reductive blaming of the father
or celebration of transgressive sexuality."[37] Likewise, the trauma theorist Kalí
Tal has denounced the tendency to blame mothers in rape narratives, where
"the responsibility of incest and rape is not placed on men who don't have to
face the consequences."[38] In fact, the inhabitants of Lancantamara describe
Chandin Ramchandin as a man who "had obviously mistaken his daughter for
his wife" (65) when he was abandoned by the latter, thus complying with
dominant, patriarchal, and heteronormative structures of power. The critique
launched at the social, cultural, and legal conditions that do not punish such
abominable acts is quite evident in *Cereus*, hence its definition of Chandin's
rape as 'a mistake'. Furthermore, the novel contests the community's "willful
ignorance"[39] because of their equation of incest and homosexuality as perverse behaviors. Definitions of what can be termed 'natural' or 'perverse' are
of the utmost importance when dealing with sexuality; thus, Tyler claims:

> I was preoccupied with trying to understand what was natural and
> what perverse, and who said so and why. Chandin Ramchandin played
> a part in confusing me about these roles, for it was a long time before I

---

[37] Ann Cvetkovich, *An Archive of Feelings: Trauma, Sexuality and Lesbian Public
Cultures* (Durham NC: Duke UP, 2003): 142.

[38] Kalí Tal, *Worlds of Hurt: Reading the Literatures of Trauma* (Cambridge: Cambridge UP, 1995): 165.

[39] Vivian May, "Trauma in Paradise: Willful and Strategic Ignorance in *Cereus
Blooms at Night*," *Hypathia* 21.3 (Spring–Summer 2006): 106–35. May defines the
concept of "willful ignorance" as "carefully crafted methods of not-knowing that are a
means of perpetuating privilege and domination. Willful ignorance entails an agree-
ment to know the world wrongly that is rewarded and encouraged because it serves to
maintain the status quo" (109).

could differentiate between his perversion and what others called
mine. (48)

Rather than seeing it as resembling Chandin's perversion, Tyler perceives his
homosexuality as being closer to Mala's queerness. By "becoming her witness" (100), Tyler testifies that, through his connection with Mala, "my own
life has finally begun to bloom" (105). Mala's queerness, however, stems not
so much from her sexuality – she is heterosexual – as from her estrangement
from normalizing discourses surrounding Indo-Caribbean women's identities
and home spaces. By positioning Mala, particularly her recovery from her
trauma, beyond the confines of the private realm, *Cereus* subverts the logic of
patriarchal diasporic discourses for which the concepts of 'home' and 'domestic space' are a sacred site of purity, tradition, and authenticity, embodied by
the figure of a subordinate woman. Accordingly, and to endorse Gayatri
Gopinath's words, the category of queer here "extends to all those bodies dis-
avowed by colonial and national constructions of home; bodies marked by
rape and incest; biologically male bodies that are improperly feminine, such
as Tyler."[40]

In a different light, 'the shared queerness' is also linked to Mootoo's central image of the cereus plant: the "rare night-blooming" cereus is an exotic,
'queer' cactus that blooms only once a year in an astonishing unfolding of
petals and sweet scent: "without blossoms, the plant appears to be little more
than an uninteresting tangle of leafage [...]. However, in bloom, it is stun-
ningly gorgeous" (22). Like the cereus, Tyler's life blossoms as he falls in
love with Otoh, the female-to-male transgender son of Ambrose Mohanty,
Mala's first and unique love, when father and son pay their only visits to
elderly Mala in Paradise Alms House. The name of Otoh, which is a nickname of Otoh-boto, the acronym for 'on the one hand, but on the other', also
exemplifies the hybridity that pervades the novel, not only in terms of crossing the boundaries of gender identity but also in its depiction of its characters,
exotic landscape, flora, and fauna. While the cereus is the epitome of metamorphosis and mutability, thus functioning as a metaphor for queer identities,
it is also attached to Mala's traumatic memories. The duality of the plant, re-
pulsive like Chandin's rape of his daughter and gorgeous like Mala's communion with nature, serves to underline other border-crossings in the novel.
Remarkably, the sexual assaults on Mala always take place inside the house,

---

[40] Gopinath, *Impossible Desires*, 184.

mostly in the kitchen, a sacred site for the maintenance and continuation of Indian women's traditional values. When, after many years of rape and humiliation, Chandin dies in a fortuitous quarrel with Mala, she dreads the idea of sleeping inside the house and spends the nights in the garden. As mentioned earlier, although much has been written on the image of the 'garden' by postcolonial and feminist criticism – i.e. either it can represent the wilderness and freedom of the colonized versus the impeccable social order of the colonizers, or it can be understood as a woman's safe space outside the violent patriarchal sphere – it plays a central role in *Cereus*. Not only do the garden's plants, animals, and trees convey the only signs of Mala's recovery, but they also show her deep concern when the children spoil the plants: "to her, the flower and the plant would be both suffering because they were separated from each other" (69).

Furthermore, this garden is as much a place of decay as it is of regeneration; it is saturated with insects, spiders, snails, different trees, plants, and smells with which Mala intermingles: "she blends into the background of its vegetation, and can imitate perfectly the cries of its birds, crickets, and frogs" (24). However, the garden is also the place where life and death meet, since the intoxicating stench of her father's corpse hovers in it. And yet, the special harmony between Mala and nature is insistently evoked by the novel as an indispensable tool for acknowledging a non-hierarchical and non-violent understanding of the world:

> Mala's companions were the garden's birds, insects, snails, and reptiles. She and they and the abundant foliage gossiped among themselves [...]. She listened to worms coiling arduously from place to place [...]. She did not intervene in nature's business [...]. Flora and fauna left her to her own devices and in return she left them to theirs. (127–28)

Mala's egalitarian relationship with the natural world contrasts with the impulse of Western colonial discourses that categorize and taxonomize, not only natural history, but also deviant sexual and racial categories.[41] The centrality of botany for colonial and nationalist regimes in their obsession to preserve the natural order of things (even as they destroy it) is sharply contested in this novel. Moreover, Mala's sense of being on an equal footing with

---

[41] See Grace Kyungwon Hong, "'A Shared Queerness': Colonialism, Transnationalism, and Sexuality in Shani Mootoo's *Cereus Blooms at Night*," *Meridians: Feminism, Race, Transnationalism* 7.1 (Spring 2006): 73–103.

nature is expressed as instinctual rather than as intellectual or scientific, as happens with Ambrose – he is an entomologist. Through the figure of Mala, then, *Cereus* calls for an ethics of reciprocity in which the subject and the community are imagined differently. Not coincidentally, readers are warned that words alone cannot tell this story, since it exceeds the boundaries of language and culture. While the failure of language to convey the horror of incest mirrors Mala's numbness, her attachment to nature opens a door to hope and renewal. Eventually

> Mala all but rid herself of words. The wings of a gull flapping through the air titillated her soul and awakened her toes and knobby knees, the palms of her withered hands. (126)

The delight that she experiences when seeing the birds and insects, and touching the plants, allows her to abandon her speechless melancholic condition and find a reconnection with life:

> As night fell she dragged her rocking chair down the back stairs into the yard under the fringes of the giant mudra tree. She sat upright like a concert director in front of the wall. As the night unwound she witnessed the slow dance of huge, white cereus buds – she counted sixty-two – trembling as they unfolded against the wall, a choreography of petal and sepal opening together, sending dizzying scent high and wide into the air. The moonlight reflected off the blossoms' pure whiteness and cast a glow over the yard. Mala basked. (134)

Like the rare night-blooming cereus, Mala is able to transform "general abasement, abjection, and soulless despair into a restorative, creative force that can mobilize the self."[42] By weaving a net of queer attachments, Mala vividly embodies both the vulnerability of an abused body and the strength of survival; in short, she is like the properties of a spider silk: "softer than cotton, stronger than steel" (214). All in all, she engages in the task of blurring rigid binaries while simultaneously remembering historical and cultural violence differently, outside the orthodox limitations of the perpetrators' ideology. It is through her queer attachment to the world of nature that Mala is able to forget her father's rape and the feelings of isolation, despair, and social abjection generated by it. These insidious forms of violence, as Cvetkovick would put it, have produced an archive of feelings which, though severely marked by self-hatred, low self-esteem, isolation, suicidal tendencies, humiliation, and

---

[42] Munt, *Queer Attachments*, 216.

shame, may be subjected to resignification and regeneration. In this vein, Mootoo's *Cereus* follows queer theory's commitment to embracing traumatic effects as "productive rather than pathological, abundant rather than lacking, social rather than solipsistic, and militant rather than reactionary."[43] By being written, these queer feelings, attachments, and emotions are revealed to be part of the shared experience of the social, thus giving rise to new productive readings and interpretations of history, memory, and culture.

WORKS CITED

Ahmed, Sarah. *The Cultural Politics of Emotion* (Edinburgh: Edinburgh UP, 2004).

Arendt, Hannah. *Eichmann in Jerusalem: A Report on the Banality of Evil* (1963; Harmondsworth: Penguin, 1977).

Canovan, Margaret. "Arendt's Theory of Totalitarianism: A Reassessment," in *The Cambridge Companion to Hannah Arendt*, ed. Dana Villa (Cambridge: Cambridge UP, 2000): 25–43.

Caruth, Cathy, ed. *Unclaimed Experience: Trauma, Narrative, and History* (Baltimore MD & London: Johns Hopkins UP, 1996).

Casteel, Sarah Phillips. "New World Pastoral: The Caribbean Garden and Emplacement in Gisèle Pineau and Shani Mootoo," *Interventions* 5.1 (2003): 12–28.

Cuomo, Chris J. *Feminism and Ecological Communities: An Ethic of Flourishing* (London & New York: Routledge, 1998).

Cvetkovich, Ann. *An Archive of Feelings: Trauma, Sexuality and Lesbian Public Cultures* (Durham NC: Duke UP, 2003).

Dias, Candice. "Shani Mootoo" (1998), http://www.english.emory.edu/Bahri/Mootoo .html (accessed 9 June 2009).

Eng, David L., & David Kazanjian, ed. *Loss* (Berkeley: U of California P, 2003).

Gopinath, Gayatri. *Impossible Desires: Queer Diasporas and South Asian Public Cultures* (Durham NC: Duke UP, 2005).

Henke, Suzette A. *Shattered Subjects: Trauma and Testimony in Women's Life Writing* (London: Macmillan, 1998)

Herman, Judith. *Trauma and Recovery: From Domestic Abuse to Political Terror* (New York: HarperCollins, 1992).

Hong, Grace Kyungwon. "'A Shared Queerness': Colonialism, Transnationalism, and Sexuality in Shani Mootoo's *Cereus Blooms at Night*," *Meridians: Feminism, Race, Transnationalism* 7.1 (2006): 73–103.

Jacobs, Janet Liebman. *Victimized Daughters: Incest and Development of the Female Self* (London & New York: Routledge, 1994).

---

[43] Eng & Kazanjian, *Loss*, ix.

LaCapra, Dominick. *Writing History, Writing Trauma* (Baltimore MD & London: Johns Hopkins UP, 2001).

May, Vivian M. "Trauma in Paradise: Willful and Strategic Ignorance in *Cereus Blooms at Night*," *Hypathia* 21.3 (2006): 106–35.

Mootoo, Shani. *Cereus Blooms at Night* (London: Granta, 1996).

Munt, Sally. *Queer Attachments: The Cultural Politics of Shame* (Aldershot & Burlington VT: Ashgate, 2008).

Sedgwick, Eve Kosofsky. *Epistemology of the Closet* (1990; Harmondsworth: Penguin, 1991).

——. *Touching Feeling: Affect, Pedagogy, Performativity* (Durham NC: Duke UP, 2003).

——, & Adam Frank, ed. *Shame and Its Sisters: A Silvan Tomkins Reader* (Durham NC: Duke UP, 1995).

Tagore, Proma. "Witnessing as Testimony: Toni Morrison's *The Bluest Eye* and Shani Mootoo's *Cereus Blooms at Night*," in *The Shapes of Silence: Writing by Women of Colour and the Politics of Testimony* (Montreal & Kingston, Ontario: McGill–Queen's UP, 2009): 24–65.

Tal, Kalí. *Worlds of Hurt: Reading the Literatures of Trauma* (Cambridge: Cambridge UP, 1995).

Tomkins, Silvan S. *Affect Imagery Consciousness*, 4 vols. (New York: Springer, 1962–92)

Vickroy, Laurie. *Trauma and Survival in Contemporary Fiction* (Charlottesville: UP of Virginia, 2002).

Warnock, Jeanie E. "'Soul Murder' and Rebirth: Trauma, Narrative, and Imagination in Shani Mootoo's *Cereus Blooms at Night*," in *Adventures of the Spirit: The Older Woman in the Works of Doris Lessing, Margaret Atwood, and Other Contemporary Women Writers*, ed. Phyllis Sternberg Perrakis (Columbus: Ohio UP, 2007): 270–98.

Williams, Raymond. *The Long Revolution* (Toronto: Broadview, 1961).

◄❖►

Haunting Wounds

Genital Alterations, Autobiography, and Trauma

CHANTAL ZABUS

I N THE LIGHT of recent developments on memory, trauma, and the body, I here wish to link various experiences of genital alterations such as female excision, male circumcision, and procedures akin to transsexual surgery, as those 'experiences' are mediated via autobiographical texts or texts with an autobiographical vestment. Such texts are haunted by a lasting wound, which is the linchpin of trauma theory, as it applies to individuals rather than a collectivity.

This reflection started as a spin-off on my work on female excision,[1] also known as 'female genital mutilation' or FGM. Many women autobiographers under scrutiny in *Between Rites and Rights* mention their excision as a wounding operation.[2] In her short story "Bahiyya's Eyes," the Egyptian Alifa

---

[1] See Chantal Zabus, *Between Rites and Rights: Excision in Women's Experiential Texts and Human Contexts* (Stanford CA: Stanford UP, 2007).

[2] Excision was and still is a rite of passage performed on women and by women in sub-Saharan Africa, the Mashreq and various other countries, regardless of their social rank or religious allegiance. It marks the initiation of the girl child, aged between four and fifteen, into adulthood. But it can also be performed on infants and on dead women. In other words, excision is, in some cases, no longer a puberty rite. Yet, as a purification rite, excision often posits an original hermaphroditism and aims at removing the allegedly vestigial masculinity of the clitoris, the way male circumcision removes the vestigial femininity of the glans but this is seldom pushed to its logical conclusion,

Rifaat recalls her excision thus: "it left me with a wound in my body and another deep inside me, a feeling that wrong had been done to me, a wrong that could never be undone."[3] Trauma, one should remember, is the Greek word for 'wound'; excision is a 'double wound' inflicted on both the body and the mind, and women's corporeal writing flows from that double wound. Significantly, Alifa Rifaat was never exposed to Western mores, yet wrote about this issue before it was conceptualized as a 'wound' in the Western psyche and as a 'mutilation' in activist and legal debates. However, Rifaat is an exception, for most women autobiographers such as Guinean Kesso Barry, Senegalese Khady (Koïta), Somali Waris Dirie, Nura Abdi, and Fadumo Korn wrote about the procedure from their Western platform in forced or chosen exile – France, Britain, the USA, Germany. Tellingly, the 'I' writes her auto-biography when the cohesion of that 'I' is most uncertain, as in exile.

Before excision was reclaimed experientially, the procedure, as in the Egyptian Nawal El Saadawi's *The Hidden Face of Eve* (1980), at first func-tioned as an 'unclaimed experience,'[4] for, in the now familiar words of Cathy Caruth, who took her cue from Freud's *Beyond the Pleasure Principle* (1919),

> [it] is not, like the wound of the body, a simple and healable event, but rather an event that [...] is experienced too soon, too unexpectedly, to be fully known and is therefore not available to consciousness until it imposes itself again, repeatedly, in the nightmares and repetitive actions of the survivor.

Caruth adds:

> Trauma is not locatable in the simple violent or original event in an individual's past, but rather in the way that its very unassimilated nature – the way it was precisely *not known* in the first instance – returns to haunt the survivor later on.[5]

---

i.e. the removal of men's nipples. As such, excision involves clitoridectomy: i.e. the removal of the clitoris, sometimes accompanied by labiadectomy: i.e. the removal of all or part of the labia minora and majora. I do not use the acronym FGM, because it pre-empts moral judgment on such culture-specific operations.

[3] Alifa Rifaat, "Bahiyya's Eyes," in *Distant View of a Minaret and Other Stories* (London: Quartet, 1983): 8.

[4] For an in-depth analysis, see Chantal Zabus, *Between Rites and Rights*, 83–96.

[5] Cathy Caruth, *Unclaimed Experience: Trauma, Narrative, and History* (Baltimore MD & London: Johns Hopkins UP, 1996): 3.

A follower of the Yale school of deconstruction, especially of Paul de Man, Caruth considers that the *knowing* of trauma is deferred and, it is implied, comes through, as in these excised women's writings, in the guise of an autobiography as 'de-facement'. Using the converse of prosopoeia, a trope by which a name is made as intelligible and memorable as a face, Paul de Man had indeed questioned the fact that autobiography depended on reference. He had instead suggested that "the autobiographical project may itself produce and determine the life [of the subject] and that whatever the writer *does* is in fact governed by the technical demands of self-portraiture" and that, the illusion of reference being more akin to fiction, this mimesis in its own turn "acquires a degree of referential productivity."[6] Whether the life of excised women produced their autobiographies or, as de Man suggests, the self-perpetuating reverse, the reclaiming process foregrounds the role of pain as the most powerful aids to mnemonics. As in pathographies to refer to autobiographies around illness, "the 'unforgettable' is etched on the body itself."[7] Pain and suffering thus play an indelible role in the creation of life-writing or self-writing out of trauma.

Caught between impulses toward exposure and concealment and hampered by a difficult access to Western-style literacy, the women autobiographers who write around their excision often resort to an amanuensis. The latter writes, often from dictation or transcription (complicated by the translation) of tapes, on behalf of the author. Without getting into the intricacies of this deferred and possibly 'de-faced' autobiography or the particulars of the quasi-ethnographic relation between taper and taped, the person who knows and the person who is known, it remains apparent that the double wound is not so elusive as one might expect, given the memorial sediments coagulating around it.

By way of coming to genital alterations proper such as infibulation,[8] I would now like to make a short detour through rape as a mode of figuration

---

[6] Paul de Man, "Autobiography as De-facement," *Modern Language Notes* 94.5 (December 1979): 920.

[7] Quoted by Gilles Deleuze, *Nietzsche and Philosophy*, tr. Hugh Tomlinson (*Nietzsche et la philosophie*, 1962; London: Athlone, 1983): 10.

[8] Infibulation involves the removal of the clitoris and the labia minora and majora, and the stitching together or suturing of the two sides so as to leave a small aperture to permit the flow of urine and menstrual discharge but this practice has never been attested as a rite.

for excision. Early in *Desert Flower* (1998), Waris Dirie, then a nomadic camel herder, remembers her rape at age four by her older cousin Guban:

> Next I felt something hard and wet pressing against my vagina. I froze at first, not understanding what was happening, but I know it was something very bad. The pressure intensified until it became a sharp pain. [...] Suddenly, I was flooded with a warm liquid and a sickening acrid odor permeated the night air. "You pee-peed on me!" I screamed, horrified. I jumped up and rubbed my scarf against my legs, mopping off the foul-smelling liquid.[9]

In *Desert Dawn*, published some four years later, Dirie adds more graphic and sartorial details about her struggle:

> he was pulling at my *guntino* and he grabbed me and untied the knots. He pulled me underneath him even though I yelled and told him to get off. Of course nobody could hear because we were so far away from the camp. He reached down and pulled up my dress and rolled on top of me. His *maa-a-weiss*, the cloth he wore wrapped around his waist, was open and he pushed my legs apart and sprawled on top of me. He was poking my vagina with this thing and I screamed, "Stop it, stop it! What are you doing?" He put his huge hand right on my little mouth and the next thing I knew he squirted something. He rolled off then started laughing and I had this sticky stuff all over me. I never smelled anything like that in my life and I still hate that smell, I hate that smell. I stood up, wiped myself and ran all the way home.[10]

When silence is forced upon her by her older cousin Guban putting his hand over her "little mouth," her early psycho-social identity is checked since the young Waris goes by the nickname "*Afdokle*, Little mouth."[11] From age four onwards, her lips are sealed.

The haunting memory of Guban's rape and betrayal lingers, like the olfactory trail of his abuse, into adulthood but even some twenty-five years after the 'event,' while settled in Europe and writing *Desert Dawn*, words, which she "didn't have" in *Desert Flower*, for she "didn't *know* what he'd done," fail her. This confirms Caruth's notion of trauma as an unknowable, unlocat-

---

[9] Waris Dirie, with Cathleen Miller, *Desert Flower: The Extraordinary Life of a Desert Nomad* (1998; London: Virago, 1999): 24.

[10] Waris Dirie, with Jeanne D'Haem, *Desert Dawn* (London: Virago, 2002): 27.

[11] Dirie, *Desert Dawn*, 69.

able occurrence or event. Dirie is thus left with abstract, quasi-academic musings about the emotional pain of being "sexually violated and hav[ing] everyone ignore it."[12] One could cynically argue that Dirie, in the second narrative of the rape, is providing additional, sensational fodder for Western consumption. But, more to our purpose, both versions of the rape illustrate Dirie's diasporic self, as it evolves towards a type of conflicting, introspective selfhood, more commensurate with European models of personal identity and Euro-American women's autobiographies which, as Elleke Boehmer has argued in another context, "tend to show greater awareness of the gaps, uncertainties, and fictions involved in the construction of identity."[13]

The same grappling with the horror of that intimate memory, which Waris Dirie exorcized publicly, holds for her varied recollections of her infibulation, which is ghosted by her earlier experience of rape. Throughout the procedure, Waris recalls her "poor mother"'s ambivalent role, as she is solicitous and caring; yet allows Waris to be "butchered with [her] mother's permission and [she] couldn't understand why."[14] From behind her mother's legs straddling her body, Waris peers at the exciser, who spits on the blood that has dried on the jagged edge of the broken razor blade. Then her mother blindfolds her, leaving Waris's other sense to record "the sound of the dull blade sawing back and forth through my skin. When I think back, I honestly can't believe that this happened to me. I feel as if I were talking about somebody else."[15] She further remembers feeling dissociated from her body and seeing herself "floating up, away from the ground, leaving [her] pain behind, and [she] hovered some feet above the scene looking down,"[16] as the exciser is sewing up the edges of her vulva up with acacia tree thorns. Waris Dire's subsequent passing out makes it difficult for her older self or present-tense identity to reincarnate that disembodied self at the time of committing things down to writing. The hiatus experienced through fainting finds its palpable corollary in the distancing of this body-beyond-pain, which is incapable of moans, groans and primordial cries. Autobiography helps name the unnamable but with a perpetual deferment, with the acknowledged impossibility of putting a face on

---

[12] Dirie, *Desert Dawn*, 25.

[13] Elleke Boehmer, *Stories of Women: Gender and Narrative in the Postcolonial Nation* (Manchester & New York: Manchester UP, 2005): 68.

[14] Dirie, *Desert Dawn*, 46, 48.

[15] *Desert Dawn*, 45.

[16] *Desert Dawn*, 45.

a name. Dirie then reports going back to the scene of the crime to look for her lost genitals as on a perverse pilgrimage to the sacred shrine of her sacrifice. With the same 'urge to know,' Nura Abdi, when entrusting her Somali experience in *Larmes de sable* (2005) to her amanuensis Leo Linder, remembers being curious about the location of "what had been sawed off all of us." She later learns that "someone had dug a hole and buried them [the severed genitals] somewhere in the courtyard."[17] Predictably, the shards of Waris's or Nura's flesh have disappeared, but not the unforgettable event.

Waris's later exposure to European, American, and African feminisms and Human Rights, as well as her work as a UN Ambassador against excision, are intervening events that have memorial consequences on her retrospective alignment of infibulation with other traumatic experiences like rape. Her aberrant memories, as evidenced by her different accounts of the same event, certainly compare with the clinical symptoms diagnosed in post-traumatic stress disorder. Clinical experience conducted at Harvard Medical School among adult survivors of childhood trauma in the early 1990s revealed that the patients who enter psychotherapy grapple with three patterns of traumatic memory, the most common one being "relatively continuous and complete recall of childhood abuse experiences coupled with changing interpretations (delayed understanding) of these experiences."[18] Although there is no clinical evidence that Dirie exhibits any such symptoms, she fixes, through her autobiographical retelling, the experience of delayed recall after years of silence and secrecy. Waris Dirie's confessional writing to her amanuensis acts as a kind of psychotherapy and, what is more, as a form of revenge, since she exposes her cousin Guban to a vast readership as a deceitful caretaker, who abused her, unbeknownst to her mother, an ally-turned-anti-mom in the employ of patriarchy.

Research by, among others, Claudette Wassill–Grimm has shown that memory is reconstructive and that we remember only the gist of things in what scientists call memory traces:

---

[17] Nura Abdi, *Larmes de sable*, tr. Gérald Messadié (Nura Abdi & Leoo G. Linder, *Tränen im Sand*, 2003; Paris: L'Archipel, 2005): 25.

[18] Mary R. Harvey & Judith Lewis Herman, "Amnesia, Partial Amnesia, and Delayed Recall Among Adult Survivors of Childhood Trauma," in *The Recovered Memory/False Memory Debate*, ed. Kathy Pezdek & Willams P. Banks (London: Academic Press, 1996): 29.

when we need to review an event from the past our brain first receives *a bare-bones image*. The actual details have often been lost, so the brain creates *a probable scenario* based on general knowledge or present-related imagery borrowed from our surroundings, or movies, books, and personal accounts we have been exposed to since the event. We fill in the gaps with more recent memories.[19]

Wassill–Grimm further elaborates a mood congruency theory according to which people do call up memories which are congruent with their present mood so that people "rewrite their personal history based on their mood at the time of recall."[20] As an older Dirie tries to flesh out the original "bare-bones image" with a "probable scenario," the remembering process confuses our expectations of linearity so that rape, infibulation and, even later, defloration are discursively aligned.

Such traumatic experiences share the same vocabulary, the same syntax, and the same grammar of pain. If, however, the reader feels sympathy, verging on empathy, with Waris Dirie's early writings, the reader of the later Dirie –or this reader in any case– has developed a carapace of cynicism. Dirie's later memories in *Desert Children* (2005) are, tellingly, "on instant recall,"[21] as if trauma, with its long, cooling deferral could be served hot. For the third time over less than a decade, Dirie rehearses her traumatic infibulation, yet adding details, which confirm the work of memory in its strenuous attempts to come to grips with this heart-wrenching event at the same time that it confirms our intuition that experience is itself interpretation and, possibly, a commodified defacement.

It remains that exile from Africa to Europe triggers off memory. As Caruth reminds us, Freud insisted, from his exile in England, on having his final book on trauma – *Moses and Monotheism* – translated into English before he died:

> For those who undergo trauma, it is not only the moment of the event, but the passing out of it that is traumatic; [...] survival itself, in other words, can be a crisis.[22]

---

[19] Claudette Wassill–Grimm, *Diagnosis for Disaster: The Devastating Truth about False Memory Syndrome and Its Impact on Accusers and Families* (New York: Overlook, 1995): 127; my emphases.

[20] Claudette Wassill–Grimm, *Diagnosis for Disaster*, 129.

[21] Waris Dirie, with Corinna Milborn, *Desert Children* (London: Virago, 2005): 10.

[22] Caruth, *Unclaimed Experience*, 9.

The function of Europe or the USA is to jolt the traumatized subject into recognition of both the trauma and the survival itself. As I have demonstrated elsewhere,[23] this recognition can start, as in the case of Somali Nura Abdi and Fadumo Korn (in *Born in the Big Rains* [2004]), and of Senegalese Khady (Koïta), when in their (respectively) British, German, and French homes for asylum seekers.

If exile in a European country is synonymous with empowerment and yet compounded with a *Spaltung* in personal identity,[24] as in the case of excised women autobiographers, can the same be said of men who have been circumcised? Compared to the panoply of experiential writings around excision, there is a tiny corpus on circumcision in the making but it is arguably disproportionate, especially if we reckon that excision concerns some 140 million women whereas male circumcision is practiced on five continents by about a billion Muslims, three hundred million Christians, sixteen million Jews and an indeterminate number of 'animists' and atheists. Therefore, a discursive type of asymmetry has set in, not only in law, medicine, and cultural anthropology, but also in first-person accounts.

This experiential void has been partly filled by, most notably, Jacques Derrida, who, in *Circumfession – Circonfession* (1991) – spoke *around* his circumcision, *circum*venting the issue, yet speaking in the first person about the procedure which he underwent when he was eight days old. Yet, it is telling that Jacques Derrida's account in *Circumfession* is thus far one of the few male experiential texts that speak autobiographically about what he construes as a traumatic bodily experience. Another notable exception is *Ma circoncision* (2004) by the French cartoonist of Syrian origin, Riad Sattouff.[25]

---

[23] Chantal Zabus, "The Afrosporic Migration of Genital Alterations to the New Europe: Trauma, the Law, and the Internet," in *Diasporic Subjectivity and Cultural Brokering in Contemporary Post-Colonial Literatures*, ed. Igor Maver (New York: Lexington & Plymouth: Rowman & Littlefield, 2009): 115–34.

[24] Françoise Lionnet mentions a "*Spaltung*, such as the one identified by psychoanalytical critics," in her *Postcolonial Representations: Women, Literature, Identity* (Ithaca NY: Cornell UP, 1995): 136.

[25] For an analysis of Riad Sattouff's circumcision, see Chantal Zabus, "Beyond Circumspection: African, Jewish, and Muslim Autobiographies Around Circumcision," in *Fearful Symmetries: Essays and Testimonies Around Excision and Circumcision*, ed. Chantal Zabus (Matatu 37; Amsterdam & New York: Rodopi, 2008): 121–24.

An increasing number of scholars dealing with circumcision have themselves been involved somewhat autobiographically in their own circumcision or that of their sons and relatives. In an interview I carried out with Sami Aldeeb Abu-Sahlieh in Lausanne in 2002, he, as a Christian Palestinian, told me that he had heard the shrill screaming of an infant in the process of being circumcised at a neighbour's house in Palestine and this prompted him to inquire about the *raison d'être* of circumcision. Leonard Glick also speaks from memory in his Preface to *Marked in Your Flesh* (2005) as a cultural anthropologist and a college professor with a medical degree, but also as the father of circumcised sons. He recounts:

> Our own three sons were circumcised [...] not ritually but in hospitals soon after birth. I accepted this without a second (or even a first) thought, assuming that it was not only medically advisable but appropriate for Jewish boys. [...] Had I known at their births what I know now, they would never have been circumcised.[26]

Glick also hints at the fact that the scholarship of Rabbi Jacob Neusner's *The Enchantments of Judaism* (1987) and Rabbi Daniel Gordis's *Becoming a Jewish Parent* (1999) functions as a cathartic device to let out anxieties about the circumcision of their own sons; he also frames the issue against a canvas of father–son filiation.

For Jacques Derrida, however, the circumcision ceremony is linked with the mother-figure and, more largely, the feminine, more so than with the *mohel*, that is, in Hebrew, the one who circumcises. In El Biar, Algeria, where Jacques Derrida was born in 1930, he reports that one did not use the Hebrew word *milah* from *berit milah* (the alliance through cutting or Covenant of the Cut)[27] to refer to circumcision but, rather, 'baptism' (Fr *baptême*), out of an '*affadissement par peur*,' a euphemistic word used out of fear – Judaism

---

[26] Leonard B. Glick, *Marked in Your Flesh: Circumcision from Ancient Judea to Modern America* (Oxford & London: Oxford UP, 2005): viii.

[27] *Berit milah* is the Covenant of the Cut referring to the Covenant between God and Abraham in Genesis 17:1–14. The latter is often invoked to justify circumcision; it spells out that "an uncircumcised male who is not circumcised in the flesh of his foreskin shall be cut off from his people; he has broken my Covenant." The second text is Leviticus 12:1–5, in which the Lord says to Moses that "on the eighth day the flesh of his foreskin shall be circumcised." For more detail, see Sami Aldeeb Abu-Sahlieh, *Circoncision masculine, circoncision féminine: Débat religieux, médical, social et juridique* (Paris: L'Harmattan, 2001).

cloaked in Catholicism – but at the same time, a translation, since Christian/
Pauline baptism was an alternative rite to replace circumcision, itself presum-
ably an alternative rite to human sacrifice.

Derrida also confesses that he does not know how to say 'circumcision' in
any other language beside the French one. Despite his avowed monolingual-
ism, he spoke about it in another medium. His entire philosophical oeuvre is
indeed traversed, ontologically haunted by his own circumcision. "Circoncision; je n'ai jamais parlé que de çà: *Eperons, Glas, Carte Postale*: la chose y
est nommée"; the very thing is named.[28] He thereby provides his own "haun-
tology," an inaugural word that opens his *Specters of Marx*[29] but whose
spectre always already limns previous writings. In *Tourner les mots: Au bord
d'un film*, the book co-authored by Jacques Derrida and the Egyptian poet and
filmmaker Safaa Fathy, around Fathy's film *D'Ailleurs Derrida* (2000),
Fathy describes Derrida's ritual entry into film as "an initiation." And Derrida, also known as the Actor, sees the editing process as the act of

> selecting [...] excluding, circumscribing, one would almost say cir-
> cumcising [...] if one wished [...] to sew back together this moment
> with all these other passages on circumcision and excision, at the core
> of the film.[30]

Almost implausibly, cutting and film cutting are sewn together.

Being thus cut and dis-membered, writing helps Derrida re-member the
primitive event in a private, confessional act, which is simultaneously public.
As Lauren Berlant would agree, "the inwardness of the intimate is met by a
corresponding publicness."[31] Derrida goes so far as to state that "le désir de
littérature est la circoncision."[32] Desire for/in literature stems from the trauma
of circumcision, for it links ink and blood. Derrida usurps the traditional role
of the *mohel* by dipping the blade-like pen in ink to make the book bleed.
With circumspection at first, Derrida turns around his own circumcision, his

---

[28] Jacques Derrida & Geoffrey Bennington, *Jacques Derrida: Circumfession*, tr.
Geoffrey Bennington (Chicago: U of Chicago P, 1993): 110.

[29] Jacques Derrida, *Specters of Marx*, tr. Peggy Kamuf, intro. Bernd Magnus & Stephen Cullenberg (*Spectres de Marx*, 1993; New York & London: Routledge, 1994): 4.

[30] Jacques Derrida & Safaa Fathy, *Tourner les mots: Au bord d'un film* (Paris:
Galilée-ARTE, 2000): 16.

[31] Lauren Berlant, "Intimacy," *Critical Inquiry* 24.2 (Winter 1998): 281.

[32] Derrida, *Circonfession*, ed. Denis Roche (Paris: Seuil, 1991): 16.

'open wound,' when he was eight days old, which he traces back to the Latin *circum-cido*: "péritomie, coupure du pourtour."[33] Circumcision or cutting of the circumference brings him through circumlocutionary acts to the practice of "*meziza(h)*," whereby the rabbi sucked the blood off the infant's circumcised penis, a practice that was abolished in Paris in 1843. Following the traditional *mohels*' distrust of a halakhic innovation for hygienic reasons,[34] *mezizah* has now been revived in some contexts. Abu-Sahlieh goes very far in castigating the revival of *mezizah* by locating it in the wider, Western context of sadism, vampirism, and, in the 2002 interview I conducted with him, paedophilia. Derrida calls his 'wound', which is, by his own reckoning, not sutured yet, an '*escarre*', which evokes, by echoic dissemination, the English *scar*, the German *Schar,* and the Greek *eskhara*, which means "the foyer," "the false foci,"[35] as if the wound should not have been on his genitals but possibly elsewhere. If Derrida mentions *mezizah* with so much harrowing trepidation, it is possibly because, as Gayatri Spivak has surmised somewhat malevolently, the mother rather than the *mohel* "sucked off the blood on the child's little penis."[36] This feminine version of *mezizah* binds Derrida, Zipporah, and his mother Esther in a perverse *religio*, adding incest to injury. Because Zipporah, Moses's wife, circumcised one of her sons in a redemptive but unexplained sacrifice in Exodus IV,[37] Derrida assimilates Zipporah to his own mother, whom he implicitly accuses of silent complicity with the *mohel*'s deed. This shift from Zipporah to Derrida's mother via (Georgette) Esther also haunts all of Derrida's philosophical works. When pronounced in French – "est-ce taire?" – as Hélène Cixous argues in her *Portrait of Jacques*

---

[33] Derrida, *Circonfession*, 115.

[34] *Mezizah*, which rabbis introduced during the Mishnah, consisted not only in circumcising the prepuce but in the rabbi swigging a bit of wine in his mouth, sucking the blood off the wounded glans, and then spewing it in a container. The *halakha* or Judaic jurisprudence stipulates that the *mohel* should do so to avoid any risk of infection but, following cases of children contracting venereal diseases through the *mohel*'s deed, a small tube was substituted for direct sucking with the mouth. See Alan Unterman, *Dictionary of Judaism* (London: Thames & Hudson, 1997): 202.

[35] Derrida, *Circonfession*, 115.

[36] Gayatri Chakravorty Spivak, "Three Women's Texts and Circumfession," in *Postcolonialism and Autobiography: Michelle Cliff, David Dabydeen, Opal Palmer Adisa*, ed. Alfred Hornung & Ernstpeter Ruhe (Amsterdam & Atlanta: Rodopi, 1998): 13.

[37] For more detail, see Bernard P. Robinson, "Zipporah to the Rescue: A Contextual Study of Exodus I V," *Vetus Testamentum* 36.4 (1986): 447–61.

Derrida as a Young Jewish Saint,[38] the mother's questioning name augurs what Derrida has called elsewhere "an amplified rhetoric of the sewn mouth"[39] and, in *Glas*, "the gaping mouth effect."[40]

In Period 14 of *Circumfession*, Derrida writes that "the restrained confession will not have been my fault but hers, as though the daughter of Zipporah had not only committed the crime of my circumcision but one more still, later, the first playing the kickoff, the original sin against me." It is as if Derrida's mother was the father and the *mohel* all in one, the one who authorized his circumcision: "Circumcised without his consent, before any word, before passivity even."[41] The purpose of circumcision being to symbolically release the male child from his mother's impure blood, Derrida practises a reverse circumcision and, out of love and forgiveness, rehabilitates his mother's "filthy," "contaminating" blood. In the process, the father figure is erased or, better, ghosted. Significantly, Derrida's *Circumfession* was written while Derrida's mother was dying and the wounds on her body, those "blackish and purulent scabs that form around the wounds," are *escarres,* from the Greek e*skharra* or false foci, deferred and displaced as in trauma. Derrida's "restrained confession" to his dying mother, binding him almost contractually as a sinner to an absolving yet usurping cleric, is a "circanalysis,"[42] which is loosely based on *Confessione* by Saint Augustine, incidentally from Souk Ahras in Algeria, Derrida's homeland. The confessional mode also shows Derrida's indebtedness to Michel Foucault's reading of Western society as a "société singulièrement avouante,"[43] where "l'aveu" hovers between avowal and confession and where "avouer" covers the notions of acknowledging, admitting, owning up (to having done something), and ultimately confessing. Even though Derrida's indebtedness to Foucault and, especially, Emmanuel Levinas lies beyond the scope of this essay, the (almost oxymoronic) collocation of 'confession'

---

[38] Hélène Cixous, *Portrait of Jacques Derrida as a Young Jewish Saint* (New York: Columbia U P, 2004): 52.

[39] Micaëla Henich & Jacques Derrida, *Lignées* (Paris: William Blake & Co-Edit, 1996): 53.

[40] Jacques Derrida, *Glas* (Paris: Galilée, 1974): 55.

[41] Jacques Derrida & Geoffrey Bennington, *Jacques Derrida: Circumfession*, 115.

[42] Geoffrey Bennington, *Interrupting Derrida* (Warwick Studies in European Philosophy; London & New York: Routledge, 2000): 93.

[43] Michel Foucault, *La volonté de savoir I: Histoire de la sexualité* (Paris: Gallimard, 1976): 79.

and 'restraint' in Derrida's "restrained confession" reveals an uneasy attempt at coming to terms with an original traumatic event linking circumcision with a barely discernible incest. Such an attempt then opens a portal to forgiving his mother or to his absolving her, as a priest would. She is the 'false focus' of his autobiography, the *escarre* around the wound of his circumcision, the one who should have confessed in the first place. Whether the amanuensis, as in excised women's accounts, or Derrida's dying mother, as in *Circumfession*, the recipient of the 'confession' remains 'someone' whom Judith Butler intuited is "one whom I presume to receive my words in some way." When giving an account of oneself, it is "always *to* someone."[44] Although the very idea of a tangible recipient has been disputed, most eloquently by De Baerdemaeker et al.,[45] the confessional mode used by such autobiographers, when "giving an account of" themselves – *auto* – and of their lives – *bio* – is partly used to cope with both the traumatic pain of a literal and figurative 'wound' and the complicit betrayal of the mother.

The spectre of an operation akin to a circumcision also haunted the life of the Canadian David Riemer, whose "survival" was indeed "a crisis," after Caruth's phrase,[46] in that he committed suicide in 2004. Born Bruce Riemer, he was, at eight months, subjected to an electrocautery on account of penile phymosis: i.e. the constriction of the foreskin which makes urination difficult. The physical result resembles a botched circumcision and therefore ghosts the often untold story of other boys whose circumcision was bungled. Bruce was then re-assigned as a girl, Brenda, whose sense of "gender identity" (the inner self of oneself as male or female) was shaped over fourteen years by the specialist on gender dysphoria, John Money of Johns Hopkins Hospital in Baltimore. John Money helped circulate the notion of "gender," and specifically "gender role," as early as the late 1950s.[47] His theories rested on the psychosexual flexibility at birth of all humans – that boys and girls are made,

---

[44] Judith Butler, *Giving An Account of Oneself* (New York: Fordham UP, 2005): 67.

[45] See the theoretical introduction on poststructuralist work on confession in Ruben De Baerdemaeker, Gert Buelens & Marysa Demoor, "notproud.com: Giving an Account of Oneself in the Cyber-era," *Textual Practice* 22.4 (2008): 757–58. Warm thanks go to Gert Buelens for drawing my attention to this excellent article.

[46] Caruth, *Unclaimed Experience*, 9.

[47] John Money, John Hampson & Joan Hampson, "Imprinting and the Establishment of the Gender Role," *Archives of Neurology and Psychiatry* 77 (1957): 333–36.

not born. Even though Money's theories applied to intersexed children, Bruce/Brenda was "a non-intersexed boy, one of a pair of monozygotic (identical) twins."[48] The story of Bruce Riemer has thus been used to illustrate a certain conception of intersexuality so that his 'case' was likened to that of someone with ambiguous or atypical genitalia, such as a micropenis or aphallia (when the penis is less than 2.5 cm stretched length in neonates).[49] Brenda was lured into thinking that she had been a girl at birth and she only came to know of her full medical history at age fourteen. Before that revelation, Brenda thought of herself as a freak and had faint intimations that she was male: "[I figured I was a guy] but didn't want to admit it. I figured. I didn't want to wind up opening a can of worms."[50] This disavowal – "I didn't want to admit it" – will not, however, lead to a confession or a full-fledged autobiography.

The relatively late discovery of such a history, buried in silence and secrecy and jealously guarded by both the Riemers and the Johns Hopkins staff, is certainly traumatic for an adolescent who has been treated as a teratological marvel. In addition to the frequent genital examinations, which Rosario deems could be "experienced as sexual molestation,"[51] Bruce–Brenda Riemer underwent orchidectomy: i.e. the surgical removal of the testes; a partial vaginoplasty: i.e. a surgical vaginal construction that was to be perfected at a later stage; and estrogen therapy. The depth of Brenda's alienation and trauma can be gauged from the painful recollections of her schooldays and her frequent suicidal attempts that culminated in her being told the circumstances of her birth. This revelation in turn prompted her to become David Riemer. David then underwent the converse of previous multiple assaults on his body such as a mastectomy: i.e. the removal of his estrogen-induced breasts; a phalloplasty:

---

[48] Vernon Rosario, "The History of Aphallia and the Intersexual Challenge to Sex/ Gender," in *A Companion to Lesbian, Gay, Bisexual, Transgender, and Queer Studies*, ed. George E. Haggerty & Molly McGarry (Oxford & Malden MA: Blackwell, 2007): 268.

[49] Rosario lists under intersexed individuals people with androgen insensitivity syndrome (AIS), congenital adrenal hyperplastia (CAH), hypospadia or the malformation of the male urinary tract. Rosario, "The History of Aphallia," 263.

[50] Quoted by Milton Diamond & Keith Sigmundsen, "Sex Reassignment at Birth: A Long-Term Review and Clinical Implications," *Archives of Pediatrics and Adolescent Medicine* 151 (March 1997): 299–300.

[51] Rosario, "The History of Aphallia," 275.

i.e. the grafting of a penis unto his body; and androgen therapy. The now renamed David's self-identified male "gender identity" and "gender role": i.e. everything he said or did to indicate to others and to himself the degree to which he felt he was a male, was at odds with the Hopkins researchers' diagnosis and, in particular, John Money's adamant use of David's 'case' to entrench the success of the gender reassignment of a boy (and a non-intersexed one, at that) into a girl. The 'shock' and 'return' ingredients of trauma theory are here given an unusual twist since the shock of discovery of David's medical history and of his 'real' sex led to the 'return' to a male body, although admittedly not the original one.

The cause of David Riemer's suicide on 4 May 2004 has been variously explained away through the loss of his job, the separation from his wife, Jane Fontane, whose children he had adopted, and the prolonged mourning of the death of his twin brother Brian in 2002. The reason is lost to history but we can safely surmise that the medical establishment's indomitable will to use David as a successful case-study played a role in his death. The Riemer twins' fate was linked in ways beyond their biology, since they both endured many traumatic humiliations. Among such humiliations, we number Money's dubious therapy through "coital mimicry" involving the six-year-old twins in "play[ing] at thrusting movements and copulation" and watching pornographic movies at Johns Hopkins,[52] which led to Brenda's satiation with such intrusive practices. Bruce–Brenda–David was later recuperated as John in the Joan/John case in the counter-theories of Milton Diamond, Money's arch-rival.

The Joan/John case is at the core of Judith Butler's chapter in *Undoing Gender* (2004) entitled "Doing Justice to Someone: Sex Reassignment and Allegories of Transsexuality." Using Michel Foucault's "politics of truth" and the "desubjugation of the subject"[53] to reflect on the assumption of a coherent gender as a presupposition of humanness, Butler surveys the theories of Milton Diamond and his belief in "the hormonal basis of gender identity";[54] of Cheryl Chase, the founder of the Intersexed Society of North America; and of Anne Fausto–Sterling, who allegedly opposed Diamond and argued for surgi-

---

[52] John Colapinto, *As Nature Made Him: The Boy Who Was Raised as a Girl* (New York: HarperCollins, 2000): 86 & 87.

[53] Michel Foucault, "What is Critique?" in *The Politics of Truth*, ed. Sylvère Lotringer & Lysa Hochroth (New York: Schizotext[e], 1997): 39.

[54] Judith Butler, *Undoing Gender* (New York & London: Routledge, 2004): 60.

cal interventions only when the child is able to make a knowing choice. Butler then reflects on the arbitrariness of gender dimorphism on the basis that "a significant percentage of children are chromosomally various"[55] and she overall posits a continuum between male and female. Because David Riemer, born with X Y chromosomes, at some point undergoes a phalloplasty, which is a construction borrowed from transsexual surgery, Butler argues that "he allegorizes transsexuality in order to achieve a sense of naturalness," by which she means "a 'return' to who he is."[56] She concludes that, in an effort to doing "justice to David, [one should] ask. What did Brenda see as Brenda looks at himself, feels as he feels himself, and please excuse my mixing of pronouns here, but matters are becoming changeable."[57] But matters are not changeable, since Brenda, at this (mirror-)stage, rejects her very metamorphosis into Brenda. What is more, the subsequent psychic re-establishment of Brenda's male core identity can develop without the presence of a penis, as shown by the f-t-ms or female-to-male, transgender individuals transitioning to male. Predictably, even prior to his phalloplasty, David quickly 'transitioned' into a male role.

According to Vernon Rosario, Butler does not "do justice" to Cheryl Chase or Milton Diamond, who is not the Y-chromosome determinist she portrays him to be, and, generally, misrepresents most of her biomedical sources in the early (2001) version in *GLQ* that was to become part of the chapter in *Undoing Gender* (2004). Despite revisions, Rosario argues, Butler insists on seeing "in the intersex condition an opportunity for destabilizing biological notions of sex and gender"[58] and, more generally, "undoing gender." In fact, David's story does the very opposite of undoing gender. The wounding of David by the medical establishment is due to its refusal to recognize that his "gender identity" could not be moulded or rendered "malleable through rearing and genital surgery."[59] If David Riemer triumphed at all beyond his death, it is in restoring to the world his profound sense of an unimpeachable male gender core identity despite various manipulations, both physical and psychical. As David Riemer supposedly said to the American journalist John Colapinto, who first visited him in Winnipeg, Manitoba in 1997,

---

[55] Butler, *Undoing Gender*, 65.

[56] *Undoing Gender*, 65.

[57] *Undoing Gender*, 69.

[58] Rosario, "The History of Aphallia," 275.

[59] "The History of Aphallia," 275.

> I'd give just about anything to go to a hypnotist to black out my whole
> past. Because it's torture. What they did to you in the body is some-
> times not near as bad as what they did to you in the *mind* – with the
> psychological warfare in your head.[60]

Significantly, the main personal pronouns are "they" and "you," and the "I"
tends to play a lesser role. It is equally significant that Colapinto's title, *As
Nature Made Him*, is excerpted from an English translation of Jean–Jacques
Rousseau's *Confessions*:

> I have entered on an enterprise which is without precedent, and will
> have no imitator. I propose to show my fellows a man as nature made
> him, and this man shall be myself.[61]

The famous Rousseau quotation – "Je forme une entreprise qui n'eut jamais
d'exemple et dont l'exécution n'aura point d'imitateur. Je veux montrer à mes
semblables un homme dans toute la vérité de la nature; et cet homme, ce sera
moi"[62] – is all the more ironical, since we do not have direct access to David
Riemer's autobiography *per se*, but only to snippets and personal vignettes
mediated through intrusive means such as journalism and medical literature.
Such vignettes are often provided by relatives or acquaintances. A case in
point is David's wife, Jane Fontane, who reportedly told Colapinto that David
"cried hysterically" when he saw in 1989 a TV documentary on CIA torture
involving electroshock to people's genitals and remembered "some things I
don't *want* to remember."[63] The shock imparted by the sudden visual corre-
lation between Money's experimentations and CIA torture resembles the
shock of recognition due to the delayed understanding of a traumatic event.
Jane's description of her husband's 'hysterical' crying is a tell-tale lapsus that
conjures up Brenda's biography, laden in silence and secrecy.

What David Riemer underwent – the irreversible alteration of his genitals –
raises the question of the future application of trauma theory to intersex and
transgender individuals, who, unlike David Riemer, are willing to undergo
sex-reassignment surgery and transition to the gender identity they feel they
have. But the present literature by or around individuals who have undergone
genital alterations, generally at an early age and without their consent, reveal

---

[60] Quoted by Colapinto, *As Nature Made Him*, xiii.

[61] Colapinto, *As Nature Made Him*, epigraph.

[62] Jean–Jacques Rousseau, *Les confessions* (Paris: Éditions Baudelaire, 1966): 5.

[63] Quoted by Colapinto, *As Nature Made Him*, 88.

that punctual wounds in one's infancy or childhood endure and are traumatic events that haunt the self and writing but also generate de-faced writing selves, let alone confessing animals.[64]

WORKS CITED

Abdi, Nura. *Larmes de sable*, tr. Gérald Messadié (Nura Abdi & Leo G. Linder, *Tränen im Sand*, 2003; Paris: L'Archipel, 2005).

Abu-Sahlieh, Sami Aldeeb. *Circoncision masculine, circoncision féminine: Débat religieux, médical, social et juridique*, preface by Linda Weil–Curiel (Paris: L'Harmattan, 2001).

Bennington, Geoffrey. *Interrupting Derrida* (Warwick Studies in European Philosophy; London & New York: Routledge, 2000).

Berlant, Lauren. "Intimacy," *Critical Inquiry* 24.2 (Winter 1998): 281–88.

Boehmer, Elleke. *Stories of Women: Gender and Narrative in the Postcolonial Nation* (Manchester & New York: Manchester UP, 2005).

Butler, Judith. *Giving an Account of Oneself* (New York: Fordham UP, 2005).

——. *Undoing Gender* (New York & London: Routledge, 2004).

Caruth, Cathy. *Unclaimed Experience: Trauma, Narrative, and History* (Baltimore MD & London: Johns Hopkins UP, 1996).

Cixous, Hélène. *Portrait of Jacques Derrida as a Young Jewish Saint*, tr. Beverley Bie Brahic (*Portrait de Jacques Derrida en Jeune Saint Juif*, 2001; New York: Columbia UP, 2004).

Colapinto, John. *As Nature Made Him: The Boy Who Was Raised as a Girl* (New York: HarperCollins, 2000).

De Baerdemaeker, Ruben, Gert Buelens & Marysa Demoor. "notproud.com: Giving an Account of Oneself in the Cyber-era," *Textual Practice* 22.4 (2008): 757–74.

de Man, Paul. "Autobiography as De-facement," *Modern Language Notes* 94.5 (December 1979): 919–30.

Deleuze, Gilles. *Nietzsche and Philosophy*, tr. Hugh Tomlinson (*Nietzsche et la philosophie*, 1962; London: Athlone, 1983).

Derrida, Jacques. *Circonfession*, ed. Denis Roche (Paris: Seuil, 1991).

——. *Glas* (Paris: Galilée, 1974).

——. *Specters of Marx*, tr. Peggy Kamuf, intro. Bernd Magnus & Stephen Cullenberg (*Spectres de Marx*, 1993; New York & London: Routledge, 1994).

---

[64] After Michel Foucault's "bête d'aveu" to describe the Western individual: "L'homme, en Occident, est devenu une bête d'aveu." In Foucault, *La volonté de savoir*, 80. See also De Baerdemaeker et al. "notproud.com," 759.

——, & Geoffrey Bennington. *Jacques Derrida: Circumfession*, tr. Geoffrey Bennington (Chicago: U of Chicago P, 1993).

——, & Safaa Fathy. *Tourner les mots: Au bord d'un film* (Paris: Galilée–ARTE, 2000).

Diamond, Milton, & Keith Sigmundsen. "Sex Reassignment at Birth: A Long-Term Review and Clinical Implications," *Archives of Pediatrics and Adolescent Medicine* 151 (March 1997): 298–304.

Dirie, Waris, with Cathleen Miller. *Desert Flower: The Extraordinary Life of a Desert Nomad* (1998; London: Virago, 1999).

——, with Jeanne D'Haem. *Desert Dawn* (London: Virago, 2002).

——, with Corinna Milborn. *Desert Children* (London: Virago, 2005).

Foucault, Michel. *The Politics of Truth*, tr. & ed. Sylvère Lotringer & Lysa Hochroth (New York: Schizotext(e), 1997).

——. *La Volonté de savoir I: Histoire de la Sexualité* (Paris: Gallimard, 1976).

Glick, Leonard B. *Marked in Your Flesh: Circumcision from Ancient Judea to Modern America* (Oxford & London: Oxford UP, 2005).

Harvey, Mary R., & Judith L. Herman. "Amnesia, Partial Amnesia, and Delayed Recall Among Adult Survivors of Childhood Trauma," in *The Recovered Memory/ False Memory Debate*, ed. Kathy Pezdek & Williams P. Banks (London: Academic Press, 1996): 29–40.

Henich, Micaëla, & Jacques Derrida. *Lignées* (Paris: William Blake & Co-Edit, 1996).

Lionnet, Françoise. *Postcolonial Representations: Women, Literature, Identity* (Ithaca NY: Cornell UP, 1995).

Money, John, John Hampson & Joan Hampson. "Imprinting and the Establishment of the Gender Role," *Archives of Neurology and Psychiatry* 77 (1957): 333–36.

Rifaat, Alifa. "Bahiyya's Eyes," in *Distant View of a Minaret and Other Stories*, tr. Denys Johnson–Davies (London: Quartet, 1983): 5–11.

Rosario, Vernon A. "The History of Aphallia and the Intersexual Challenge to Sex/ Gender," in *A Companion to Lesbian, Gay, Bisexual, Transgender, and Queer Studies*, ed. George E. Haggerty & Molly McGarry (Oxford & Malden MA: Blackwell, 2007): 262–81.

Robinson, Bernard P. "Zipporah to the Rescue: A Contextual Study of Exodus IV," *Vetus Testamentum* 36.4 (1986): 447–61.

Rousseau, Jean–Jacques. *Les confessions* (Paris: Éditions Baudelaire, 1966).

Spivak, Gayatri Chakravorty. "Three Women's Texts and Circumfession," in *Post-colonialism and Autobiography: Michelle Cliff, David Dabydeen, Opal Palmer Adisa*, ed. Alfred Hornung & Ernstpeter Ruhe (Amsterdam & Atlanta: Rodopi, 1998): 7–22.

Unterman, Alan. *Dictionary of Judaism* (London: Thames & Hudson, 1997).

Wassill–Grimm, Claudette. *Diagnosis for Disaster: The Devastating Truth about False Memory Syndrome and Its Impact on Accusers and Families* (New York: Overlook, 1995).

Zabus, Chantal. "The Afrosporic Migration of Genital Alterations to the New Europe: Trauma, the Law, and the Internet," in *Diasporic Subjectivity and Cultural Brokering in Contemporary Post-Colonial Literatures*, ed. Igor Maver (New York: Lexington & Plymouth: Rowman & Littlefield, 2009): 115–34.

——. *Between Rites and Rights: Excision in Women's Experiential Texts and Human Contexts* (Stanford C A : Stanford U P, 2007).

——. "Beyond Circumspection: African, Jewish, and Muslim Autobiographies Around Circumcision," in *Fearful Symmetries: Essays and Testimonies Around Excision and Circumcision*, ed. Chantal Zabus (Matatu 37; Amsterdam & New York: Rodopi, 2008): 99–128.

The Australian Apology
and Trauma of Unbelonging

Personal Trauma/Historical Trauma in Tim Winton's *Dirt Music*

BÁRBARA ARIZTI

U NLIKE OTHER AUTHORS who pour their own traumatic experiences into their fiction, the Australian Tim Winton does not seem
to have had more than the average share of trauma in his life. It is
true that his father, a policeman and the son of a policeman, would bring
home stories of abuse, crime, and road accidents – he was badly injured himself while on duty when a drunk driver pushed him off his motorbike.[1] However, as the trauma scholar Dominick LaCapra cautions,[2] it is one thing to go
through trauma yourself and quite a different one to be a witness – or to be
told – of the traumatic experiences of others. Perhaps the nearest Winton has
been to trauma were the two years (1987–88) he spent touring Europe with
his family. "The first 24 hours in Paris were the most traumatic in my life," he
remembers.[3] There, he felt snubbed by Europeans, dislocated from his land,
and totally unwilling to increase the long list of Australian expats: "I knew the

---

[1] Michael McGirr, *Tim Winton: The Writer and his Work* (South Yarra, Victoria:
Macmillan, 1999): 7.

[2] Dominick LaCapra, *Writing History, Writing Trauma* (Baltimore MD & London:
Johns Hopkins UP, 2001): xi and passim.

[3] Quoted in Salhia Ben–Messahel, *Mind the Country: Tim Winton's Fiction* (Crawley: U of Western Australia P, 2006): 11.

moment I set my foot down that I wasn't European," he says; "I felt torn, almost, like torn out of the soil from home."[4] In 1988 he returned to the coastal area of Western Australia and has remained there ever since, apparently unaffected by the cultural cringe or the feeling of provincialism and suffocation that have made many an Australian author choose to live abroad. In fact, Winton seems to be leading a fairly happy life of simple pleasures. A full-time writer since he was sixteen, he is a celebrity in his own country and is also well known in countries like the USA and the UK, where two of his adult novels[5] – *The Riders* (1994) and *Dirt Music* (2002) – made it onto the Booker Prize short-list.

In marked contrast to Winton's story of self-confidence and success, the lives of his fictional creatures are often scarred by trauma in various shapes. His novels and short stories are populated by deserted or widowed husbands and wives, terminally ill characters, neglected children, alcoholic fathers, nasty episodes of wife-battering, gory descriptions of road accidents, etc. *Dirt Music*, Winton's seventh novel, is no exception to this. The book tells the story of Georgiana Jutland (Georgie) and Luther Fox (Lu), a story of love-at-first-sight, which is short-circuited but also fuelled by their own and other characters' unresolved traumas. Although the emphasis in *Dirt Music* lies on individual trauma, it is also my intention to delve into the connections between personal and historical traumatic events. As I see it, Lu's working through his personal trauma relies on elements that both expose and play down the foundational trauma of the Australian nation: namely, the appropriation of the Aboriginal land.

In an interview with Richard Rossiter,[6] Winton stresses the role of the past in his fiction: "the presence of the past is unavoidable, it's there in all my work. The past has its consolations but often it's just a knife twisting in an old wound." The impinging of unassimilated past events upon the present and the image of the wound – trauma means 'wound' in Greek – are key elements in trauma theory. In *Beyond the Pleasure Principle*, Freud reproduces the story

---

[4] Quoted in Richard Rossiter & Lyn Jacobs, *Reading Tim Winton*, ed. Rossiter & Jacobs (Sydney: Angus & Robertson, 1993): 13.

[5] Winton, a very prolific writer, is the author of three short-story collections, eight adult novels, seven novels for children and adolescents, three books of photography and travel, and countless essays and newspaper articles.

[6] Richard Rossiter, "The Writer and the Community: An Interview with Tim Winton," *Westerly* 49 (2004): 38.

of Tancred, told by Tasso in his *Jerusalem Liberated.* Tancred's actions, Cathy Caruth glosses

> wounding his beloved in a battle and then, unknowingly, seemingly by chance, wounding her again, evocatively represent in Freud's text the way that the experience of a trauma repeats itself, exactly and unremittingly, through the unknowing acts of the survivor and against his very will.[7]

As Salhia Ben–Messahel suggestively puts it, in *Dirt Music,* "memories unexpectedly rebound on the individual like a boomerang."[8] Georgie, the female protagonist, is a forty-year-old nurse who quit her job some years before, after an obscure incident with a terminally ill patient. Mrs Jubail, who suffered from a particularly nasty form of cancer that colonized her face, still haunts her in the form of recurrent dreams, like the three instances reproduced below:

> The nightmare pursued her from Saudi Arabia and on to the States, to Indonesia and home to Australia. [...] She recognized the creeping sense of dread. She thought of how epileptics and vertigo sufferers could feel episodes approaching.[9]

> She woke in a panic and went through the house and turned on lights. (195)

> At White Point Georgie had Mrs Jubail come visiting in her sleep. Down hardlit corridors with her veil thrown back and her grisly face out-thrust behind those arms. Sister! Sister? Georgie ran and used the steel trolley to batter her way through stone and glass in a shower of paper cups and ampoules. The sweet smell blew on her. And there was always a wall, a blind alley she couldn't broach. (197)

Repetition concerning language, imagery or plot is one of the commonest strategies for translating trauma into narrative. In the words of Anne Whitehead,[10] repetition "mimics the effects of trauma, for it suggests the insistent return of the event and the disruption of narrative chronology or progression." Georgie's trauma, triggered off by the Mrs Jubail episode, dates back to her

---

[7] Cathy Caruth, *Unclaimed Experience: Trauma, Narrative, and History* (Baltimore MD & London: Johns Hopkins UP, 1996): 2.

[8] Ben–Messahel, *Mind the Country,* 80.

[9] Tim Winton, *Dirt Music* (London: Picador, 2001): 123. Further page references are in the main text.

[10] Anne Whitehead, *Trauma Fiction* (Edinburgh: Edinburgh UP, 2004): 86.

childhood. The eldest daughter of an upper-class couple, she felt neglected by her mother, a compulsive shopper, and estranged from her father, who abandoned his wife and family for a younger woman. Georgie grows up a rebel, embraces the label of the family black sheep, and gets involved in a series of unsatisfactory relationships with men. Her feeling of dissatisfaction increases after turning forty, extends to her current partner – a widower with his own traumatic past – and comes to a peak with the sudden death of her mother and her reunion with her father and sisters.

A founding moment in trauma studies was the acknowledgement by the American Psychiatric Association in 1980 of "Post Traumatic Stress Disorder" (PTSD), summarized by Caruth[11] in the following way:

> a response, sometimes delayed, to an overwhelming event or events, which takes the form of repeated, intrusive hallucinations, dreams, thoughts of behaviours stemming from the event, along with numbing that may have begun during or after the experience, and possibly also increased arousal to (and avoidance of) stimuli recalling the event.

Lu Fox is the only survivor of a car accident that killed his brother and sister-in-law and their two children. They were, in fact, Lu's only relatives, since his mother and father also suffered traumatic deaths: the former was killed by a falling branch when he was only a kid and the latter died of a mesothelioma provoked by his mining of asbestos. After the accident, Fox decides to turn his living into "a project of forgetting" (103). He burns his papers and moves into a marginal position in White Point, the fishing town where both Georgie and Lu live. He is, in his own words, "The Ghost Who Walks" (99). Proof of Lu's marginality is the fact that he completely drops music – he and his family played professionally in a band – and now earns his living as an illegal fisherman. Fragmentary memories of the accident resurface at various points in the narrative. They generate a tension between remembering and forgetting characteristic of trauma narratives and corroborate Caruth's contention that "the accident [...] does not simply represent the violence of a collision but also conveys the impact of its very incomprehensibility."[12]

The resistance to understanding offered by the traumatic memory is reflected in *Dirt Music* in a series of textual strategies that echo the characters'

---

[11] Cathy Caruth, "Introduction" to *Trauma: Explorations in Memory*, ed. Caruth (Baltimore MD & London: Johns Hopkins UP, 1995): 4.

[12] Caruth, *Unclaimed Experience*, 6.

disorientation, emphasize disruption, and question the linearity, coherence, and sense of closure of traditional realism. The novel is written as a discontinuous narrative in which fragments of various lengths – most of them focalized by Georgie and Lu – alternate, presenting flashbacks, digressions, and events in parallel, and bringing about a certain degree of confusion in readers. Typography also contributes to the whole. Dashes and suspension points evoke psychological gaps in characters;[13] there are passages without punctuation, italicized and capitalized sections, and words in bold that disrupt the smooth unobtrusive surface of the conventional text. Winton makes heavy use of direct speech and Western Australian lingo, unmarked by inverted commas, which gives the story a strong oral flavour.[14] Extradiegetic, heterodiegetic narration blends with passages of free indirect style, providing access to the characters' innermost thoughts and feelings in the manner of modernism. In fact, modernist and postmodernist texts are, in the opinion of many a critic, privileged sites for the narrative rendition of the complex experience of trauma.[15] Readers not only read about trauma, they sort of experience it as well in the syncopated disjointed rhythms of these two modes. (Post)modernist strategies particularly suit Winton, who has often voiced his discomfort with realism for leaving important areas of experience unattended.[16]

The emphasis in my analysis so far has been on what LaCapra has labelled 'denial' and 'acting-out', two usual ways of coping with trauma. The traumatized subject is seized by a form of amnesia that partially or completely glosses over the traumatic moment, or is trapped in the compulsive repetition of the event. Neither of these strategies, however, succeeds in fully freeing the victim from the effects of trauma. It is as if victims were weighed down by the heavy burden of an invisible backpack or remained tied to an elastic band that forced them back to the traumatic experience, preventing them from leading a normal life. There is a third way of handling trauma, 'working

---

[13] Ben–Messahel, *Mind the Country*, 143.

[14] *Mind the Country*, 159.

[15] Whitehead, *Trauma Fiction*, 87; Stef Craps, *Trauma and Ethics in the Novels of Graham Swift: No Short-Cuts to Salvation* (Brighton & Portland OR: Sussex Academic Press, 2005): 11.

[16] Quoted in Ben–Messahel, *Mind the Country*, 14; in Elizabeth Guy, "A Conversation with Tim Winton," *Southerly* 56.4 (Summer 1996): 127; in Beth Watzke, "Where Pigs Speak in Tongues and Angels Come and Go: A Conversation with Tim Winton," *Antipodes* 5.2 (December 1991): 97.

through', on which LaCapra, unlike other theorists, confers particular importance, especially when dealing with instances of historical trauma. LaCapra
refers to it in the following terms:

> Working through is an articulatory practice: to the extent one works
> through trauma [...] one is able to distinguish between past and pres-
> ent and to recall in memory that something happened to one (or one's
> people) back then while realizing that one is living here and now with
> openings to the future.[17]

Working through the traumatic experience enables the individual to fully re-
engage in life.

The accidental meeting and subsequent involvement between Georgie and
Lu trigger off their working through their traumatic experiences. According to
Judith Herman, recovery cannot take place in isolation:

> In her renewed connections with other people, the survivor re-creates
> the psychological faculties that were damaged [...] by the traumatic
> experience [:] the basic capacities for trust, autonomy, initiative, com-
> petence, identity, and intimacy.[18]

As modern psychotherapy has proved, the figure of the listener can play an
important role in the process of overcoming trauma:

> Fox finds himself uncoiling somehow, as though he can't pull back
> once he's started. He babbles at her about how they practised to tapes
> and LPs on the verandah instead of doing their homework. [...] He
> tips back against the sink appalled at this outburst. (96, 97)

Their encounter, however, will also make things difficult for them, especially
for Lu. His poaching is discovered, his dog is shot and his truck smashed to
pieces. As Jim Buckridge, Georgie's partner, happens to be the head fisherman, he is suspected of the deed. Fox fears for his farm and his life and sets
off on a journey up north to an isolated place called Coronation Gulf Georgie
once mentioned as being her favourite place. The interruption of their relationship brings about new traumatic symptoms in them, symptoms that co-
incide with those that Kalí Tal describes as typical of PTSD:

---

[17] LaCapra, *Writing History, Writing Trauma*, 21–22.

[18] Judith Herman, *Trauma and Recovery: From Domestic Abuse to Political Terror*
(1992; London: Pandora, 2001): 133.

panic attacks or startle reactions; a preoccupation with the traumatic
event in the form of nightmares, flashbacks, or persistent thoughts
about the trauma that intrude into everyday affairs; and a general dysphoria, a numbness that takes the meaning out of life and makes it hard
to relate to other people.[19]

Notice how Georgie is described in the following passages: "Georgie stayed
on at Jim's in a state of sober, confounded lethargy. [...] She felt cauterized
inside" (189); "She'd become so disembodied, so abstracted in the last six
months. She decided to view it as a digression" (260). After a sudden and
intense episode of backache, she starts to get over. Her working through is
presented in more modest terms than Lu's: she gives first aid and nurses a
neighbour who has been badly injured in a car accident (279), kills Mrs
Jubail's ghost in a dream (343), and progressively takes possession of Lu's
farm, cleaning every single room down, and sorting things out for him. This
last stage in her return to normality is very significant indeed, as it involves a
series of tasks traditionally associated with women. This seems to confirm
Winton's difficulties in portraying independent females: on the one hand, they
are often strong, unorthodox, and outspoken characters, like Georgie; on the
other, they find it difficult to cast off their traditional roles, or are punished in
subtle ways for doing so.

While Georgie's working through reaches its climax indoors, Lu's happens
almost completely in the great outdoors of Australia. His recovery rests on
two main pillars: an intimate connection with the landscape and his renewed
interest in music, or, as Kylie Crane wittily puts it, a combination of "*Dirt*, or
place, presence, nature on the one hand, and *Music*, or emotions, past, culture
on the other."[20] Up in the wilderness of Coronation Gulf, Lu makes himself a
primitive instrument by tying a nylon line to a fig tree:

> It makes a nice drone, a sound just outside nature but not dissimilar to
> it. He clears his throat uncertainly and hums the note. [...] you're
> whacking this thing into a long, gorgeous, monotonous, hypnotic note
> and it's not killing you, it's not driving you into some burning scream-
> ing wreck of yourself – listen! (368)

---

[19] Kalí Tal, *Worlds of Hurt: Reading the Literatures of Trauma* (Cambridge: Cambridge UP, 1995): 137.

[20] Kylie Crane, "The Beat of the Land: Place and Music in Tim Winton's *Dirt
Music*," *Zeitschrift für Anglistik und Amerikanistik* 54.1 (2006): 21.

His recovery through music will not be complete till he finds an audience in
the figure of Georgie, who eventually tracks him down in his hiding place:

> It had something to do with music. The string in the tree had con-
> firmed it. [...] Lu was pure, hot feeling [...]. Music wants to be heard.
> Feeling wants to be felt. He'd always wanted to be found, even if he
> didn't know it. (415–16)

What interests me here, however, is the 'dirt' rather than the 'music': i.e.
Lu's dependence on the Australian land in his working through his personal
traumas. Anne Whitehead has looked into how the constituent components of
the landscape – water, wood, and rock, primarily – can help absorb and transform the shock of trauma.[21] These three elements are overwhelmingly present
in Coronation Gulf and it is through them that Lu manages to re-found his
traumatized identity:

> His days are lived according to the tide. [...] Amongst the rocks he
> jogs for mangrove jacks, fingermark, bluebone and pikey bream. [...]
> On the island there are so many unexpected pleasures, like the hot
> warm boles of the young boab trees he brushes with his fingertips in
> passing. (352–53)

The reference to local species unknown to Europeans before colonization,
reveals the parasitic nature of Lu's relationship with the Australian landscape
and wildlife. Fox's history of displacement and dispossession, the killing of
his dog, and the destruction of his means of living, though painful indeed,
bear no comparison with the historical trauma of the Aborigines.

There are two passages in the novel that clearly connect the personal and
the historical sides of trauma through the image of dirt:

> Darkie [Lu's brother] gives the old Holden some throttle and the tray
> slides into a drift, kicks back while the kids shriek with pleasure.
> Behind them the ruts of the drive yaw in and out of view.
>
> And then there's dirt in his mouth. The sky gone completely. (116)

> As she tilted the envelope up to make sure, a trickle of dust fell be-
> tween her fingers onto the scrubbed table. [...] When she dipped a
> finger in and put it to her tongue she knew it was nothing more than
> red earth.
>
> The envelope with its boab tree stamp was postmarked Broome a
> few days before. [...] she stared at the little mound of dirt a while

---

[21] Whitehead, *Trauma Fiction*, 10.

> until, wetting a finger, working dab by dab, she ate it. [...] When
> Georgie rinsed her mouth at the basin it was like spitting blood. She
> brushed her teeth and wiped the basin down. Gone. (214)

The first passage is part of Lu's memories of the accident that killed his
brother, sister-in-law, nephew, and niece. The moment of the accident is
glossed over through an image of dirt in his mouth. The second passage concerns Georgie, who has just received an anonymous letter containing a blank
fold of notepaper and a handful of red earth. Later in the novel we are shown
Lu in the process of sending it. The dirt also finds its way to the protagonist's
mouth. The fact that Georgie eats the red earth and that it looks like blood
when she rinses her mouth point to Lu's and her own personal traumatic experiences. However, the connection of earth and blood signifies at a further
level as well, pointing to the history of genocide and dispossession endured
by the Australian Aborigines.

The fictional name Coronation Gulf corresponds to the remote Kimberly
region, the northern tip of Western Australia. In her monograph on Winton,
Salhia Ben–Messahel reproduces the words of B. Sibree after the release of
Dirt Music:

> For seven years [Winton] explains, "the novel has existed only as a
> series of handwritten notebooks. I was going to work every day and I
> was working on them, and they were the book, but they weren't the
> story. I started travelling in the north because I could just smell some-
> thing." Like the smell of rain. Only then did he begin to find out what
> the story was about. Only then did its key characters emerge. "Stuff
> started to arrive," he says, ... "It was nice, but it was odd."[22]

The documentary film *The Edge of the World* by Geoffrey Bennett and Don
Featherstone (1997) roots Winton's life and work in the Western Australian
landscape and follows him on his journey up north. There are several allusions to the plot and characters of *Dirt Music* – then a work in progress – and
spectacular views of the island where the last part of the novel is set. Winton
has often voiced his intimate quasi-mystical connection with the landscape of
Western Australia. He is a white Australian with a strong sense of place and
belonging. For Winton, landscape is intimately connected to identity. "If you
know your landscape you know yourself," he told Elizabeth Guy in an interview back in 1996:

---

[22] Quoted in Ben–Messahel, *Mind the Country*, 112.

> I think it's an idea that's very difficult to apprehend any more, you
> know? In the Sixties it was a given and people understood that state-
> ment. People were born into the house and lived there for the whole of
> their lives. The patch that they were born on became part of the whole
> canvas of their lives. And they had their bearings from that. They be-
> longed. Now people are very unsure about themselves. [...] The notion
> of knowing your ground and your country is almost a religious thing. I
> suppose if my skin were dark this would have more credibility.[23]

As can be deduced from the last two lines, Winton associates his sense of belonging with the native inhabitants of Australia: "The great Aboriginal tenet is
that the land does not belong to you, but that you belong to the land."[24] The
prominent role the Western Australian landscape plays in Lu's recovery from
his personal trauma can be read as Winton's tribute to his native land, but also
as a case of white settler envy or trauma envy, a condition posited by Marc
Delrez.[25] Most critics of Winton to date have praised his fiction in terms of
how beautifully it portrays the landscape of Western Australia. The author's
strong feeling for it seeps out of both his novels and short stories. Ben–
Messahel is a clear case in point, as her following comment on *Dirt Music*
shows:

> The story arises from the music of the land and is a symphony on the
> theme of Western Australia. It emphasizes the need for protection of
> the environment and the oppressed, Indigenous rights and reconcilia-
> tion – current Australian issues that become part of the life of the fic-
> tional characters, who stand as reminders of history. [26]

Dirt Music shows awareness of the Aboriginal cause. As Ben–Messahel
notes, the novel "is set in the years that witnessed the *Mabo* judgment, the
Native Title Bill and the South African Truth and Reconciliation Commis-

---

[23] Guy, "A Conversation with Tim Winton," 128.

[24] Richard Rossiter, "In His Own Words: The Life and Times of Tim Winton," in
Reading Tim Winton, ed. Richard Rossiter & Lyn Jacobs (Sydney: Angus & Robertson, 1993): 12.

[25] I am indebted to the doctoral seminar taught by Delrez at the Department of English and German Studies (University of Zaragoza) in February 2009 and to his insight-
ful paper delivered at the international conference "Between the 'Urge to Know' and
the 'Need to Deny': Ethics and Trauma in Contemporary Narrative in English," held in
Jaca in March, 2009.

[26] Ben–Messahel, *Mind the Country*, 12.

sion"; "its impetus," she adds, "is towards reconciling white Australians to the land and its original inhabitants."[27] She also draws attention to the frequent insertion of the word 'sorry' in bold letters, which in her opinion "not only relates to the characters' own troubled past but also to the country's historical treatment of Aboriginal people," in an attempt to make up for the insensitivity towards the issue on the part of earlier governments. Again, personal and historical trauma come together in *Dirt Music*. Up in Coronation Gulf, Lu Fox meets and befriends two Aborigines, Menzies and Axle. The reaction of the latter when he sees Lu's maps of the area – he grabs them angrily and throws them into the fire – is explained by his companion in the following terms: "Can't blame a blackfulla not likin a map, Lu" (312). "Go on the country [...] not on the map," suggests Axle, "almost pacified now" (312). The maps, the presence on the road up north of Landcruisers and Cherokee four-wheel-drives, and the fact that the characters have to be flown in to Coronation Gulf, all point to various forms of colonization, which range from violent conquest to scientific exploration. They also invoke ways of relating to the native land that differ strongly from that of its rightful inhabitants. Plumwood[28] has drawn attention to the "purely instrumental status that nature has been assigned in Western thought":

> In 1973 the Norwegian philosopher Arne Naess and Richard Routley of the Australian National University almost simultaneously proposed that the problem with the Western view of nature lies mainly in its anthropocentrism and its denial that the non-human world has any moral status or other significance that is not reducible to usefulness to humans, their ends and purposes.

Winton has also commented on how Europeans are "always doing things to the land": "We do things to objects, mould them into our image. We do not allow ourselves to be done by."[29] Lu's attitude towards the land in *Dirt Music* is undoubtedly more akin to the Aborigines' than to the Europeans'. In fact, he is eventually and almost literally undone by the elements, and it is his intimate contact with nature that cures him of his traumatic past:

> he gets a glimpse of himself in the shaving mirror and stops dead. His hair is a dirty spinifex snarl and when he steps back involuntarily

---

[27] Ben–Messahel, *Mind the Country*, 13.

[28] Val Plumwood, "Plato and the Bush," *Meanjin* 3 (1990): 527.

[29] Rossiter, "In His Own Words," 12.

> he sees the colourless rag of his shirt. He looks more closely at the
> scabs and scales of his brow, at the festering beard and those wet,
> red eyes, and he feels himself searching out his own face in these
> features with a desperation that soils the pleasure of all the food in
> his belly and the feeling he's had that this could be it, the day he
> might come in out of the bush and make peace. But this. You can't
> come in as this *thing*. (425)

Nevertheless, Lu's going native or, rather, 'going bush', can also be interpreted as cultural appropriation of the Aborigines' special bond with the land
and thus as an instance of what Marc Delrez has labelled 'white settler envy'.
After all, and as the previous passage makes clear, his is a temporary state
which he can enter and exit at will, and not a permanent condition.

While I definitely acknowledge Winton's commitment to the Australian
landscape and people – he has been actively involved in and has generously
donated to various environmental causes – I also see the need to stand at a
certain distance from the general laudatory tone in order to explore the fis-
sures in his interest in the land. Delrez has pointed to the ambivalence of
trauma studies in Australia, where the idea of trauma is often displaced from
the native Australians to the settlers, who compete with the former for the
possession of the wound. What white Australians seem to be envious of is the
Aborigines' emotional link with the land and the legitimacy of their relationship with it. As an early passage in *Dirt Music* in which Lu sells illegal fish to
a Vietnamese restaurateur demonstrates, Winton is aware of the need to differentiate between victims:

> I don't call cops.
> Me neither. We're both in the same position, you know.
> Bullshit! I been through a war. And then South China fuckin Sea
> and Malaysia camps and Darwin. And fifteen people looking up to me,
> Lu. Not the same! (29)

What Winton fails to acknowledge as clearly in his novel is the huge gap
separating the traumatic experience of the Aborigine from that of the white
settler.

In "The Colonizing Victim: Tim Winton's Irish Conceit," Jennifer Rutherford analyzes Winton's earlier novel *The Riders* in the context of Anglo-
Celtic Australian nationalism. Scully, a white Australian touring Europe with
his family, is deserted by his wife after they have decided to sell their house in
Fremantle and settle in the Irish countryside. In his desperate search for

Jennifer through Paris, the Greek island of Hydra, and Amsterdam, Scully – a portrait of the innocent Australian abroad – is snubbed by continental Europeans, endangers the life of his nine-year-old daughter, and reaches a point of physical and psychological exhaustion. Eventually, father and daughter abandon their search and find a second home in Ireland, where Scully befriends the local postman. In drawing an affinity between the two countries, Winton equates the history of colonization and resistance of the Irish with Australia's position with respect to Europe. His denunciation of the hierarchies and snobbism of Europe ruling (post)colonial relations works in the way of legitimizing white Australian narratives of nation.[30] It is my contention here that *Dirt Music* represents a further step in Winton's attempt to 'shake off the cultural cringe' and endorse his narrative of white Australian identity, this time by grounding it on the Aboriginal cause. By making the male protagonist, the perfect combination of the outlaw and the bushranger, share his conception of the land with the native Australians, Winton is setting Australia in opposition to Europe, where, he affirms, nature has been replaced by civilization and architecture.

In his book *Palimpsestes*, Gérard Genette explores the relationship between a literary work and what he calls its *paratext*: i.e. those elements and sections that lie outside the bulk of the text, such as the title, preface, epilogue, acknowledgements, etc. The relationship established between *Dirt Music* and the sections "Acknowledgements" and "Permissions," which come right after the novel's text is, in my view, very telling. The last words in the novel, "She's real" are instantly contradicted by the "Acknowledgements": "This is a work of fiction and its characters are imaginary" (463). In *Dirt Music*, the fictional love story of Georgie and Lu unfolds against the background of the real history of Aboriginal trauma on which Australia was founded. Ironically, the "Permissions" section dutifully pays homage to copyright laws, by acknowledging the sources of all borrowings in the novel, from song lyrics to Emily Dickinson's poetry, while missing the most important point of all: the right of the native peoples to a peaceful – or perhaps not – existence on their homelands. As Kevin Rudd, the recently displaced Prime Minister of Australia, put it in his momentous 2008 "Sorry Speech": "we are

---

[30] Jennifer Rutherford, "The Colonizing Victim: Tim Winton's Irish Conceit," in *Flight from Certainty: The Dilemma of Identity and Exile*, ed. Anne Luyat & Francine Tolron (Amsterdam & New York: Rodopi, 2001): 153, 155.

the bearers of many blessings from our ancestors; therefore we must also be the bearers of their burdens as well."[31]

WORKS CITED

Ben–Messahel, Salhia. *Mind the Country: Tim Winton's Fiction* (Crawley: U of Western Australia P, 2006).

Bennett, Geoffrey, dir./screenplay, & Don Featherstone, prod. *The Edge of the World* (Lindfield, N S W: A Film Australia National Interest Program, 1997; 56 min.).

Caruth, Cathy. *Unclaimed Experience: Trauma, Narrative, and History* (Baltimore M D & London: Johns Hopkins U P, 1996).

——, ed. & intro. *Trauma: Explorations in Memory* (Baltimore M D & London: Johns Hopkins U P, 1995).

Crane, Kylie. "The Beat of the Land: Place and Music in Tim Winton's *Dirt Music*," *Zeitschrift für Anglistik und Amerikanistik* 54.1 (2006): 21–32.

Craps, Stef. *Trauma and Ethics in the Novels of Graham Swift: No Short-Cuts to Salvation* (Brighton & Portland O R: Sussex Academic Press, 2005).

Genette, Gérard. *Palimpsests: Literature in the Second Degree* tr. Channa Newman & Claude Doubinsky (*Palimpsestes: La littérature au second degré*, 1962; Lincoln: U of Nebraska P, 1997).

Guy, Elizabeth. "A Conversation with Tim Winton," *Southerly* 56.4 (Summer 1996): 127–33.

Herman, Judith. *Trauma and Recovery: From Domestic Abuse to Political Terror* (1992; London: Pandora, 2001).

LaCapra, Dominick. *Writing History, Writing Trauma* (Baltimore M D & London: Johns Hopkins U P, 2001).

McGirr, Michael. *Tim Winton: The Writer and his Work* (South Yarra, Victoria: Macmillan, 1999).

Plumwood, Val. "Plato and the Bush," *Meanjin* 3 (1990): 524–35.

Rossiter, Richard. "In His Own Words: The Life and Times of Tim Winton," in *Reading Tim Winton,* ed. Richard Rossiter & Lyn Jacobs (Sydney: Angus & Robertson, 1993): 1–15.

——. "The Writer and the Community: An Interview with Tim Winton," *Westerly* 49 (2004): 29–38.

——, & Lyn Jacobs, ed. *Reading Tim Winton* (Sydney: Angus & Robertson, 1993).

---

[31] Kevin Rudd, "Sorry Speech," *Sydney Morning Herald* (13 February 2008): 5, http://www.smh.com.au/news/national/kevin-rudd-says-sorry/2008/02/13/120276034 2960.html (accessed 25 July 2010).

Rudd, Kevin. "Sorry Speech," *Sydney Morning Herald* (13 February 2008): 1–9, http://www.smh.com.au/news/national/kevin-rudd-says-sorry/2008/02/13/12027 60342960.html (accessed 25 July 2010).

Rutherford, Jennifer. "The Colonizing Victim: Tim Winton's Irish Conceit," in *Flight from Certainty: The Dilemma of Identity and Exile*, ed. Anne Luyat & Francine Tolron (Amsterdam & New York: Rodopi, 2001): 153–64.

Tal, Kalí. *Worlds of Hurt: Reading the Literatures of Trauma* (Cambridge: Cambridge UP, 1995).

Watzke, Beth. "Where Pigs Speak in Tongues and Angels Come and Go: A Conversation with Tim Winton," *Antipodes* 5.2 (December 1991): 96–98.

Whitehead, Anne. *Trauma Fiction* (Edinburgh: Edinburgh UP, 2004).

Winton, Tim. *Dirt Music* (London: Picador, 2001).

——. *The Riders* (Sydney: Pan Macmillan, 1994).

◄❖►

"Twisted Ghosts"

Settler Envy and Historical Resolution in Andrew McGahan's *The White Earth*

MARC DELREZ

I N A RECENTLY PUBLISHED SURVEY of contemporary Australian fiction, Andrew McGahan's *The White Earth* (2004) is found to be exemplary of the "rural apocalypse novel," a specific subgenre which typically registers anxieties about political and religious extremism in outback Australia – usually by associating a Gothic element with the sedate routines of life in the country. It is the kind of literature where "remote country towns are imagined as parochial to the point of paranoia,"[1] often with the consequence that an eruption of violence comes to disturb the mundane life-patterns or the natural rhythms apparently favoured by small-town communities. This category of apocalypse fiction in the country can be seen to encompass a number of significant recent Australian novels, such as Alexis Wright's *Carpentaria* (2006), Tim Winton's *Dirt Music* (2001), and Janette Turner Hospital's *Oyster* (1996), but also to gesture further backwards to such classics as Randolph Stow's *Tourmaline* (1963), most of Thea Astley's production, as indeed most of Patrick White's. What is possibly distinctive, however, about McGahan's particular treatment of the rural-apocalypse theme in *The White Earth* is

---

[1] Ken Gelder & Paul Salzman, *After the Celebration: Australian Fiction 1989–2007* (Carlton: Melbourne UP, 2009): 23.

that the book actually *begins* with the description of a catastrophe, as if the repressed violence implicit in the hidden tensions constitutive of rural society were shown also to have already erupted. This raises the possibility that some at least of Australia's contemporary violence in fact echoes an earlier disruption, thus bringing into play a pattern of endless repetition which is interestingly reminiscent of trauma.

Indeed, the novel contains a "Prologue" which focuses on a character called William, a young boy said to be "halfway between his eighth birthday and his ninth," who stands on the veranda of his home and contemplates, "huge in the sky, the mushroom cloud of a nuclear explosion." The narrator's comment, to the effect that "William said nothing, for there was no one to tell," suggests that all of the book that follows ought perhaps to be understood as one of those attempts in writing to bear witness to the unspeakable, whether this is Hiroshima or the Holocaust. The mushroom cloud "casting a vast shadow upon the hills beyond"[2] can then be read as a signal that the shadow of genocide will somehow darken the microcosmic world of the pastoralists which constitutes the setting for the novel about to unfold. This being said, it becomes clear at once that what the boy takes to be a disaster of major proportions, partly as an aspect of his inability to comprehend the event in the moment of its occurrence, boils down to a mere instance of family drama, since what he is witnessing is the death by fire of his own father – the latter is consumed in the blaze ignited by an electrical fault in his combine harvester while he is reaping a tinder-dry paddock of wheat. The fact that dozens of other farmers, having seen the smoke from the vantage-point of their surrounding properties, know "instantly what it [is]" (3), amounts to placing the accidental casualty into another kind of narrative, that of the common heroism implicit in the long march of settlement, whereby an intractable environment is slowly domesticated through sheer hard work and against terrible odds. The novel's prologue thus serves the purpose of creating an ambiguous framework in which the well-rehearsed myth of the heroic pioneers is pitted against an altogether darker context, one that possibly subtends the former and subliminally points to the genocidal foundations on which the history of settlement was constructed in the first place.

Also, the fact that the larger apocalypse recedes as the novel proceeds seems in keeping with an important aspect of McGahan's characterization of

---

[2] Andrew McGahan, *The White Earth* (Crows Nest, N S W : Allen & Unwin): 1. Further page references are in the main text.

his boy-protagonist. When William's unhinged mother discovers that he silently witnessed the death of his father, she strikes him a vicious blow which catches "his right ear in a painful, piercing smack" (4) and which causes the beginnings of an ear infection that will subsequently impair his hearing. William is then literally going deaf in one ear as he becomes engrossed in the lesson in Australian history that the novel takes him through. The suggestion is clearly that the familiar version of history which is going to be inculcated in the boy by his uncle John McIvor, a local land-owner who takes a new interest in this orphan nephew as a potential heir to his property, ought to be seen as essentially truncated and, in all senses of the term, partial. Now, it so happens that, in the words of a commentator, *The White Earth* "captures a moment when non-Aboriginal settlement in Australia – *white* settlement – began to panic: when the assumptions non-Aboriginal people in rural Australia, pastoralists in particular, held about their rights to ownership seemed no longer to be watertight."[3] This is the period in the early 1990s when "Aboriginal claims for sacred sites such as Coronation Hill and Hindmarsh Island galvanized the nation's attention";[4] and it is significant that all of the novel leans towards a denouement that will unfold at the very moment when the Native Title Act will be passed in December 1993. As we know, this represented a major legislative landslide, in keeping with the 1992 Mabo ruling by the High Court of Australia, which effectively dislodged the doctrine of *terra nullius* – Latin for 'nobody's land'– that had been invoked ever since first contact to justify the settlers' refusal to acknowledge native title when claiming ownership of the 'new' continent on behalf of the British Crown. The Mabo case, by upholding the view that native title continued despite the European annexation of Australia, unleashed a wave of anxiety among the freeholders – as would the 1996 Wik decision, which further ruled that pastoral leases did not extinguish native title.[5] The conservative hysteria triggered by these momentous decisions is what the novel sets out to explore, but, again, it is noteworthy that this descent into the turpitude of redneck politics depends for the boy on his gaining mastery of a knowledge that remains halved, or skewed, by an historical

---

[3] Gelder & Salzman, *After the Celebration,* 24.

[4] *After the Celebration,* 25.

[5] For a cogent survey of the legal and political decisions which marked the years of Reconciliation in Australia, see Garth Nettheim, "Reconciliation and Unfinished Business in Australia," in *Reconciliations,* ed. Agnes Toth & Bernard Hickey (Perth: A P I Network, 2005): 3–39.

tradition essentially determined by the stakes of ownership. This is the kind of knowledge envisaged by William as he ponders that, "when he knew every-thing about the station there was to know, he too would be ready to own it in his turn" (181). Such ownership, however, is relativized by the novel's frame, which looks to the Mabo decision as a way of undoing apocalypse, and which simultaneously begs the question of whether William, the reasons for his ear-ache finally diagnosed, can ever wholly recover his sense of hearing.

It can, then, be argued that *The White Earth*, no less than Kate Grenville's highly controversial novel *The Secret River*, which came out in the following year (2005), is responsible for shifting the focus of the "History Wars"[6] from the discourse of historiography, where they had been waged so far, to that of Australian fiction. The sort of decentering of history that occurs in McGa-han's book certainly appears as a major breakthrough, which underscores the difficulty of achieving a truly postcolonial position in a place like Australia where most cultural and political self-representations inevitably rely on die-hard colonialist parameters. Indeed, *terra nullius* makes one think of Adorno's quip that no true life is possible in a wrong world (or, alternatively, that poetry is impossible after Auschwitz). It has now been recognized that settler litera-tures occupied an uneasy position within an institutionalized postcolonial dis-course premised on a principle of analogy between discrete approaches to de-colonization. Whereas they were originally included in the postcolonial corpus as a matter of course, in a way that potentially elided the proximity to those imperialist paradigms which continued to inform them,[7] increasingly settler cultures have subsequently tended to be disqualified from consideration in the postcolonial debate, precisely on account of their inherited closeness to a European mind-set. Thus, in the name of a growing historicism and of the need for greater attention to the specificities of context, such critics as Gillian Whitlock have voiced the following complaint:

---

[6] On this controversy, which has dominated debates about Australian identity and its cultural and historical origins, see especially Stuart Macintyre & Anna Clark, *The His-tory Wars* (Melbourne: Melbourne UP, 2006), and various essays in *Lighting Dark Places: Essays on Kate Grenville*, ed. Sue Kossew (Cross/Cultures 131; Amsterdam & New York: Rodopi, 2010), particularly Brigid Rooney, "Kate Grenville as Public In-tellectual" (17–38), Elizabeth McMahon, "Author! Author! The Two Faces of Kate Grenville" (39–54), Eleanor Collins, "Poison in the Flour: Kate Grenville's *The Secret River*" (167–78), and Sarah Pinto, "History, Fiction, and *The Secret River*" (179–97).

[7] See Bill Ashcroft, Gareth Griffiths & Helen Tiffin, *The Empire Writes Back: Theory and Practice in Post-Colonial Literatures* (London & New York: Routledge, 1989).

> Thinking about settlers is deeply unfashionable in postcolonial criticism. Settlers have always been unpalatable subjects. Their writings [...] rest uncomfortably on the cusp of coloniality, writings which work with rather than against European models and feature difficult and sometimes ambiguous engagements with a history of invasion and dispossession.[8]

The point is in part that, more often than not, the urgency of calls "to redress the balance of focus and retrieve a space for the consideration of the settler cultures"[9] conceals an unsavoury propensity for representing white settler citizens as the victims rather than the beneficiaries of conquest. Thus, it has been possible to claim that "settler colonialism is [...] an ongoing relationship that is impervious to formal decolonization"[10] – indeed, one that can be traced through to the present day. For some, in a place like Australia, only the Aborigines can lay claim to some kind of unproblematic postcolonial condition, which is why a critic like Simon During – and others after him – found it useful to distinguish between such categories as the postcolonized and the postcolonizers.[11] In this kind of context, it may be argued that *The White Earth* emerges as a postcolonizing novel, precisely by virtue of its determination to dislodge settlers' pretensions to postcoloniality, while the question remains by what means a book that remains tied to the narrative of settler history can itself enter into any kind of stable postcolonial condition.

Along the same line of thought, it is my suggestion that a deep ambivalence also characterizes the emergence of trauma studies in Australia, together with the perception that the foundation of the nation itself was inseparable from the experience of a communal trauma which continues to reverberate through the anxieties of belonging frequently expressed in Australian literature today. It is symptomatic that the terminology of trauma was utilized to describe the settler population's growth of awareness of the more blemished chapters in the national history, whereby, in the years of Reconciliation (roughly, the 1990s), "a once-certain sense of being-in-the-nation, that feeling

---

[8] Gillian Whitlock, *The Intimate Empire: Reading Women's Autobiography* (London & New York: Cassell, 2000): 41.

[9] Cynthia vanden Driesen, *Writing the Nation: Patrick White and the Indigene* (Cross/Cultures 97; Amsterdam & New York: Rodopi, 2009): xxi.

[10] Patrick Wolfe, "The Limits of Native Title," *Meanjin* 59.3 (2000): 131–32.

[11] See Simon During, "Postcolonialism and Globalization," *Meanjin* 51.2 (1992): 339–53.

flowing from the authority of colonial possession, [suddenly] seem[ed] to be irretrievably delegitimized."[12] Thus, the somehow belated discovery that the foundation of Australia coincided with an act of dispossession and genocide resulted, for the settlers' descendants, in a traumatic sense of the loss of "a properly constituted national selfhood," accompanied by a corresponding urge to repair the damage by offering a proper apology to the Aborigines. It may not be the least of ironies that the perception of a "seemingly irreparable rupture in the settler's sense of a place in the nation"[13] in fact echoed, across the centuries, the trauma of dispossession suffered by the Aborigines at the time of invasion. There is, then, a sense in which the quality of trauma, just like the postcolonial condition itself, emerges as an aspect of Aboriginal experience which is typically displaced onto the settlers, as the latter histrionically claim for themselves the kind of history that will display "a kind of indigenous equivalence," and consequently legitimate their "reconstituted attachment to the nation."[14] It is not irrelevant that, as has now been shown, this "white [...] mimicry of indigenous expressions of belonging" has formed a far from negligible dimension of Australian literary production during and after the Reconciliation years.[15]

This take on the contemporary situation in Australia is offered in full recognition of the fact that, historically, the settlers were once themselves the underprivileged rejects of British society, and that transportation may well have represented some sort of trauma, too, which subsequently had to be overcome. But this originary condition, which had encouraged Australians to think of themselves as deserving survivors, only enhanced the surprise-effect unleashed by the revelations of the Reconciliation years, which indirectly drew attention to the relative affluence enjoyed by the average Australian citizen today even as they historicized the conditions of its emergence. In a sense, Australia's attachment to its convict past only confirms the view that

---

[12] Haydie Gooder & Jane M. Jacobs, "'On the Border of the Unsayable': The Apology in Postcolonizing Australia," *Interventions: International Journal of Postcolonial Studies* 2.2 (2000): 236.

[13] Gooder & Jacobs, "'On the Border of the Unsayable'," 235.

[14] "'On the Border of the Unsayable'," 237.

[15] Gelder & Salzman, *After the Celebration*, 25; see also Marc Delrez, "'The Spirit of the Land': The Purposes of Mysticism in Recent Australian Literate Culture," in *Bernard Hickey, a Roving Cultural Ambassador: Essays in His Memory*, ed. Maria Renata Dolce & Antonella Riem Natale (Udine: Forum, 2009): 101–108.

suffering tends to be invested with the value of moral capital; while the Aborigines' credentials for treading the stage as the dispossessed of today served to signal the urgency of displacing the model currently in use for the business of national identity-construction. Also, in this context it ought to come as no surprise that Australia's identity politics should typically favour a dichotomous mode of conceptualization schematically differentiating between 'us' and 'them', to designate non-Indigenous and Indigenous Australians respectively. This duality was identified as a consequence of the shift, in recent cultural discourse, "from speaking about multiculturalism to speaking of nationhood." Thus, the same commentator continues:

> The Australian state is no longer one which can be positively transformed culturally, politically, economically, linguistically, socially, by the arrival of immigrants and refugees. Instead, the Australian state is a monolithic institution, Anglo-Celtic, Judaeo-Christian, so much so that a citizenship test can now be constructed to articulate the unchanging, fixed nature of this thing called 'Australianness.'[16]

This reminds us, if need be, that myths of identity entertain only the most vexed of relations with the complexity of actual sociological configurations, and promote grids of reading in which "the very stuff of living history is abandoned."[17]

Therefore, tempting as it may be to approach the sociology of the post-colonizing settler culture in terms of the dynamics of trauma, this can be done only on condition that it be recognized that we would then be dealing with a collective trauma, shared across the generations and across the racial groups. By this token, the destabilized settlers under Reconciliation can indeed be seen to be suffering from a sense of the traumatic, painful disruption of their earlier sense of belonging in the nation, though this perception, together with the displacement of suffering that it enables and naturalizes, simultaneously signals the problematic nature of any facile analogy between decolonization and psychotherapy. Importantly, ever since Frantz Fanon's suggestion (in *The Wretched of the Earth*) that colonialism is a nervous condition, this sort of link has tended to underlie descriptions of anticolonial struggle, whenever the latter was seen in terms of working oneself through the cultural symptoms

---

[16] Christos Tsiolkas, "On the Concept of Tolerance," in Christos Tsiolkas, Gideon Haigh & Alexis Wright, *Tolerance, Prejudice and Fear*, intro. J.M. Coetzee (Crows Nest, NSW: Allen & Unwin, 2008): 13.

[17] Tsiolkas, "On the Concept of Tolerance," 13.

produced in the subordinated subject by the experience of protracted colonization. A relatively recent occurrence of the trope, at the start of Leela Gandhi's
Postcolonial Theory, has the merit of being explicit:

> The colonial aftermath calls for an ameliorative and therapeutic theory
> which is responsive to the task of remembering and recalling the colonial
> past. The work of this theory may be compared to what Lyotard de-
> scribes as the "psychoanalytic procedure of *anamnesis*, or analysis –
> which urges patients to elaborate their current problems by freely asso-
> ciating apparently inconsequential details with past situations – allowing
> them to uncover hidden meanings in their lives and their behaviour." In
> adopting this procedure, postcolonial theory inevitably commits itself to
> a complex project of historical and psychological "recovery."[18]

While this sort of statement may seem optimistic and even epistemologically
naive in its analogical recourse to psychoanalysis in order to come to grips
with political realities, this is even more the case in the context of the settler
colonies, where, as suggested above, any condition of "trauma persists in and
as a differential relation of power between the perpetrator and the victim."[19]
One should, then, remain cautious lest trauma theory, which acknowledges
the possibility that people may sometimes "face the task of grieving not only
for what was lost but for what was never theirs to lose,"[20] be used manipu-
latively as a way of levelling down, in the name of communal suffering, those
political and economic disparities which often continue to characterize the
postcolonizing society.

A further paradox is that, even as they provide the template of the founding
traumatic experience, the Aborigines tend to be invested with precisely those
qualities, construed in terms of authenticity and continuity of occupation of
the land, of which the impoverished settlers are now feeling deprived. This is
why it has been argued that the latent spirit of Reconciliation may well be a
form of envy.[21] Even after the then Labour Prime Minister of Australia, Kevin

---

[18] Leela Gandhi, *Postcolonial Theory: A Critical Introduction* (New York: Columbia UP, 1998): 8.

[19] David Lloyd, "Colonial Trauma/Postcolonial Recovery?" *Interventions: International Journal of Postcolonial Studies* 2.2 (2000): 214.

[20] Judith Herman, *Trauma and Recovery: From Domestic Abuse to Political Terror*
(New York: HarperCollins, 1992): 198.

[21] See Anthony Moran, "Aboriginal Reconciliation: Transformations in Settler
Nationalisms," *Melbourne Journal of Politics* 25 (1998): 101–31.

Rudd, eventually offered an official apology on behalf of the nation, it is disturbing that settler envy continues to flourish, although the vast injustices suffered by the indigenous population have hardly so much as begun to be addressed. There is, then, a sense in which the settlers, under Reconciliation and by dint of their very empathy with Aboriginal suffering, exhibit the desire to take possession of the wound itself, fantasized as that which allows the victims to entrench their entitlement to full Australian citizenship. In other words, there may well be, as an aspect of settler envy, such a thing as "trauma envy," a notion actually envisaged by John Mowitt who refers to "the gain of pain"[22] that accrues as an effect of the link established between traumatic injury and moral authority. In the context of the Australian predicament, it seems evident that trauma has come to provide such a seal of authority and legitimacy that it elicits a desire to have suffered from it, albeit at a remove of several generations. It is just as well if, once cut off from its historical provenance and thus hypostatized, trauma is no longer seen to result from the misdeeds of its perpetrators. To the contrary, such a situation authorizes the emergence of a moralizing discourse which obfuscates the materiality of exploitation and allows the speaker to achieve legitimacy by proxy, through the pursuit of a spiritual equivalence with the victims.

It could be shown that a form of trauma envy traverses an incredibly large proportion of today's discursive production in Australia. Suffice it here to suggest that it even crops up where one was least expecting it, as in Germaine Greer's pamphlet entitled *Whitefella Jump Up*, which offers an implacable reading of settler history, as well as, among other things, a caustic castigation of the Australians' catastrophic mismanagement of their environment. Greer links contemporary ecological disasters to a whole history of settler alienation from the place, concluding polemically:

> In Australian literature, the Europeans' corrosive unease expresses itself in a curious distortion of the pathetic fallacy, which characterizes the land as harsh, cruel, savage, relentless, the sky as implacable, pitiless and so forth. The heart of the country is called "dead." […] It was not the country that was damned but the settler who felt in his heart that he was damned. His impotent cursing, which has left a legacy in the unequalled degree of profanity in Australian speech, was a classic

---

[22] John Mowitt, "Trauma Envy," *Cultural Critique* 46 (Fall 2000): 276.

piece of transference. We hate this country because we cannot allow
ourselves to love it. We know in our hearts' core that it is not ours.[23]

What Greer is really saying, in a sense, is that the wilful destruction of the
land by the settlers is a consequence of envy, in keeping with Melanie Klein's
contention that envy, defined as "the angry feeling that another person possesses and enjoys something desirable,"[24] can take the form of spoliation of the
desired object. However, the irony of the matter is that Greer herself considers
that the only way for the nation to outgrow this attitude would be by embracing Aboriginality wholesale, which testifies to the intensity of her own
settler envy, of the kind that consists in a wish to *take away* the coveted object. Indeed, the book's epigraph makes it clear that 'jump up', in the Kriol
language, means to 'leap up to a higher level', and therefore, 'to be resurrected or reborn'. Accordingly, the main argument of *Whitefella Jump Up* is that
settler society ought to espouse Aboriginality if it is to rise from its 'dead'
condition, to become rejuvenated and redeemed of its current spiritual exhaustion. The ultimate paradox is, then, that a sense of settler envy – hence,
an acquisitorial or neocolonial impulse – can be seen to characterize even the
most radical condemnations of white exactions in Australia.

In contrast, part of the distinction of *The White Earth* is that McGahan's
novel, by dint of showing up the resentment which informs so much of contemporary Australian cultural and political discourse, creates the conditions
whereby it might be seen for what it is – a neocolonial avatar – and consequently criticized. This is clearest in those passages when John McIvor, William's
uncle, constructs Australia as a "sacred site" (209) open for spiritual consumption by the settlers: indeed, along lines of apprehension which closely replicate
what is usually understood about the Aborigines' mode of connection to the
land. Witness the following diatribe, addressed to William by his uncle:

> "There are folk out there who believe that the Aborigines are the only
> ones who understand the land, that only the blacks could have found a
> place like this and appreciated what it was. They think that the blacks
> have some magical connection that whites can never have, that we're
> just stumbling around here without any idea, that we don't understand
> the country, that we just want to exploit it. But that's not true. We can

---

[23] Germaine Greer, *Whitefella Jump Up: The Shortest Way to Nationhood* (London: Profile, 2004): 10–11.

[24] Melanie Klein, *The Selected Melanie Klein*, ed. Juliet Mitchell (New York: Free Press, 1986): 212.

have connections with the land too, our own kind of magic. This land
talks to me. It doesn't care what colour I am, all that matters is that I'm
here. And I understand what it says, just as well as anyone before me,
black or white." (181)

Clearly, the novel offers a condemnation of this sort of whipped-up spirituality professed by the settlers, by explicitly associating it with the rabid politics
of William's uncle, but also by showing that these magic "connections with
the land," obviously derived though they are from Aboriginal religious models, can only enter into a regime of competition with their own source of inspiration. If magical connections are "the essence of ownership" (181), then
indigenous magic must be denied even as it is recuperated. This is why Mc-
Ivor goes out of his way to conceal the presence on his station of a waterhole
and a bora ring, "a circle of stones within a circle of trees," which never
ceased to draw Aborigines as an appointed site for their most "important
rituals" (179), so that, under the emerging legislation, they might justify a land
claim on their part.

Intriguingly, however, while the novel proves unambiguous in its indict-
ment of settler envy of an Aboriginal mode of spirituality, so that the half-
deaf William refuses to step into the shoes of his uncle when the latter claims
that "the land speaks to [him]," by contrast it would appear that a form of
"trauma envy" may nevertheless continue to affect the boy, who does not
cease to be visited by nightmarish visions of fire in the night. The novel thus
appears to embrace the conventions of the 'post'colonial ghost story – documenting as it does the "fantasies of white spiritual relationship with place"[25] –
especially when it turns out that William is granted sights of a dreadful phan-
tom who stalks the property in the guise of a man burning in the night. Because quite a number of characters (including William's own father, but also
his great-uncle's step-father) indeed died in a fire, the narrative plays riddles
and tends to make the figure of the ghost overdetermined to the point of undecidability. Thus, for a long time it remains unclear whether the burning
ghost emanates from the depths of settler history or whether it bespeaks the
horrors of the Aborigines' decimation at the hands of the first pastoralists. The
latter hypothesis gains in plausibility in view of the exertions of some right-
wing activists, the Australian Independence League, whose political rally,

---

[25] David Crouch, "National Hauntings: The Architecture of Australian Ghost
Stories," in *Spectres, Screens, Shadows, Mirrors*, ed. Tanya Dalziell & Paul Genoni
(*JASAL* Special Issue 2007): 100.

held on the grounds of Kuran Station, degenerates into a racist rite reminiscent of Ku Klux Klan iconography and choreography. Moreover, the black ascendancy of William's magical vision seems reinforced when, in a fit of delirium induced by fever, he catches sight of the legendary bunyip about which "the Aborigines had warned the early settlers" (316). This creature issues a piercing cry which is "the sound of death and cold and age" (317), and which prepares William for the later discovery that his ancestors were involved in the massacre of the Kuran people – indeed, those who used to inhabit the land – whose mortal remains had to be cremated by murderers only too eager to conceal their crime. In the end, the suggestion seems to be that white and black magic coalesce into one and the same "dream haunted with flame" (269) – indeed, in proportion to the degree of enmeshment which makes settler and Aboriginal histories inextricably dependent on each other. In this sense, William's haunting visions can be interpreted as an expression either of white guilt or of black mourning, or indeed of both at the same time: trauma envy.

Such a sense of the mutuality of trauma seems in tune with the settler confidence that the "country will speak to you, if you listen." These are, of course, the words of William's uncle, who, unaware of his nephew's failing hearing, congratulates him on his supernatural gifts of perception, insisting that this sort of blessing is neither "an Aboriginal thing" nor "a white thing," but a "human thing" (295) available to whomever can strain their ears and become attuned to the secret sounds of the land. However, this rhetoric is ultimately displaced by the author–narrator, who reveals that, if William is indeed the rightful recipient of the land's dreams, somebody who "*bear[s] the mark*" (317), this is in the first place because all through his meandering peregrinations across the bush he has been wearing, by way of protection from the sun, an old and musty hat found among family relics and fitted with the badge, QMP. Indeed, it turns out that his uncle's father used to belong to the Queensland Mounted Police, and more particularly to an infamous special troop called the Native Police, whose job it was to 'disperse' any troublesome Aborigines in the early days of settlement. It is this ominous badge, "the Australian equivalent of an SS uniform" and a symbol of darkest authority, that had prompted the response of the bunyip – for the latter "had regarded it with ancient hostility" (336). Only with this revelation does it become clear why the apparition of the burning man, "flame streaming over his face" (230), had been felt by William to contain a personal warning, meant for him alone, and heralding a disaster still to come.

Eventually it will dawn on him that the cautionary message spoken by the "twisted ghosts" of the past can hardly be heard as an indication of his belonging: "The inheritance was no gift. It was a burden" (327). Such is his own role in the unfinished inheritance business narrated by the book, that he feels "his own ghost [will] eternally haunt this place, bearing its burden back and forth amidst the shadows" (365). Thus, McGahan sets out to decentre the traditional ghost story in Australia, which usually denotes *possession* in all senses of the term. Indeed, by being possessed by the ghosts of History's Aboriginal victims, the settlers may well evince their responsiveness to the foundational trauma of Australia, and in this way they possibly show that they, too, belong in the nation. But the ghost of a burning man which haunts William in *The White Earth* turns out to be pointing not to the past but to the future, and more specifically to the moment when his uncle will try to cremate, yet another time, the bones of the Aborigines massacred on 'his' property, in an attempt to negate the genocide which took place as an aspect of settlement. In terms of the genealogy of the magic illustrated in the book, it is significant that the boy should thus be possessed not by the traumas of another culture but by the denials of his own. In this sense, McGahan writes against, and thus steps outside of, a literary tradition which celebrates mystery or mysticism so as to legitimize settler claims to belonging. Needless to say, William will remain deaf to the end. What the novel therefore recommends is that one should descend into one's own history instead of appealing to magic in order to short-circuit the strenuous intellectual efforts and lucid self-analysis that the settler inheritance today requires.

WORKS CITED

Ashcroft, Bill, Gareth Griffiths, & Helen Tiffin. *The Empire Writes Back: Theory and Practice in Post-Colonial Literatures* (London & New York: Routledge, 1989).

Caruth, Cathy. *Unclaimed Experience: Trauma, Narrative, and History* (Baltimore MD & London: Johns Hopkins UP, 1996).

Crouch, David. "National Hauntings: The Architecture of Australian Ghost Stories," in *Spectres, Screens, Shadows, Mirrors*, ed. Tanya Dalziell & Paul Genoni (*JASAL* Special Issue 2007): 94–105.

Delrez, Marc. "'The Spirit of the Land': The Purposes of Mysticism in Recent Australian Literate Culture," in *Bernard Hickey, a Roving Cultural Ambassador: Essays in His Memory*, ed. Maria Renata Dolce & Antonella Riem Natale (Udine: Forum, 2009): 101–108.

During, Simon. "Postcolonialism and Globalization," *Meanjin* 51.2 (1992): 339–53.

Fanon, Frantz. *The Wretched of the Earth*, tr. Constance Farrington, preface by Jean–Paul Sartre (*Les damnés de la terre*, 1961; tr. 1963; New York: Grove Weidenfeld, 1967).

Gandhi, Leela. *Postcolonial Theory: A Critical Introduction*. (New York: Columbia UP, 1998).

Gelder, Ken, & Paul Salzman. *After the Celebration: Australian Fiction 1989–2007* (Carlton: Melbourne UP, 2009).

Gooder, Haydie, & Jane M. Jacobs. "'On the Border of the Unsayable': The Apology in Postcolonizing Australia," *Interventions: International Journal of Postcolonial Studies* 2.2 (2000): 229–47.

Greer, Germaine. *Whitefella Jump Up: The Shortest Way to Nationhood* (London: Profile Books, 2004).

Herman, Judith. *Trauma and Recovery: From Domestic Abuse to Political Terror* (New York: HarperCollins, 1992).

Klein, Melanie. *The Selected Melanie Klein*, ed. Juliet Mitchell (New York: Free Press, 1986).

Kossew, Sue, ed. *Lighting Dark Places: Essays on Kate Grenville* (Cross/Cultures 131; Amsterdam & New York: Rodopi, 2010).

Lloyd, David. "Colonial Trauma/Postcolonial Recovery?" *Interventions: International Journal of Postcolonial Studies* 2.2 (2000): 212–28.

Macintyre, Stuart, & Anna Clark. *The History Wars* (Melbourne: Melbourne UP, 2006).

McGahan, Andrew. *The White Earth* (Crows Nest, NSW: Allen & Unwin, 2005).

Moran, Anthony. "Aboriginal Reconciliation: Transformations in Settler Nationalisms," *Melbourne Journal of Politics* 25 (1998): 101–31.

Mowitt, John. "Trauma Envy," *Cultural Critique* 46 (Fall 2000): 272–97.

Nettheim, Garth. "Reconciliation and Unfinished Business in Australia," in *Reconciliations*, ed. Agnes Toth & Bernard Hickey (Perth: API Network, 2005): 3–39.

Tsiolkas, Christos. "On the Concept of Tolerance," in Christos Tsiolkas, Gideon Haigh & Alexis Wright, *Tolerance, Prejudice and Fear*, intro. J.M. Coetzee (Crows Nest, NSW: Allen & Unwin, 2008).

vanden Driesen, Cynthia. *Writing the Nation: Patrick White and the Indigene* (Cross/Cultures 97; Amsterdam & New York: Rodopi, 2009).

Whitlock, Gillian. *The Intimate Empire: Reading Women's Autobiography* (London & New York: Cassell, 2000).

Wolfe, Patrick. "The Limits of Native Title," *Meanjin* 59.3 (2000): 129–44.

❖

The Trauma of Immigration and the Ethics of Self-Positioning in Richard Flanagan's *The Sound of One Hand Clapping*

HEINZ ANTOR

I N 1997, the Australian writer Richard Flanagan published his novel *The Sound of One Hand Clapping*, in which he critically engages with some of the traumatic aspects of his country's history as well as with the traumas suffered by many of those who came to Australia to begin a new life there. The book describes the fortunes of the Buloh family, who emigrate from Slovenia to the fifth continent in the aftermath of the Second World War in order to build up a better existence there. But the ravages of war as well as the experience of migration and its consequences have traumatized the whole family. Flanagan impressively depicts what the wounds[1] of the Buloh family members consist in, how they try to deal with them, and to what extent there can be a process of healing. The depiction and analysis of traumatization is thus combined with the narrative construction of attempts at reconstructing an orientational framework in a situation in which things seem to have fallen apart, and this tentative self-repositioning of the traumatized characters adds an ethical dimension to the novel, which deals with the putting together again of the broken fragments of *ethos* in the Greek sense of the word: i.e. 'char-

---

[1] 'Trauma' derives from the Greek word τραύμα 'wound'.

acter',[2] and which opens up the history of postwar immigration to Australia to an ethical evaluation that critically undermines official contemporary historiography.[3]

All three members of the Buloh family are severely traumatized in this novel. They had to suffer the invasion of their home country by the military forces of the Nazis and they had to witness the destruction of houses and the killings of relatives, friends, and neighbours before they managed to leave war-ravaged Slovenia and emigrate. Transplanted to a new world on the other side of the planet, the Bulohs have to experience how all their habitual orientational markers are either useless or severely flawed, in a world in which neither their language nor their previous cultural patterns play any significant role. The mother, Maria Buloh, is unable to cope with the physical as well as psychological hardships created by her European experiences[4] and by the alterity of her new surroundings in Tasmania, which traumatize her a second time[5] so that she commits suicide by hanging herself one winter night in 1954. This, in turn, traumatizes Bojan Buloh, Maria's husband, all over again, as well as his little daughter, three-year-old Sonja. She witnesses the moment her mother leaves the family's modest home in order to hang herself in the snow-covered winter forest of Tasmania, and she is severely traumatized by this experience of loss.

---

[2] See Wayne C. Booth, *The Company We Keep: An Ethics of Fiction* (Berkeley: U of California P, 1988): 8, and Charles Taylor, *Sources of the Self: The Making of the Modern Identity* (Cambridge: Cambridge UP, 1989): 27.

[3] See Mirko Jurak, "Slovene Immigrants in Australia in Richard Flanagan's Novel *The Sound of One Hand Clapping*," *Acta Neophilologica* 34.1–2 (2001): 28. Flanagan's novel is just one example of a whole spate of Australian literary texts dealing with immigration and displaced persons, the most famous fictional DP probably being Himmelfarb in Patrick White's *Riders in the Chariot*. Flanagan could have chosen examples of forced migration from other ethnic contexts, but deals with post-World War II immigrants to Australia because of his wife's Slovene background. *The Sound of One Hand Clapping* is the second volume of Flanagan's Tasmanian triptych, which opened with *Death of a River Guide* in 1994 and was completed with *Gould's Book of Fish* in 2001.

[4] Richard Flanagan, *The Sound of One Hand Clapping* (New York: Grove, 1987): 253. Further page references are in the main text.

[5] "Maria [was] seeing only the night sky which was nothing and explained nothing and offered nothing and her despair was total and utter [...]" (262).

The novel begins with a telling statement which adumbrates the nature of what is to come:

> All this you will come to understand but can never know, and all of it took place long, long ago in a world that has since perished into peat, in a forgotten winter on an island of which few have ever heard. It began in that time before snow, completely and irrevocably, covers footprints. As black clouds shroud the star and the moonlit heavens, as an unshadowable darkness comes upon the whispering land. (1)

This poetic passage already spells out some of the main problems dealt with in the novel. The problems of knowing and of understanding are alluded to, and the issues of annihilation and of forgetting and, by implication, remembering, are mentioned. Just as the footprints are rubbed out and not seen any longer, so does the deep darkness referred to in the last sentence add an ominous note to the opening lines of this novel. The very first sentence sets the task ahead: i.e. that of understanding in the face of the unknowable, of getting to grips with what can never be wholly managed and assimilated.

When Maria Buloh leaves her wooden hut in Tasmania to walk out into the snow-covered forest and hang herself, her little daughter Sonja calls after her in a whimper, and Maria tries to calm her with words uttered in Slovenian:

> "Aja, aja," said Maria Buloh, attempting to soothe the child with the words mothers of her country always used to put children to sleep.
> "Aja, aja." (2–3)

This is just one instance of many in this book that point to the importance of language in making humans comfortable and allowing them to feel well and at home in the world. When language does not function any longer or when the characters move in a linguistically alien environment, this means a rupture between themselves and their surroundings, from which they feel dissociated and isolated, which is also what happens to Bojan Buloh, as we shall see.[6]

Maria Buloh's leaving her hut in order to commit suicide is described in the first chapter of the novel from her own point of view so that the reader is allowed an insight into Maria's wounded state. She is unable to link up with her environment and thus unable to securely place herself in it. When she looks around her, she is "seeing it all anew, as if it had no connection with

---

[6] See also Jaroslav Kušnír, "Post-Colonial Space and Australian Identity in Richard Flanagan's *Sound of One Hand Clapping*," *Zeitschrift für Australienstudien* 23 (2009): 69–80.

her" (3). One of the reasons for her inability to situate herself in the context of Tasmania is that her new Australian surroundings are associated with memories of what caused the psychic injuries of many of the refugee immigrants, memories that she does not want to face and prefers to suppress:

> She saw how the whole black and white scene was lit up by the stark electric lights [...], how on either side of the street were crude vertical-board huts with corrugated-iron roofs and corrugated-iron chimneys, and how to some who lived there it brought back all too painful memories of forced labour camps in the Urals or Siberia. But she knew it wasn't Stalin's USSR. Knew it wasn't Kolyma or Goli Otok or Birkenau. Knew it wasn't even Europe. Knew it to be a snow-covered Hydroelectric Commission construction camp called Butlers Gorge that sat like a sore in a wilderness of rainforest.
>
> In this land of infinite space, the huts were all built cheek by jowl, as if the buildings too cowered in shivering huddles before the force and weight and silence of the unknowable, that might possibly be benign, might possibly even not care about people, but which their terrible histories – chronicles of centuries of recurring inhumanities and horrors which they carried along with a few lace doilies and curling photographs and odd habits and peculiar ways of eating – could only allow them to fear.
>
> Because not to fear was to imagine a world beyond experience.
>
> And that was too much for anybody. (4)

Even though Maria here thinks about the other immigrants' traumatizations, the problem she contemplates is her own as well. Her new surroundings, in their stark appearance, conjure up memories of a past of loss, horror, and destruction, they re-awaken what she tries to forget and suppress, and, at the same time, these terrible memories force her to see her new Australian environment as a threatening one. She is thus unable to feel at home in Tasmania, to assimilate her new experiences to an acceptable framework of understanding, because her previous life history only allows her to conceptualize Australia as something dangerous, something to be afraid of. She evinces the symptoms of the "generalization of threat" which is typical of post-traumatic stress disorder (PTSD).[7] Maria is unable to live such a life under the constant stress of fear and determines to put an end to her existence,

---

[7] Bessel A. van der Kolk & Alexander C. McFarlane, "The Black Hole of Trauma," in *Literary Theory: An Anthology*, ed. Julie Rivkin & Michael Ryan (Oxford: Blackwell, 2004): 496.

which has become insufferable to her. She thus appears to those observing her as "the strange woman who was staring […] as if she saw a future akin to the past when they would all once more be scattered with the wind and nothing of this horrible time and place would remain" (6–7). Thus, the experience of flight, emigration, and diaspora is also a part of Maria's trauma, and this, together with the horrors of the past, relentlessly undermines her confidence in the possibility of a more benign future.

Maria's view of the world as described here is typical of traumatized people in several respects. For example, van der Kolk and McFarlane describe avoidance and numbing as a common reaction to re-experiencing trauma:

> Once traumatized individuals become haunted by intrusive reexperiences of their trauma, they generally start organizing their lives around avoiding having the emotions these intrusions evoke.[8]

To Maria, the sight of the wooden huts with corrugated-iron roofs and corrugated-iron chimneys that make up the settlement of the immigrant labourers working on the hydroelectric dam in Tasmania, where she lives with her family, is the medium of a constant re-experiencing of her own traumatic emotions created during and in the aftermath of the Second World War. Thus, since she has to live in the settlement and cannot avoid confrontation with that wounding sight, the strategy of organizing her life around what is unbearable for Maria is denied to her, and since she cannot stand the resulting strain, she breaks and commits suicide. She is thus an example of traumatized "people's inability to come to terms with real experiences that have overwhelmed their capacity to cope."[9] Maria thus slides into what is referred to as 'post-traumatic decline,' a state in which trauma victims "experience a progressive decline and withdrawal, in which *any* stimulation […] provokes further detachment. To feel nothing seems to be better than feeling irritable and upset."[10] Maria takes the ultimate step in detaching herself from her real life and in reducing feeling by killing herself. This is due to the fact that she is not capable of overcoming the experience of her world falling apart, which is at the core of her psychic wound. Her war experiences, as well as the ordeals of migration and diaspora, make it impossible for her to live on. As Reiker and Carmen have shown,

---

[8] van der Kolk & McFarlane, "The Black Hole of Trauma," 494.

[9] "The Black Hole of Trauma," 488.

[10] "The Black Hole of Trauma," 495.

confrontations with violence challenge one's most basic assumptions
about the self as invulnerable and intrinsically worthy, and about the
world as orderly and just. After abuse, the victim's view of self and
world can never be the same again: it must be reconstructed to incorporate the abuse experience.[11]

Maria's thoughts as she leaves her hut for the forest to commit suicide there
illustrate her persistent feeling of vulnerability, her insuperable belief in the
injustice and threatening, as well as chaotic, quality of the world, and thus her
inability to perform the reconstructive work of incorporation that Reiker and
Carmen consider to be essential for a healing of trauma. This is why "aggression against self," one of the "complex adaptations to trauma,"[12] is Maria's
only and ultimate way out.

    Maria's family, her husband Bojan and her little daughter Sonja, are trau-
matized in turn by her suicide or, in the case of Sonja, her unexplained disappearance. Bojan seeks refuge in work,[13] drink, and violence. Drink allows him
to forget and thus practise a strategy of post-traumatic avoidance, while the
violence he shows in beating his daughter when in a state of inebriation is
another symptom of his wounded state. In a scene in which he beats up the
sixteen-year-old Sonja, he accuses her of going out with boys:

> "I bet you been out with the bloody boys, I know, I know, you bloody
> slut, you little tart, you are just like your whore of a mother carrying on
> with – " (12)

The unfinished implication expressed here by Bojan: namely that Maria left in
1954 with another man, is merely another strategy of avoidance, an alternative
story made up by the traumatized man in order not to have to face the memory of his wife's suicide, as well as to spare his daughter the harrowing knowledge of what really happened. This unfaced and only dimly remembered
reality – Sonja was only three years old when she saw her mother for the last
time as Maria left the hut and disappeared – is something Sonja experiences
as "some huge unknowable enigma at [her father's] centre" (11), and again, as
in the opening paragraph of the novel and in Maria's ruminations on the

---

[11] P.P. Reiker & E.H. Carmen, "The Victim-to-Patient Process: the Disconfirmation
and Transformation of Abuse," *American Journal of Orthopsychiatry* 56 (1986): 362.

[12] van der Kolk & McFarlane, "The Black Hole of Trauma," 499.

[13] In fact, Bojan's job in the forestry/dams context and the frenetic way in which he
performs his work seem to serve a redemptive purpose.

unknowable, the issue of knowing and of understanding experience: i.e. of making it intelligible, placeable, and manageable, is at the centre of the question of how to overcome trauma and live a satisfying life in Australia.[14] What Sonja can discern, however, is that due to her father's outbursts of drunken fury, her world is falling apart, which again reinforces her traumatized state as one in which the world can no longer be perceived as good and ordered:

> It was not him. It was not.
> But in the far distance she saw her home and her home was break-
> ing into pieces and a giant was exploding out of it and the giant would
> not stop growing and the sun was eclipsing behind his back and the
> world was darkness and the giant's anger had become a frenzy. (12)

The image of something breaking into pieces becomes a central one in the novel, symbolizing the traumatizing effects of being confronted with something one cannot cope with. It applies both to her traumatized father's violent and strange behaviour and to the loss of her mother. With reference to Bojan, we are told that "she did not cry, but he was breaking something and she could not put it back together no matter how she tried, and the hurt opened up like an abyss within her heart" (13).

In another scene, which takes the reader back to 1954, Sonja is taken away for an afternoon from Bojan, who is still utterly crushed by his wife's suicide, and again we are given a vivid description of the extent of Sonja's traumatization, which turns into a harrowing rendering of how, to the little girl, a whole world is falling apart and declines into utter chaos:

> it was commented upon how blank was her face. [...] She appeared
> neither happy nor sad. [...] In front of her the women had set up an up-
> turned gelignite box, covered with a makeshift red chequered table-
> cloth, upon which was arrayed her toy china tea-set for her to play
> with.

---

[14] See Roger Luckhurst, "Mixing Memory and Desire: Psychoanalysis, Psychology, and Trauma Theory," in *Literary Theory: An Oxford Guide*, ed. Patricia Waugh (Oxford: Oxford UP, 2006): 499, summarizing Sigmund Freud's and Joseph Breuer's "On the Psychical Mechanism of Hysterical Phenomena": "a psychical trauma is something that enters the psyche that is so unprecedented or overwhelming that it cannot be processed or assimilated by usual mental processes. We have, as it were, nowhere to put it, and so it falls out of our conscious memory, yet is still present in the mind like an intruder or a ghost."

Sonja picked up the teapot, moved it past the tablecloth, and let the
teapot fall to the ground where it smashed.

There was no energy in what she did, rather an absence of energy,
an absence of emotion, desire. There was no joy in the pot smashing
nor anger in the dropping of it. And so she continued in a methodical,
entirely impassive manner, smashing the tea-set. Though her face be-
trayed no such emotion she felt momentarily surprised that the sound
of the smashing porcelain could not overwhelm the other sounds she
carried within her. First the teapot, then the milk jug, then the saucers
and the cups, all fell to the ground and broke into dozens of fragments.
But no matter how many tea-set pieces fell to the ground the other
noises always returned like a howling inside her head that would not
leave: sounds of her father sobbing, of the blizzard wind that had
beaten up their shack-home the night before, of her mother singing, of
her mother singing. Teapot and milk jug, saucer and cup upon con-
crete. Porcelain, pearl-smooth on the outside, sharp as glass and dry as
death upon breaking. Had they broken? Had they?

Tea pot and milk jug smashing. Her mother singing. Her father sobbing. Saucer and cup breaking. A howling inside that would not leave.
Her father and her mother.

Saucer and cup.

Singing.

Saucer and cup.

Breaking. (45–46)

This is a scene of central importance in our context because it quintessentially
demonstrates just how seriously traumatized three-year-old Sonja is. The
blankness of her face and the absence of emotion are typical symptoms of the
"inability to modulate arousal" connected with post-traumatic stress disorder.[15] The systematic, almost automatic breaking of her teapot and the china
set it was part of paradoxically signifies two seemingly mutually exclusive
symptoms of trauma: namely, "compulsive reexposure to the trauma"[16] and
"avoiding and numbing."[17] In breaking the pot, Sonja practises "the compulsive reexposure of some traumatized individuals to situations reminiscent of
the trauma";[18] the teapot has acquired special significance in a prior scene

[15] van der Kolk & McFarlane, "The Black Hole of Trauma," 495.

[16] "The Black Hole of Trauma," 493.

[17] "The Black Hole of Trauma," 494.

[18] "The Black Hole of Trauma," 493.

between Sonja and her mother in which, when asked why they have switched to drinking tea, Maria answers her little daughter: "Because it is Tasmania and not Slovenia. Because our world is upside down" (31). The teapot thus acquires symbolic significance and becomes the objective correlative of the experience of things falling apart, of the disintegration of the known world in the act of forced emigration. By shattering the teapot, Sonja exposes herself afresh to the experience of the breaking-up of order and normality, while at the same time destroying the symbol of that experience and creating a noise which she hopes in vain might cancel out the auditory memory of noises she associates with her trauma, from her mother's singing when leaving her family before committing suicide to her father's sobbing at finding himself a widowed migrant with a small child to care for. It is also symptomatic that Sonja's attempt at avoiding this accoustic re-exposure to trauma is to no avail. This is also expressed on a formal level in the increasing syntactic fragmentation and staccato repetition of the key words denoting what causes Sonja's trauma, so that the very prose produced here by Flanagan to describe the girl's experience re-creates her circular and endless traumatic exposure to what she cannot cope with. Sonja is thus caught up between the urge to reenact and the need to deny, and this seems to turn into a catch-22 situation for her, a situation that offers no way out of the trauma. It will be decades before such a way can be found and before the teapot can become whole again.

The scene in which Maria explains to her little daughter that they drink tea now in an upside down version of the world, in which nothing is any more as it should be, finishes with a reference by Maria to the need to forget the past in order to be able to look forward and live a satisfying life in Australia:

> [...] as if to accentuate her point Maria grasped Sonja's hand firmly and then slowly turned it over revealing Sonja's palm. Maria ran her ring finger around Sonja's small palm, raising white circles upon the child's soft puffy flesh.
> Maria saying: "Because to have a future you must forget the past, my little knedel."
> Then she took Sonja's four small fingers in her hand and folded them shut over Sonja's palm. (31)

This is taken up again in chapter sixteen, which is set five years later and in which we are told about what Sonja remembers. That memory is problematic in traumatic persons is hinted at right from the beginning of that chapter, where we learn that "Sonja ought have [sic] remembered more things than she did. [...] Foolish things, [...] dumb things – that's all she remembered" (80).

Apparently, the essential is missing in Sonja's memory; she does not know what is central. Sonja can remember things like her first communion dress or feeling like an angel in it. As the Polish Mrs Michnik (in whose care Sonja now spends most of her time) claims, "What does the past matter? The mother is long gone, and the girl wouldn't remember her. She was too small, and nobody talks about it" (83). This seems to confirm Maria Buloh's earlier remark about the necessity to forget the past in order to have a future. However, Sonja's reaction to Mrs Michnik's remarks is a telling one insofar as it casts serious doubt on the validity of a strategy of oblivion:

> As she listened to them talk about her mother, she slowly turned the back of her left hand over, revealing her open palm. Then she ran the index finger of her right hand around her palm.
> [...]
> Then with her right hand Sonja took the four fingers of her open left hand and very slowly folded them shut over her palm.
> So: a dress, an angel, and playing games with her fingers. That's all she remembered [...]. Stupid things, dumb things.
> Not the things that matter. (82–83)

Sonja here re-enacts the very action performed by her mother in that earlier scene in which, explaining about the need to forget the traumatizing past, Maria runs her own finger around her three-year-old daughter's palm. This element of repetition in the novel is a textual equivalent of the practice of re-exposure described by van der Kolk and McFarlane as typical of traumatized persons. Sonja cannot and does not want to forget her mother and the harrowing story of her disappearance. The girl's action constitutes an act of remembering and a revolt against Mrs Michnik's spurious claim concerning the irrelevance of the past, but also against Maria's own very similar claim. The latter's suicide provides the best evidence for the impossibility and the dangerous quality of any attempt at forgetting. Maria's need to deny is here countered by Sonja's implied urge to know, hinted at by the last sentence of the above passage about the things Sonja can clearly remember not being the things that matter. The imprecision of this sentence also points to just how difficult and hard it is to remember and to understand what matters: i.e. what lies at the core of Sonja's trauma. The image constructed here by Flanagan of the fingers of one hand folding shut over the traces left earlier on the palm of the other hand thus ingeniously encapsulates the paradoxical and ambiguous tension created by the simultaneity of the need to deny, symbolized by the covering up of the traces on the palm, and the urge to know, expressed through the very quality of Sonja's gesture as a re-enactment and thus an act of memory as well as an as yet unsuccessful attempt at understanding.

That coping with trauma is essentially an epistemological as well as a hermeneutic problem, confronting the traumatized person with the task of domesticating the negative experience by placing it in a meaningful framework and, by doing so, making it manageable, is emphasized right at the beginning of chapter seventeen, which immediately follows:

> If Sonja could remember more she might have been able to call to mind how it all began. But really, she recalled only broken pieces, fragments of lucidity that emerged sharp and hard only to disappear back into meaninglessness, the moment she tried to focus upon them. (84)

Understanding what caused the events that triggered the trauma is part of the work of coping, we are told here, but the incompleteness and the elusiveness of Sonja's memory, a symptom of her need to deny, an unconscious version of the trauma patient's strategy of avoiding, renders impossible such a hermeneutic act. Significantly, Sonja's partial memories are referred to as sharp-edged shards, reminiscent of the image of the teapot, which thus takes on yet another semantic function by referring to the painful work of establishing knowledge and understanding through the unearthing, reconstruction, and putting together again of the fragments of a past that can seriously hurt.

The novel depicts the process of coping with trauma as one in which neither the past nor the future can be denied at the other's expense. Rather, the two have to be brought together, because only in a recognition and an understanding of the traumatic past can there be a positive post-traumatic future beyond suffering, fixation, and neurosis.

> the posttraumatic syndrome is the result of the failure of time to heal all wounds. The memory of the trauma is not integrated and accepted as a part of one's personal past; instead, it comes to exist independently of previous schemata (i.e., it is dissociated).[19]

Neither Bojan nor Sonja are able to integrate their traumatic memories by constructively merging past, present, and future during most of the action of the novel.

It is only in the 1989 scenes that such a solution gradually emerges. Sonja undertakes a trip back to Tasmania to meet her father again, and possibly to

---

[19] van der Kolk & McFarlane, "The Black Hole of Trauma," 491.

tell him about her pregnancy. In one scene, Sonja is back at Butlers George, and frantically unearths the porcelain pieces of the tea set she smashed in 1954 after the suicide of her mother, "as if trying to give birth to that land lost within her skull" (34). The imagery used here is significant, because Sonja is actually expecting a baby but is uncertain about whether or not to have it. During her years in Sydney she has had a series of sexual relationships, all of which were either completely casual and meaningless or were terminated by her as soon as the man showed a more serious interest in her and suggested starting a proper long-term relationship, as was the case with the father of Sonja's unborn child. This inability of hers to have a lasting relationship with a man is a long-term effect of her childhood traumatization. Van der Kolk and McFarlane describe "a generalized numbing of responsiveness to a whole range of emotional aspects of life" as part of the strategy of "dissociation"[20] practiced by PTSD patients; in Sonja's case, this makes her unable to have a normal relationship with a man. Dissociation is practised "to keep unpleasant experiences from conscious awareness,"[21] and this is precisely what Sonja tries to do as well. She isolates herself and refuses to engage intensely with others for fear of being hurt in the process. This is a typical symptom of PTSD – "disturbed affect regulation" and "altered relationships with self and others."[22] This also explains why Sonja sets out on her trip back to Tasmania with the firm resolve to have an abortion after her return to Sydney (99).

It is Sonja's older friend Helvi, who, when Sonja is about to return to Sydney, at the airport first makes her rethink her decision to have an abortion by pointing out that "sometimes an abortion is right. [...] But sometimes [...] it is wrong. Sometimes a baby can help heal" (139). Healing is exactly what Sonja is in need of, and through Helvi's wise words Sonja becomes aware of the fact that she will have to accept her past, thus overcoming the trauma caused by it and paving the way for a better future by having her baby. In a crucial moment of recognition and decision,

> Suddenly she came to her senses, picked the handbag up, flashed an embarrassed, awkward smile at the security officer and muttered an apology. [...] But instead of heading into the departure lounge she turned and started walking away from it, at first with measured steps,

---

[20] van der Kolk & McFarlane, "The Black Hole of Trauma," 494.

[21] "The Black Hole of Trauma," 494.

[22] "The Black Hole of Trauma," 499.

> then with a canter, finally breaking into a run. [...] Sonja was in flight,
> not away from what she was, but back toward it. (141)

This is not the end of Sonja's troubles yet, however, but merely a turn in the right direction. At least she has begun to turn towards her past, which is a prerequisite for the memory-work of recovery in a double sense: i.e. the archaeological recovery of the fragments of the past hidden beneath the debris of incomplete memories and the thick layers of wilful forgetting, and the recovery of the trauma patient on the way to a new wholeness and mental health. Sonja finally realizes that the love between her and her father is the only thing that can rescue both of them from the isolation their traumatized state has left them in:

> All that remained, she thought, was her. And him. But apart, they were
> nothing more than a home become a barn, an orchard ploughed under
> to become a paddock. [...] The sound of one hand clapping. (236)[23]

This realization not only makes Sonja visits her father again after all her Sydney years but also contributes to her decision to have her baby, because she has become aware of the importance of love, affection, and family bonds as counterforces to be pitted against the contingency and cruelty of the world.

One decisive step, then, towards the healing of Bojan and Sonja's trauma is their coming together again after years of separation and after a rather troubled father–daughter relationship caused by Bojan's bouts of drunkenness and the beatings he frequently gave Sonja. Both have to overcome their strategies of numbing, their self-isolating reflexes, and this is triggered when Sonja

---

[23] The concept of the sound of one hand clapping here sounds rather negative, but it was chosen by the author for the title of his novel "because of its openness to interpretation" (Mirko Jurak, "Slovene Immigrants in Australia in Richard Flanagan's Novel *The Sound of One Hand Clapping*," 27), as Flanagan pointed out in an interview on TV Slovenija in 1999. And indeed, the Indian philosopher Osho, in his book of the same title, links the concept with a state of greater self-awareness and a surpassing of alienation, which is what Sonja achieves at the end of the novel (see Jurak, "Slovene Immigrants in Australia in Richard Flanagan's Novel *The Sound of One Hand Clapping*," 27–28), so that the idea of the sound of one hand clapping can also be interpreted in a positive way. The concept is also a typical example of a *kōan* in Zen Buddhism: i.e. of an idea the meaning of which cannot be understood by rational thinking but only by intuition or by the heart, just as Sonja, at the end of Flanagan's novel, reaches a new understanding of herself and of her place in Australia through her love for her Australian-born child.

writes to Bojan telling him about her pregnancy. He uses his creative energy
as a carpenter to express his (grand)fatherly love by making a cradle and a
high chair for the baby and giving them to Sonja. At first, Sonja is shocked
when she feels that, confronted with these simple gifts from her father, she is
"letting love in" (357), a reaction which at first fills her with fear and loathing.
This is the conventional reaction of a trauma patient, but it soon turns into its
opposite:

> Sonja stood there caught between smiling and crying, between love
> and contempt. These offerings – so silly, so futile – and yet they had
> been made in good faith.
> So … *so* beautiful.
> [...]
> That wet awful evening Sonja saw innocence in her father, it was as
> though she was seeing her father for the first time, as if for the first
> time their love was both naked and visible and it stood before them as
> a cot and a high chair and a cradle.
> [...]
> She wished to say: "I love you.
> I love you, you bastard, you bastard, you bastard." (358–59)

In this scene, what has been lost through traumatization is re-established and
thus turns into a remedy against trauma: i.e. the ability to believe in something
such as good faith, innocence, beauty, and the good. The reconstitution of a
belief in the possibility of a moral scale in human endeavour is also an inherently ethical re-awakening because it allows Sonja and Bojan to place
themselves again in a meaningful framework which can replace the heap of
broken images and fragments left behind by the old shattered frameworks
blown to pieces by the harrowing events recounted in the novel.

That this also means the overcoming of trauma becomes clear in chapter
seventy-six, in which Sonja gives birth to her child and, while doing so, remembers the past again, and with it everything she has avoided and consigned
to oblivion for decades. Sonja here recovers her hitherto repressed memory of
the fatal night in which her mother Maria committed suicide, and this ends her
tormented vacillating between the need to know and the urge to deny. It ter-
minates her state of traumatization by putting an end to her strategies of
numbing and avoidance; in giving birth to her baby, she gives birth to a new
life for herself.

To Bojan, becoming a grandfather also turns out to be a healing event. He
even repairs the teapot his daughter smashed to pieces thirty-six years earlier,

and when he hands the pot to Sonja, she in turn passes her new-born daughter to Bojan, who comments: "I think there are some things that matter more than words" (417). Bojan has overcome the isolation he felt was reinforced by his incomplete mastery of English, and through the link with his granddaughter he can feel rooted in the world again. The effect on Sonja of having seen her daughter on her father's arm is quite remarkable, too:

> And after Bojan left, a small miracle took place. For the first time and not the last time in this new lifetime, Sonja cried and her tears fell like summer rain upon her baby's head. (418)

These are not tears of woe and pain, but tears as fertile as the rain they are compared to. They signify Sonja's return into the world of feelings after decades of numbness and emotional deprivation. Her trauma is healed.

The novel ends with a scene in which Sonja takes her daughter out to the site of the former workers' camp at Butlers Gorge, where they have a picnic together. Significantly, it is only now, on the last page of the novel, that the reader learns the name she has given her baby:

> And as she lay so on the ground she would hold her child close and whisper her daughter's name. Her beautiful name.
> "Maria," she would say to the earth, "my Maria." (424)

In the baby, the other Maria, Sonja's mother, has been symbolically resurrected, and her death and its traumatizing effects have thus been overcome, although the knowledge of the past will always remain hard to retrieve and hard to communicate. We leave Sonja wondering at the end of the book: "how would she ever tell her daughter of what only those who lived it can ever know?" (425).

WORKS CITED

Booth, Wayne C. *The Company We Keep: An Ethics of Fiction* (Berkeley: U of California P, 1988).

Flanagan, Richard. *The Sound of One Hand Clapping* (New York: Grove, 1987).

Jurak, Mirko. "Slovene Immigrants in Australia in Richard Flanagan's Novel *The Sound of One Hand Clapping*," *Acta Neophilologica* 34.1–2 (2001): 17–29.

Luckhurst, Roger. "Mixing Memory and Desire: Psychoanalysis, Psychology, and Trauma Theory," in *Literary Theory: An Oxford Guide*, ed. Patricia Waugh (Oxford: Oxford UP, 2006): 497–507.

Reiker, P.P., & E.H. Carmen. "The Victim-to-Patient Process: The Disconfirmation and Transformation of Abuse," *American Journal of Orthopsychiatry* 56 (1986): 360–70.

Taylor, Charles. *Sources of the Self: The Making of the Modern Identity* (Cambridge: Cambridge UP, 1989).

van der Kolk, Bessel A., & Alexander C. McFarlane. "The Black Hole of Trauma," in *Literary Theory: An Anthology*, ed. Julie Rivkin &. Michael Ryan (Oxford: Blackwell, 2004): 487–99.

Inside Out in the Land Down Under

Reading Trauma through Janette
Turner Hospital's *Oyster*

ISABEL FRAILE

W HILE A THOROUGHLY ENJOYABLE and gripping experience, reading Janette Turner Hospital's *Oyster* (1996) often
manages to feel, at the same time, like reading a handbook of
trauma theory. It is not only that trauma appears on the level of the plot in
every imaginable form (young Mercy Given is raped by the cult leader Oyster, and her brother Brian is also raped and subsequently murdered at the
same sinister hands; the schoolteacher Susannah Rover is kicked to death and
then fed to a feral pig; Jess has to murder a man herself to avoid being raped;
and Major Miner is a survivor of the Singapore disaster). It is also that every
single topic dwelt upon by trauma theorists is there, from the depiction of
feelings of guilt and shame as a consequence of trauma[1] to a detailed description of the phases of trauma (213–14), including its (relative) resolution via
mourning (443). Attention is also paid to the complex ways in which trauma
can be transmitted within the family. Nick, for example, feels that "disaster
[runs] in our blood" (119), and, most poignantly, Sarah realizes that "it is as
though something has required that she should live the nightmares of relatives

---

[1] Janette Turner Hospital, *Oyster* (London: Virago, 1996): 174. Further page references are in the main text.

she never knew, nightmares that all her life she has tried to flee." As a Jew whose ancestors died in Nazi camps, Sarah suddenly feels that, in spite of the fact that the turn of the century is approaching, she is "in an oven," and the worst thing is not having inherited this trauma but the suspicion that she may have transmitted it to her step-daughter:

> What she cannot bear, what she cannot bear, is that Amy should have been trapped in the same web. How could that be, that doom should be passed on not only to the third and fourth generation, but across blood-lines to a step-generation, across faith boundaries, across traditions? Is harm as deadly in the breath as in the blood? (433)

Another relevant aspect of the trauma experience reflected by the novel is the trap in which the victim / survivor is caught between the need to talk and the clear consciousness that talking is to no avail: "Mercy thinks: there is the fact that talk can change nothing. And there is the need to talk bearing down like a river in flood, unstoppable" (148). To make things worse, and in a way which is again fully characteristic of trauma, young Mercy is unable to talk even if she wants to:

> 'Jess, I want to tell you…'
> But mirages assailed her.
> 'Except I can't,' she said. 'I want to tell you what happened at the Reef, but I can't.' She covered her face with her hands. Her sobbing was very quiet and came from a long way down. (86)

Again, what Cathy Caruth has repeatedly referred to as that "complex rela-tionship between knowing and not knowing,"[2] and which is one of the clear-est tokens of trauma, constitutes a real obsession in the text. About the inhabitants of Outer Maroo, the little outback town where the story unfolds, we are told that "knowing nothing and being untraceable was everybody's goal, though no one mentioned such matters aloud" (64). This tension is per-haps most movingly depicted when Mercy

> feels that soon she will be able to build a fence […], no, not a fence, a wall, that soon she will have enough pieces of… pieces of…? – what are they? – enough pieces of these things that cannot be turned into darkness, these pieces of light, enough of them to build a wall, four walls, and the walls will be high enough and potent enough to contain

---

[2] Cathy Caruth, *Unclaimed Experience: Trauma, Narrative, and History* (Baltimore MD & London: Johns Hopkins UP, 1996): ix.

> everything she knows about Oyster's Reef, and there will be no win-
> dows and no door at all in this room that she will make, this shining
> bunker [...], and then Mercy will be able to walk away and will no
> longer have to know what she knows. (23)

Mercy's feeling would in all likelihood be shared by many Outer Maroovians who suffer, as she does, from what Soshana Felman has labelled "the sickness of the one who 'knows'."[3] Readers of Hospital are indeed familiar with such an ailment, which recurs throughout much of her Australian short fiction and is the centre and forefront of her 1992 novel *The Last Magician*, a novel about which Kate Temby has made a statement which is also fully applicable to *Oyster*:

> it is not an absence of answers that engenders the arduous journey to
> the centre of the labyrinth, but the impossibility of accepting the
> answers which on one level have always been known, yet which are
> constantly denied.[4]

This sickness was already well known to Freud, who, in his own words, was "not aware [...] that [many patients suffering from traumatic neuroses] [were] much occupied in their waking lives with memories of their accident." "Perhaps," he concluded, "they are more concerned with *not* thinking of it."[5]

I would just like to briefly note that traumatic features, which I have pointed out so far in individual characters, can also be traced on the communal level. For example, the fact that trauma can pass (as explained by critics such as Ann Cvetkovich[6]) through opposing phases of numbness and anxiety, or hyperarousal, is exemplified in *Oyster* by the movement outlined by the town of Outer Maroo as a whole, from the drowsiness into which it sinks at the beginning of the story, when Susannah writes in her diary that "the whole town seems drugged" (85), to the feverish agitation that precedes the final

---

[3] Shoshana Felman, "Education and Crisis, or the Vicissitudes of Teaching," in *Trauma: Explorations in Memory*, ed. Cathy Caruth (Baltimore MD & London: Johns Hopkins UP, 1995): 21.

[4] Kate Temby, "Gender, Power and Postmodernism in *The Last Magician*," *Westerly: A Quarterly Review* 40.3 (1995): 52.

[5] Sigmund Freud, *Beyond the Pleasure Principle*, tr. & ed. James Strachey (*Jenseits des Lustprinzips*, 1920; tr. New York: Bantam, 1961): 12.

[6] Ann Cvetkovich, *An Archive of Feelings: Trauma, Sexuality, and Lesbian Public Cultures* (Durham NC & London: Duke UP, 2003): 15.

catastrophe. At this point, Godwin's men, ready to start a spree of destruction and death by setting the Given house on fire, are portrayed as "drunk," "high on the thrill of aggression" (422), to such an extent that they cause Major Miner to think of the prison camps and how "the worst things, the things that even nightmares shied away from, occurred in the last days before Liberation" (421).

The issue of trauma is therefore given full coverage in *Oyster*, in such a way that one cannot but recall that Hospital is an academic as well as a creative writer, and this shows: here and there, the reader perceives the keen awareness with which she handles her material. This is perhaps particularly true of her treatment of time, to which Jess, the narrator of the novel, draws our attention in a variety of tones, from the more scientific "Time is elastic, a function of the mind" (195) to the half comic, half-cynical "Time is a joke" (163). And the reader can hardly disagree with her, at least as far as the treatment of time in the novel is concerned. To begin with, *Oyster*'s temporal structure is highly convoluted, as can be noticed by just looking at the titles of the sections into which the novel is divided. After the prologue, we move to the section entitled "Last Week – Monday: High Noon," after which we come across "This Week," only to come back, through "Two Years Ago," to "Last Week – Monday Afternoon"; the temporal labyrinth continues to make the reader dizzy until the very end, thus exemplifying Anne Whitehead's observation that, in trauma fiction, "temporality and chronology collapse."[7]

It is not only the reader who feels dizzy with such temporal jumps; the characters have an even harder time of it:

> Time played its usual games with Mercy: it was not a line, not a circle, but a fog. Things happened, but it was difficult to fix them in a sequence. Her brother Brian, for instance, moved out to the Reef, she found it hard to be precise about when. And then Mercy herself, without intending to, went there briefly, but when was that? She was looking for Brian. She kept seeing her visit again, she kept seeing the Reef,

---

[7] Anne Whitehead, *Trauma Fiction* (Edinburgh: Edinburgh UP, 2004): 3. – I feel very grateful to the editor who, as Donald J. Greiner informs us, "persuaded [Hospital] to add title heads [...] to guide the wandering reader through the mirage of the time shifts," because her original intention was "to avoid using chapter titles to suggest what she calls 'a narrative mirage'." Greiner, "Ideas of Order in Janette Turner Hospital's *Oyster*," *Critique: Studies in Contemporary Fiction* 48.4 (2007): 382.

it kept appearing to her, she kept seeing Brian, she kept seeing Susannah Rover... (85)

The above passage perfectly illustrates what Whitehead means when talking
about "the irruption of one time into another,"[8] and which Caruth first referred
to as a "possession by the past," "in which the overwhelming events of the
past repeatedly possess, in intrusive images and thoughts, the one who has
lived through them."[9] This possession is emphasized by the use of verbal
tenses, as the narrator herself points out: "Singapore falls and falls in the present continuous" (240). Dominick LaCapra also has words on the subject
when discussing the process of post-traumatic acting out,

> in which one is haunted or possessed by the past and performatively
> caught up in the compulsive repetition of traumatic scenes – scenes in
> which the past returns and the future is blocked or fatalistically caught
> up in a melancholic feedback loop. In acting out, tenses implode, and
> it is as if one were back there in the past reliving the traumatic scene.[10]

This is many times exemplified throughout the novel, but perhaps nowhere
more succinctly, and for that very reason so powerfully, than very near the
ending, when Jess addresses Major Miner, only to discover that "he is somewhere else, and where he is, Singapore still burns" (447).

The disruption of time categories has, in fact, become a staple of trauma
criticism. Not so many critics have, to my knowledge, paid attention to the
disruption of space. One of those who has is Ronald Granofsky,[11] who includes space in his list of "categories of understanding which we use to assimilate new experiences" and which are "often challenged" in the literature
of trauma,[12] as Jess readily confirms again: "Time is a trickster, and so is
space" (7). Taking the similarity pointed out by Jess as a point of departure,
the novel often carries out a space–time conflation, which, as Granofsky again
informs us, is also fully characteristic of the trauma novel:

Whitehead, *Trauma Fiction*, 6.

[9] Cathy Caruth, *Trauma: Explorations in Memory* (Baltimore MD & London: Johns
Hopkins UP, 1995): 151.

[10] Dominick LaCapra, *Writing History, Writing Trauma* (Baltimore MD & London:
Johns Hopkins UP, 2001): 21.

[11] Ronald Granofsky, *The Trauma Novel: Contemporary Symbolic Depictions of
Collective Disaster* (New York & Washington DC: Peter Lang, 1995): 21.

[12] Granofsky, *The Trauma Novel*, 22.

it is the encapsulating aspect of the temporal which […] tends to break
down in the literature of trauma. The spatialization of time […] is one
method by which this can be done. That is to say, a temporal conven-
tion may be used to mime a spatial representation in order to under-
mine the category of time itself.[13]

Thus, the deep confusion the characters feel is expressed in terms like the
following: "the shores of the Ice Age, with nothing between then and now but
rusted and powdering rock" (153); or, in the final scenario of destruction by
fire: "it is impossible, from this vantage point, to pin down where time ends
and where space begins" (154). Terms are sometimes coined by the characters
themselves in order to voice an experience which language as it is fails to express, as when Sarah is presented as "falling away into the neverwhere between her slack index finger and thumb" (179).

But the disruption of space is carried out in many ways other than its conflation with time. Among them, there is one that I find particularly significant:
the dialectic *Oyster* constantly establishes between inside and outside. It is on
this aspect that I would like to concentrate in what follows. This concern is, in
fact, shown from the very title, which already suggests an alternative opening
and closing on to the external world, by evoking the process by means of
which the pearlers "insert foreign matter, *grit*, a small seed pearl, a little nub
of nacreous substance" (336) into the oyster in order to obtain "the cultured
pearl of great price" which "men will die for" (337–38). Even more con-
spicuously than in the title, however, this dialectic is embodied in the very
name of the town where the story takes place: Outer Maroo. The first of the
two elements that make up this name looks fairly common at first sight, since
the adjective 'outer' often accompanies the name of a town in order to designate simply the part that is farthest from the centre, as opposed to the 'inner
city', which indicates the oldest part of a city, near or at its centre. What is
striking about this case is that it works exactly the other way round: Inner
Maroo is to be found, not at the centre, not even on the outskirts, but outside
the town. It may well prove interesting, therefore, to revise a few basic facts
about the history of Outer Maroo in order to try and understand this paradox.
To achieve this, I would like to look at a couple of passages from the novel in
some detail:

---

[13] Granofsky, *The Trauma Novel*, 22.

Aladdin's Rush is abandoned, it has been worked out, but opals still hide here. I have found three opalized seashells – from a million years ago, Miss Rover said, when Outer Maroo was under the sea. If that is true, fish have slithered and silvered where I'm sitting, and the great slow waves of the ocean floor have washed these walls. That is the *long* history of Outer Maroo, Miss Rover says. She showed us photographs of the *plesiosaurus* that miners found at Lightning Ridge. (77)

"The long history of Outer Maroo" is thus concerned exclusively with factors that are other than human, basically geological and zoological, since it goes back to a very remote point in the past, "a million years ago." What I find interesting here is the contrast that the text establishes between this "long history" and what we could label 'short-term history', a period about which sixteen-year-old Mercy Given, one of the central characters in *Oyster*, tells us the following:

I know it is less than sixty years since a Beresford, some older relation of Ma's, found opal floaters at Aladdin's Rush and built the house that is the oldest in Outer Maroo. That was in 1938.

But before that there was Maroo, a handful of miners and a few opal shafts in the 1870s. The miners set up camp and sank the first shafts inside a bora ring, not far from where Oyster's Reef is today. There was trouble. The miners blamed the Murris [that is, the Aborigines] and there was a massacre of their camp. Everyone knows this. It's still a junkyard of bones out there, not far from the Reef. [...] After the massacre, the old town, the town of Maroo, prospered on opal for three years, and then it was burned to a crisp. Everyone says that the Murris who escaped the massacre came back and did it. That was in 1873. Maroo sank into the earth until Outer Maroo was built to the east of it. We call the oldest shafts, the 1870s shafts, Inner Maroo, because all that is left is holes in the ground. (79–80)

It is true that there is a marked contrast between the amount of information we are offered about this short-term history, which goes only as far back as the 1870s, and the "long history." This is only natural, since human history is much easier to document than geological history, which is far more remote. In spite of this contrast, many parallelisms can be traced between the ways in which both kinds of history are presented. To begin with, the events they comprise are not only labelled "history" but in every sense depicted as such: dates that we can re-order as a chronological table, place names, beginnings and endings, samples of historical evidence, even documents and photographs. It must be noted, however, that this air of historical reconstruction only affects, in fact, a part of history. There is a beginning (the first house built in Outer Maroo) preceded by a previous beginning ("but before that there was Maroo…"), which is presented as the original one. Before that, the only traces of life are those left by the plesiosaurus. This account sounds as if nothing is missing between very remote geological (pre)history and recent human history. But, of course, there is a tremendous gap between both: the extremely long intervening period of Aboriginal inhabitation is simply skipped. Only Jess reminds us that

> they have been here, the bora rings, for over twenty thousand years, it is believed; it is only in the past hundred, a hiccup in time, that indifferent graziers and the threads of their four-wheel drives have scattered the stones and have imprinted zippered scars across their sacred clay skin. (44)

Otherwise, not a thought is given to a period which is considerably longer than Jess herself points out, since it is generally accepted nowadays that the span of time during which Aborigines are likely to have inhabited Australia is at least 40,000 years, and even this period could fall short of the truth, since "there are strong arguments for 60,000 years, and a still longer presence cannot be ruled out."[14] It is not strange, from this point of view, that Ethel, the only Aboriginal woman whose voice we can hear in the course of the novel, should label white people as "you just johnny-come-latelies" (45).

Official history, as depicted in *Oyster*, tells a very different story, one in which the Aboriginal point of view is altogether absent. The area where the story develops is, as I hope the previous quotations have made clear, presented very differently before and after colonization took place. It could, in fact, be said that it is first envisaged as mere space and seems to acquire the category of place only once white colonization is well under way in Australia. If, as the geographer Yi-Fu Tuan holds, place differs from space, in that "what begins as undifferentiated space becomes place as we get to know it better and endow it with value";[15] if "place is space to which meaning has been

---

[14] Stuart Macintyre, *A Concise History of Australia* (Cambridge: Cambridge UP, 1999): 9.

[15] Quoted by Rick van Noy, *Surveying the Interior: Literary Cartographers and the Sense of Place* (Reno & Las Vegas: U of Nevada P, 2003): 7.

ascribed,"[16] it is fairly clear that Mercy Given, despite the fact that she is consistently presented as a progressive character, willing to change the world she lives in, has still not been wholly able to accept, albeit on a deeply unconscious level, that the area where her hometown lies fully became a place long before the 1870s.[17] Aboriginal inhabitation does not seem to be human enough for her, though she would, in all probability, hotly deny this.

It may be useful to recall here Bill Ashcroft's salutary warning that

> in many cases a sense of place may be embedded in cultural history, in legend and language, in art and dance, without becoming a concept of contention and struggle, until colonization disrupts a people's *sense* of place.[18]

As opposed to what used to be commonly accepted, then, white colonizers did not create but, on the contrary, destroyed or at least deeply unsettled the sense of place of Aboriginal peoples. What really matters is, as Ashcroft points out, not so much the ability to conceptualize place in a particular way (that is, the European way) as the actual experience of place. And, in this sense, few peoples in the world could be said to have as strong a bond to their land as Australian native peoples. This bond is embodied in precisely the kind of cultural manifestations Ashcroft refers to, since "ancestral events, as recorded in stories, songs and rituals, have a particular significance in Aboriginal lives,

---

[16] "Introduction" to *Text, Theory, Space. Land, Literature and History in South-Africa and Australia*, ed. Kate Darian–Smith, Liz Gunner & Sarah Nuttall (London: Routledge, 1996): 3.

[17] It is this difficulty to accept certain aspects of the history of Outer Maroo that justifies the fact that Mercy fails to ask certain questions, if we take into account how restless her mind is otherwise. For instance, "there was trouble" – but what sort of trouble? caused by whom? This constitutes a strong contrast to the many dates and data that, as has been seen, she provides the reader with for other purposes. If Mercy avoids even thinking of these questions, this is because, by not formulating them, she is also at liberty to forget how painful it must have been for the Murris to see how these "first shafts" were sunk, precisely, "inside a bora ring." No wonder, from this point of view, that the novel contains so many negative neologisms, such as "unknow" or "unhappen," because these are, in fact, highly revealing of the way the history of Australia has been written … and unwritten. As so often, it seems that the traumatic story of the black community in Australia can only be written here by means of silence.

[18] Bill Ashcroft, *Post-Colonial Transformations* (London: Routledge, 2001): 125.

for they express a particularly close relationship to the land."[19] And yet, all we
are offered in the passages under analysis is the white side of history. Aborigines, as a matter of fact, are mentioned only when they come into conflict
with the white people. Before that point, the text omits mention of them even
if, for the sake of geographical accuracy, bora rings have to be brought up.
But, even then, they are mentioned in passing in such a way that, were the
reader not to know what they are, they could be mistaken for geographical
features, as if the text meant that the camp was planted in a deep valley. Aborigines are thus presented as if, rather than constituting a form of human
agency in their own right, they were just an inert part of the surrounding
nature. This may sound very attractive from a Romantic, or romanticized,
point of view, but is not very practical when it comes to attending to Aboriginal claims on the land or any other political vindication or, for that matter,
when it comes to regarding Aborigines as human beings.

We are now in a position to interpret the name of the town in a different
light by relating it to its deeply traumatic history. Inner Maroo is not called
Inner Maroo for any standard reason but, rather, because the inhabitants of the
town want to keep its history hidden, to turn their backs on its traumatic past
of racist murder and destruction – which, by the way, is but a thinly disguised
version of the true history of the Australian nation. Everyone in Outer Maroo,
just as happened in Australia for many decades, has always done their best to
forget the massacre that took place there, which is why Inner Maroo lies outside Outer Maroo. As a result, everything in the town has become de-centred:
the original centre has been banished to the outside of the town. What was
once just "Maroo" has become "Inner Maroo" as an indication that, in the best
interests of all the inhabitants of Outer Maroo (or, rather, of all of its white inhabitants), it is necessary to forget the past, thus bearing witness to Professor
Bill Stanner's contention that "racism in Australia often takes the form of
forgetting."[20] It is necessary to keep the past out of sight, to build a

---

[19] Bill Ashcroft, Gareth Griffiths & Helen Tiffin, *Post-Colonial Studies: The Key
Concepts* (London: Routledge, 2000): 9.

[20] Quoted by Melissa Lucashenko, "'But You Don't Look Like a Metaphor': Migaloo Thinking About Aboriginal People," in *Changing Geographies. Essays on Australia*, ed. Susan Ballyn (Barcelona: Centre d'Estudis Australians, 2001): 121. See,
inter alii, W.E.H. Stanner, "Introduction: Australia and Racialism," in *Racism: The
Australian Experience*, vol. 1: *Prejudice and Xenophobia*, ed. F.S. Stevens (1971; Sydney: Australia & N.Z. Book Co., 2nd ed. 1974): 7–14.

completely independent new town so as to start everything anew, to evade the Levinasian responsibility of 'looking at', and to be able to 'look away' instead.

These two opposite attitudes of 'looking at' and 'looking away' can also be analyzed in ways that are relevant to our understanding of the novel, apart from their strictly ethical meanings. As I see it, they may also be regarded as being embodied in the second element of the name of the town, which has not yet been analyzed. Why "Maroo," indeed? Disregarding considerations of an Aboriginal-language origin for the name,[21] and instead taking a eurocentric approach to narrative onomastics, one might assume that the name can be associated with 'maroon'. 'Marooned' is certainly what the European colonists must have felt when they first arrived on the Australian shores, to say nothing about the feelings of the convict inmates of the penal colony Australia was transformed into by its first white inhabitants. All the nuances of the verb 'to maroon' must have been experienced by these first European inhabitants: abandoned, at a loss, unable to escape, even if, for many of them, this was precisely the place they had already escaped to.[22] Utter outsiders to a country they did not feel to be their own, they constantly looked away to Europe for points of reference: a cultural attitude that has persisted, and in many senses, in Australia. Inheritors of this cultural dead-weight, the inhabitants of Outer Maroo feel 'marooned' both in the town and at Oyster's Reef, as Mercy's desire to escape constantly illustrates.

---

[21] There is nothing of topographical significance in today's Australia relating to 'Maroo' in an Aboriginal context, and that is most probably how Turner wanted things to be – a place that is not 'on the map'. Nevertheless, in Charles de Boos's novel *Fifty Years Ago: An Australian Tale* (1867), a white settler family is massacred by members of the Maroo tribe, and there was, in the 1890s, a sheep station called Maroo in Queensland. There is a tiny settlement called Maroo near the Koorawatha Nature Reserve in New South Wales, and an Australian-bred black grape is called Maroo. Furthest from the opal diggings in *Oyster* but perhaps of some consequence is the fact that the New South Head Road in Sydney's Eastern Suburbs was built on an Aboriginal foot track, called Maroo (= 'hand'), that ran through the land of the Cadigal people – an instance of the 'archaeological' obliteration of Aboriginal presence through European colonialist incursion.

[22] A clear reference in the novel to this historical reality is the fact that most of the inhabitants of Outer Maroo are reported to have abandoned the places where they used to live because of their obscure pasts. This is the case with, for example, Jess and Major Miner.

But there is a second way in which the name 'Maroo' may be interpreted, because the reference may be not only to the verb 'to maroon' but also to the adjective. While the first meaning may relate to the white side of Australian history, as I have just suggested, the second sends us back to an Aboriginal perspective. As an adjective, 'maroon' simply suggests the brownish red colour of the Australian desert. This is quite a descriptive meaning, as opposed to the interpretative nature of the previous one, and this, too, may be linked to an Aboriginal sort of attitude. 'Looking at' the here and now, this is what there is to be seen, this is all there is: not interpretation, just sheer perception. The feeling one gets here is pretty different from the one before: it is one of rootedness and of acceptance, of deep links with the land, not of analysis and objectification. 'Maroo' turns out to be a name that sticks to the earth, that just contemplates. It is only if you look away, if you persist in looking at other countries for points of reference, that you can really feel 'marooned' in Australia. What is at stake here is but another way of being an insider or an outsider to the country. Being an insider, though, involves taking responsibility for the country's past, and many of the inhabitants of Outer Maroo would rather forget all about that.

But, as trauma theory teaches us, the past dies hard, and "traumatic events refract outwards."[23] This is metaphorically suggested by the motif of the bones that appear to emerge obsessively from the heart of *Oyster* (those of murdered Aborigines, those of the members of a religious sect).[24] No matter how hard we try to forget or eliminate traumatic events, there is always a trace that betrays their presence. Even if, as in the extreme case of the schoolteacher in *Oyster*, not even her bones are left, there is always, as Pete says, her perfume, which is everywhere. As Freud already declared, repression leads to repetition, the compulsion to repeat being in fact "the manifestation of the power of the repressed."[25] A silenced past will therefore do its best to get itself re-enacted. Which is precisely what it insists on doing in *Oyster*: the massacre of Aborigines will find a replica in the slaughter of the members of Oyster's sect who, incidentally, had previously made friends with the Murris,

---

[23] Cvetkovich, *An Archive of Feelings*, 19.

[24] Of the many parallelisms which can be found between *Oyster* and *The Last Magician*, this obsession with bones is among those I find most significant. The motif is perhaps even more striking in the latter, since Cat's bones literally insist on resurfacing from the earth after having been buried there for a long time.

[25] Freud, *Beyond the Pleasure Principle*, 21.

and who, besides, were basically foreigners. The connection between both groups of people is more intimate than might appear at first sight, as the following passage suggests:

> Foreigners have meant trouble no matter where they came from: whether they were from Charleville or Quilpie, whether they were teachers from Brisbane or bright kids from Sydney or Perth, whether they were from the Murri camps that came and went along the river-beds, or from countries where they speak another tongue. (10)

Strange as it may seem, this is a typically white Australian viewpoint, as suggested by John Barnes:

> Fearful of the power of authority, Daisy Corunna and her daughter Gladys denied their Aboriginality. When Sally, having been challenged by her schoolfellows, asked her mother Gladys, "Are we Aussies, Mum?," she was told "Tell them you're Indian." There was no possibility of their claiming to be Aussies because they were too dark-skinned. Australians were assumed to be white; coloured people must be from somewhere else – or worse still, Aborigines.[26]

The result of all this is that those who should be considered innermost to the country, if only because they were there long before anybody else was, are considered either as non-existent, by virtue of what Cvetkovich has called "the amnesiac powers of national culture," or as foreigners.[27] 'Native' has therefore become 'foreigner', 'Inner' has changed places with 'Outer', Oyster's Reef is an opal mine, and is sometimes referred to as being "out there" (79–80), in spite of the fact that it is actually something like an underground town, and is, moreover, "almost as far inland as you can go" (181). To this list of contradictions must be added the fact that Maroo is called "Outer" when nobody outside it knows about its very existence, thus exposing the fallacy of the name in yet another way.[28] To say nothing of the fact that, as Richard Carr

---

[26] John Barnes, "Questions of Identity in Contemporary Australia," in *Australian Nationalism Reconsidered: Maintaining a Monocultural Tradition in a Multicultural Society*, ed. Adi Wimmer (Tübingen: Stauffenburg, 1999): 65.

[27] Cvetkovich, *An Archive of Feelings*, 16.

[28] An interesting parallelism can here be established between the history of Outer Maroo, the town which, in the best, though not very legal, interests of its inhabitants, "by cunning intention, and sometimes by discreet bribery (or other dispatch) of government surveyors [...] has kept itself off maps" (4), and the history of Australia. For, as Daniel Dorling and David Fairbairn inform us, "although the Dutch are credited

has pointed out, Outer Maroovians feel intense "fears regarding outside intervention in their lives"[29]: fear of that outside that they bear in their very name.
Something has gone very wrong, something primordial has been altered; the
internal logic of Outer Maroo seems to work in reverse, just like mirages,
which turn everything upside down, and which are, of course, a fundamental
part of the landscape of *Oyster* (see, for example, 7–8, 246). This is perhaps
due to the fact that, as Judith Zur has shown, trauma may well have the effect
of actually redrawing inside/outside boundaries.[30] In unveiling these contradictions, in thus reversing the inside/outside positions, *Oyster* illustrates Sel-
tzer's view that "trauma discourse challenges the distinction between the external and the internal as locations of pain."[31]

It must be noted that, whenever inside and outside change places, it is to
the advantage of the white invader, who feels powerful enough to claim, as
Jess the narrator does at one point in the novel, that "foreigners are all much
the same. They are not us. The arrival of any foreigner changes the map, and
foreigners spell the beginning of the end" (10–11). Bearing in mind that, as
has been said, Aborigines have also traditionally been included in the category of "foreigners," Freud's curious contention that trauma is a "foreign
body" in our psyche inevitably comes to mind here, since it betrays the same
desire to avoid certain painful aspects of reality.[32] Both of these positions are,
it seems to me, attempts to externalize or disown one's own history, be it a
traumatic personal past or a country's history of racist bloodshed. Nothing can
be more intimate to a person than his or her own wounds, or to a country than
its first inhabitants. Yet, what Freud seems to suggest by means of this terminology is that the foreign body of trauma should be expelled, rather than in-

---

with the first encounter in 1606, it is suggested that the Portuguese, considerably earlier, were the first Europeans to arrive in Australia, leaving its shore off their charts for
reasons of secrecy and fear of rival European nations." Dorling & Fairbairn, *Mapping:
Ways of Representing the World* (Harlow: Prentice Hall, 1997): 16.

[29] Richard Carr, "Just Enough Religion to Make us Hate," *Antipodes* 18.1 (2004): 11.

[30] Judith Zur, "Remembering and Forgetting: Guatemalan War Widows' Forbidden
Memories," in *Trauma: Life Stories of Survivors*, ed. Kim Lacy Rogers & Selma
Leydesdorff, with Graham Dawson (New Brunswick NJ & London: Transaction,
2004): 48.

[31] Quoted by Cvetkovich, *An Archive of Feelings*, 18.

[32] Sigmund Freud, *Studies in Hysteria*, tr. James Strachey (*Studien über Hysterie*,
1895; London: Hogarth, 1955): 185.

tegrated, so as to regain mental health. In a similar fashion, white Australians tried either to simply do away with surviving Aborigines or to push them away from sight and therefore from consciousness. And here we face the same contradiction once again: in attempting to do this, what they simultaneously managed to do was to place Aborigines in the very heart of the country, the red centre, the innermost area so paradoxically called 'the outback'. This serves as a symbolic reminder that, unless we attend to our traumas, they will remain there, radiating out from our hearts and showing through our silences.

Oyster, however, is not content with just illustrating or even denouncing the existence of racial and historical traumas. It also attempts to show ways in which these can effectively be attended to. It may be suggested that, if the novel conveys trauma by means of the breach between inside and outside that has just been analyzed, it also hints that it is possible to do away with that and with other related polarities, and thus overcome the effects of trauma. A first approach to the undoing of polarities in the novel is provided by Major Miner and his opinions about Bugger Harvey and about the Aborigines, to whom the Bugger is shown to be closely related:

> Sometimes he took on the world; and sometimes he just curled up and drank himself legless and blind, and it was this ambivalence, this dual way of living, Major Miner had decided, that made the Bugger so at ease with the Murris, and the Murris so at ease with him. (350)

It is true that, in some senses, this passage does not offer a very positive portrayal of the Murris, but it still opens up the possibility of a way out of contradictions. Ambivalence, though indeed risky if pressed too far, may also be productive, especially where too much rigidity has existed. In a society that has so aggressively, and for so long, segregated the black from the white, ambivalence brings about the welcome discovery that, to some questions at least, "there [is] no black-and-white answer," as Major Miner has to acknowledge, "smiling grimly at the way language itself made bad jokes" (348). This statement must, I think, be understood both in the racial sense intended by Major Miner and as an indication that what Barthes, and trauma theoreticians after him, have called the 'middle voice', one of whose defining characteristics is, precisely, undecidability, is at play here.[33] It is this concept of the

---

[33] Roland Barthes, "To Write: An Intransitive Verb?" in *The Structuralist Controversy: The Languages of Criticism and the Sciences of Man*, ed. Richard Macksey & Eugenio Donato (Baltimore MD & London: Johns Hopkins UP, 1970).

middle voice that I would like to address now. It must be made clear that I am
not thinking so much of those stylistic devices that Barthes and Derrida have
called 'the style of middle-voicedness' as of an attitude that seems to underlie
the way the middle voice works. In contrast with both the active and the passive voices, where the subject is considered external to the action, in the middle voice it is presumed to be interior to the action. To clarify what is meant
by this, Barthes provides an example that I find quite illuminating:

> According to the classic example, given by Meillet and Benveniste, the
> verb *to sacrifice* (ritually) is active if the priest sacrifices the victim in
> my place for me, and it is middle voice if, taking the knife from the
> priest's hands, I make the sacrifice for myself. In the case of the active,
> the action is accomplished outside the subject, because, although the
> priest makes the sacrifice, he is not affected by it. In the case of the
> middle voice, on the contrary, the subject affects himself in acting; he
> always remains inside the action, even if an object is involved.[34]

Now, there are certain passages in *Oyster* that, to me at least, are strongly reminiscent of this definition. One of them is the story Major Miner was told by
one of his mates in Singapore, and which is worth reproducing at length:

> Prince Wen Hui, touring his kitchens one day, admired his cook's
> flawless ease as a butcher. Beneath the cook's hands and beneath his
> blade, the carcass of an ox seemed to fall apart, neatly segmented, as
> though it were made of softened butter.
>   'That is amazing,' Prince Wen Hui exclaimed. 'What is your
> method?'
>   'I have no method,' the cook said. 'I follow the Tao.'
>   'A good cook,' he explained, 'needs a new cleaver once a year. He
> cuts. A poor cook needs a new one every month. He hacks. I have used
> the same cleaver, O prince, for nineteen years, and it has carved up a
> thousand beasts. That is because I see nothing with my eye, but
> instead, with my whole being, I give myself attentively to the mystery
> of the body of the ox. Then I let the blade follow its instinct. It finds
> the secret openings and the fine spaces between joints. I cut through no
> joint, Your Highness, I chop no bone. The ox falls apart. I clean the
> blade and put it away.' (242)

What the cook is absolutely interior to is, as the middle voice requires, the action of cutting. Otherwise, his position here is one of utter undecidability. He

---

[34] "To Write: An Intransitive Verb?" 142.

places himself in a space which is neither exactly interior to the object (total identification is, of course, impossible as well as undesirable) nor totally exterior to it (since this is the secret of his success) and which is, on the other hand, both things at the same time. The boundaries between inside and outside have, in this instance, all but disappeared, producing a new panorama which in some ways recalls that of Bhabha's 'third space'. On the other hand, this fragment seems to leave but little space for worries like those Dominick LaCapra has expressed about the middle voice: namely, that by virtue of its undecidability, it "would seem to undercut the problems of agency and responsibility in general"[35] – hardly could anybody be more entirely present, more aware, more attentive to the task, and therefore more responsible for it, than Prince Wen Hui's cook. The same could be said of this second example, whose protagonist is Major Miner right after blasting his explosives in order to uncover

> a vein of pipe opal like vivid blue-green lightning [...]. Chuang-tzu and Joe Blow were watching, as always. You have done well, they said. Truly, a great cutter does not cut. The finest work is effortless.
> The Tao does all by doing nothing, they said. (350)

This passage also illustrates another aspect of the middle voice put into practice: the active voice is explicitly renounced ("a great cutter does not cut") in favour of the middle voice: the subject is so engaged in the action that no effort has to be made, since the whole process seems to flow spontaneously. And all the while, the subject willingly assumes full responsibility for his actions. This is, at any rate, what he believes until his self-complacency is suddenly interrupted in the following way:

> 'Hack work,' growled Bugger Harvey from behind him. 'Completely unnecessary violence. Completely senseless.'
> [...]
> 'That,' said Bugger Harvey mournfully, studying the cliff face as though he felt its ravages in his gut, "is what I would call mutilation.'
> [...]
> 'Of a very beautiful mesa.' (350–51)

Bugger Harvey is here shown to be several steps ahead of Major Miner in his practical understanding of what the middle voice means. Listening to his voice, Major Miner's attitude appears in a new light: he has not penetrated the

---

[35] LaCapra, *Writing History, Writing Trauma*, 26.

mysteries of nature as deeply as Bugger Harvey has. In spite of appearances, his action has been "accomplished outside the subject," since he has not been able to feel the destruction produced by his action, while the Bugger has indeed "always remained inside" the process, so much so that he indeed feels "the ravages in his gut." Interestingly, the Bugger declares that it is from the Murris that he learned to develop these abilities:

> 'If that pipe opal is meant for you," the Bugger said, "there'll already be a way in. You could learn a thing or two from the Murris, you destructive clod.'
>
> '[...] They've taught me that anything that can't be reached with a pointed stick doesn't belong to us, and I say they are bloody well right.'
>
> '[...] The earth is our mother, like the Murris say, and you can't cut her up and get away with it. [...] And you don't *need* to tear her up, you stupid oaf, because she's generous. I'll show you.' (351)

And, just as he says, he shows the Major the way in which opal can be got hold of without in any way damaging the surrounding landscape, by making oneself one with nature, in a new metaphorical realization of the meaning of the middle voice. Here, however, the middle voice is not read as being symptomatic of trauma, which is the way in which most theoreticians read it. If the middle voice means "remaining inside the action," in these examples this is realized, not as trauma, but as a beautiful way of being centred, in contact with oneself, totally present in and through whatever one is doing, and totally in contact, at the same time, with the world around. To me, it sounds like a meditative state that counteracts all alienation. And alienation, as Mudrooroo's fictional account in *Doctor Wooreddy* reminds us, is entirely absent for Aboriginal peoples even as a concept,[36] as opposed to the Western view of the world, where this concept is very much at home (and, unfortunately, not for the traumatized mind alone). Thus, the text establishes a very direct relationship not between the middle voice and trauma, but between the middle voice and Aboriginality. This relationship is especially clear where nature is concerned. Aborigines are more intimate with the mysteries of the earth, since, as

---

[36] The protagonist of the novel says about the Aborigines at one point: "Then he realized that they could not comprehend the destruction of a whole community and the severing of the link between individual and earth. The very concept of alienation was beyond them." Mudrooroo, *Doctor Wooreddy's Prescription for Enduring the Ending of the World* (Melbourne: Hyland House, 1983): 84.

the Bugger says, "they know a damn sight more than we do" because "they've been around longer" (352). Put another way, they have an inside view of landscape, as opposed to the European, external view. Judith Wright has very clearly explained this difference:

> The very word 'landscape' involves, from the beginning, an irreconcilable difference of viewpoint, and there seems [to be] no word in European languages to overcome the difficulty. It is a painter's term, implying an outside view, a separation, even a basis of criticism. We cannot set it against the reality of the earth-sky-water-tree-spirit-human complex existing in spacetime, which is the Aboriginal world. We have unravelled the original continuum into many different elements. [...] To add the further elements of prehistory, history, and future that are bedded in the Dreamtime is to realize how far our world has been fragmented.[37]

As the previous extract suggests, there are many other ways, apart from its use of the middle voice, in which the novel can be connected to an Aboriginal type of sensibility,[38] such as the space–time continuum I mentioned earlier in relation to trauma theory. But detailed analysis of these parallelisms would fall outside the scope of this essay. Suffice it to say that the few white characters who are saved from the final catastrophe at the end of *Oyster* are those who have learnt to come into contact with their inner selves, having learnt the lesson that the Bugger teaches on the Murris' behalf. Major Miner, for example, has come to understand the old lesson that "freedom is an inner condition" (242), and has been able to put that knowledge to practical use: by listening with his "inner ear" (244), he is now able to locate opal without having to destroy the environment. He has even "ceased to require explosives" because of his increased capacity for internalization, "and he owed it also to the Murris who camped in the riverbeds and who were the Bugger's mates" (244).

---

[37] Judith Wright, "Landscape and Dreaming," in *Australia: The Daedalus Symposium*, ed. Stephen R. Graubard (Sydney: Angus & Robertson, 1985): 32.

[38] Donna J. Davis has already paid attention to some of the ways in which Hospital's fiction reflects an Aboriginal perspective. See Davis, "Postmodern Issues in Janette Turner Hospital's Nature-Dominated Short Stories 'The End-of-the-Line End-of-the-World Disco' and 'Our Own Little Kakadu'," in *Postmodern Approaches to the Short Story*, ed. Farhat Iftekharrudin et al. (Westport C T: Praeger, 2003): 65–75.

As for the rest of the characters who manage to survive, they all do so by escaping in the first place from Outer to Inner Maroo: i.e. by returning to the first origins, to the time when the white township did not exist and only the Aboriginal peoples camped freely: "The Reef, [Major Miner] thinks, driving towards the breakaways. He knew it would all come back to the Reef, back to Inner Maroo, back to the bora rings, back to the beginning again" (426). This is not to say that the novel advocates any simplistic preference for the Aborigines (commonly identified with what I've called 'inside positions') and against white people (more often related to 'outside positions'). In fact, this polarity is the last one the text undoes as the ending approaches. Or this, at least, seems to me to be the import of the two opposite or, rather, complementary movements that take place towards the end of the novel. On the one hand, Mercy, with Nick and Sarah, is now moving towards the coast, towards the outside of the country, where, free from the paradoxically named Outer Maroo, she will see, for the first time in her life, the sea and the wide world:

> And Mercy imagines Brisbane, the golden city. She imagines the great
> river with water in it. She thinks of grass, ferns, trees, ocean, sand. She
> imagines herself running into the ocean as into the world. She will let
> the world crest and froth about her. (453)

On the other hand, the Aborigines are on their way back to the red centre to recover their land once again. Both of these movements are equally supported by the text; neither is privileged over the other. What is upheld here is neither the coast nor the interior, neither the white nor the black, but, rather, inclusiveness. The point is that, once the truth, no matter how traumatic it may be, has been known and accepted, once it has come out into the open instead of remaining buried, hidden inside, one can move fluently from one extreme of the polarity to the other, and so keep oneself open to growth and development. Aborigines, after all, have always remained open to the world outside, as long as theirs is respected. In fact, they are even shown as ready to learn about the Bible, and to mix with other people:

> In the beginning, a lot of Murris moved into the burrows and tunnels
> of Oyster's Reef. They gave their hearts to the Lord, they sang hymns,
> they listened to Oyster's Bible lessons, they showed Oyster where the
> opal ran. And then all those camp followers, all those young kids from
> Brisbane and Sydney and Melbourne, from New York and Timbuctoo,
> from God knows where, all those kids began to arrive. It seemed to be
> all one big happy family, black and white, white and black, at the
> Reef. (353)

Mercy, for her part, and despite her desire to know the sea and the city, is ready to go back to Outer Maroo for her parents, of whose death she still has not learnt. Jess and Major Miner, however, decide to stay in Inner Maroo forever. What the text is saying, as I see it, is that as long as you remain centred inside, positions may be freely shifted. But, in any case, one must first be able to contact one's own, personal or national, Inner Maroo. One must be able to delve into one's traumatic past in order to fully grasp the present. In the case of the Australian plight, this may be the only available way to, as David Malouf would put it, "see that there might be another and more inward way of possessing a place, and that in this, as in so much else, the people we dispossessed had been there before us."[39]

WORKS CITED

Ashcroft, Bill. *Post-Colonial Transformations* (London: Routledge, 2001).

——, Gareth Griffiths & Helen Tiffin. *Post-Colonial Studies: The Key Concepts* (London: Routledge, 2000).

Barnes, John. "Questions of Identity in Contemporary Australia," in *Australian Nationalism Reconsidered: Maintaining a Monocultural Tradition in a Multicultural Society*, ed. Adi Wimmer (Tübingen: Stauffenburg, 1999): 63–71.

Barthes, Roland. "To Write: An Intransitive Verb?" in *The Structuralist Controversy: The Languages of Criticism and the Sciences of Man*, ed. Richard Macksey & Eugenio Donato (Baltimore MD & London: Johns Hopkins UP, 1970): 134–56.

Carr, Richard. "'Just Enough Religion to Make us Hate': The Case of *Tourmaline* and *Oyster*," *Antipodes* 18.1 (2004): 9–15.

Caruth, Cathy. *Unclaimed Experience: Trauma, Narrative, and History* (Baltimore MD & London: Johns Hopkins UP, 1996).

——, ed. *Trauma: Explorations in Memory* (Baltimore MD & London: Johns Hopkins UP, 1995).

Cvetkovich, Ann. *An Archive of Feelings: Trauma, Sexuality, and Lesbian Public Cultures* (Durham NC & London: Duke UP, 2003).

Darian–Smith, Kate, Liz Gunner & Sarah Nuttall, ed. *Text, Theory, Space: Land, Literature and History in South-Africa and Australia* (London: Routledge, 1996).

---

[39] David Malouf, *A Spirit of Play: The Making of Australian Consciousness* (Sydney: ABC Books, 1998): 16.

Davis, Donna J. "Postmodern Issues in Janette Turner Hospital's Nature-Dominated Short Stories 'The End-of-the-Line End-of-the-World Disco' and 'Our Own Little Kakadu,'" in *Postmodern Approaches to the Short Story*, ed. Farhat Iftekharrudin et al. (Westport CT: Praeger, 2003): 65–75.

Dorling, Daniel, & David Fairbairn. *Mapping: Ways of Representing the World* (Harlow: Prentice Hall, 1997).

Felman, Shoshana. "Education and Crisis, or the Vicissitudes of Teaching," in *Trauma: Explorations in Memory*, ed. Cathy Caruth (Baltimore MD & London: Johns Hopkins UP, 1995): 13–60.

Freud, Sigmund. *Beyond the Pleasure Principle*, ed. & tr. James Strachey (*Jenseits des Lustprinzips*, 1920; tr. New York: Bantam, 1961).

——, with Josef Breuer. *Studies In Hysteria*, in *The Standard Edition of the Complete Psychological Works of Sigmund Freud*, vol. 2, ed. & tr. James Strachey (*Studien über Hysterie*, 1895; London: Hogarth, 1955): 1–305.

Granofsky, Ronald. *The Trauma Novel: Contemporary Symbolic Depictions of Collective Disaster* (New York & Washington DC: Peter Lang, 1995).

Greiner, Donald J. "Ideas of Order in Janette Turner Hospital's *Oyster*," *Critique: Studies in Contemporary Fiction* 48.4 (2007): 381–90.

Hospital, Janette Turner. *The Last Magician* (London: Virago, 1992).

——. *Oyster* (London: Virago, 1996).

LaCapra, Dominick. *Writing History, Writing Trauma* (Baltimore MD & London: Johns Hopkins UP, 2001).

Lucashenko, Melissa. "'But You Don't Look Like A Metaphor': Migaloo Thinking about Aboriginal People," in *Changing Geographies: Essays on Australia*, ed. Susan Ballyn et al. (Barcelona: Centre d'Estudis Australians, 2001): 127–34.

Macintyre, Stuart. *A Concise History of Australia* (Cambridge: Cambridge UP, 1999).

Malouf, David. *A Spirit of Play: The Making of Australian Consciousness* (Boyer Lecture Series; Sydney: ABC Books, 1998).

Mudrooroo. *Doctor Wooreddy's Prescription for Enduring the Ending of the World* (1983; Melbourne: Hyland House, 1992).

Noy, Rick van. *Surveying the Interior: Literary Cartographers and the Sense of Place* (Reno & Las Vegas: UP of Nevada, 2003).

Stanner, W.E.H. "Introduction: Australia and Racialism," in *Racism: The Australian Experience*, vol. 1: *Prejudice and Xenophobia*, ed. F.S. Stevens (1971; Sydney: Australia & N.Z. Book Co., 2nd ed. 1974): 7–14.

Temby, Kate. "Gender, Power and Postmodernism in *The Last Magician*," *Westerly* 40.3 (1995): 47–55.

Whitehead, Anne. *Trauma Fiction* (Edinburgh: Edinburgh UP, 2004).

Wright, Judith. "Landscape and Dreaming," in *Australia: The Daedalus Symposium*, ed. Stephen R. Graubard (Sydney: Angus & Robertson, 1985): 29–56.

Zur, Judith. "Remembering and Forgetting: Guatemalan War Widows' Forbidden Memories," in *Trauma: Life Stories of Survivors*, ed. Kim Lacy Rogers & Selma Leydesdorff, with Graham Dawson (New Brunswick NJ & London: Transaction, 2004): 45–59.

Notes on Contributors

MEENA ALEXANDER was born in Allahabad, India, and raised in India and Sudan. When she was eighteen she went to study in England. She now lives in New York City, where she is University Distinguished Professor of English at Hunter College and the Graduate Center at the City University of New York. She is a 2008 Guggenheim Fellow in Poetry. Her six books of poetry include *Illiterate Heart*, which won the PEN Open Book Award, *Raw Silk*, and the recently published *Quickly Changing River*. She is the editor of *Indian Love Poems* (2005). She is the author of the acclaimed memoir *Fault Lines* (1993), chosen as one of *Publishers Weekly*'s Best Books of 1993, and revised in 2003 to incorporate significant new material. She has also published two novels, *Nampally Road* (1991) and *Manhattan Music* (1997); a book of poems and essays, *The Shock of Arrival: Reflections on Postcolonial Experience* (1996); and two academic studies, one of which is *Women in Romanticism: Mary Wollstonecraft, Dorothy Wordsworth, and Mary Shelley* (1989). Her book of reflections on poetry, migration, and memory, *Poetics of Dislocation*, appeared in 2009. She is the recipient of the 2009 Distinguished Achievement Award in Literature from the South Asian Literary Association for contributions to American Literature.

HEINZ ANTOR studied at the Universities of Erlangen (Germany) and Oxford (UK). He has taught at George Mason University (Fairfax VA) and at the Universities of Düsseldorf and Bremen, and is currently Professor of English Literatures at the University of Cologne. He is editor of the journal *Anglistik* and serves on the editorial boards of *Canadian Literature* and *Symbolism*. His interests include world literatures in English, postcolonial studies, the English novel, and literary and critical theory. Among his books are *The Bloomsbury Group* (1986); *Die Narrativik der Angry Young Men* (1989); *Text – Culture – Reception: Cross-Cultural Aspects of English Studies* (1992); *Der englische*

Universitätsroman (1996); *Shakespeare alternativ* (1997); *Intercultural Encounters: Studies in English Literatures* (1999); *English Literatures in International Contexts* (2000); *Refractions of Germany in Canadian Literature and Culture* (2003); *Refractions of Canada in European Literature and Culture* (2005); *Inter- und Transkulturelle Studien* (2006); and *Fremde Kulturen verstehen – fremde Kulturen lehren* (2007).

BÁRBARA ARIZTI is Senior Lecturer at the University of Zaragoza. She is the author of the book *'Textuality as Striptease': The Discourses of Intimacy in David Lodge's "Changing Places" and "Small World"* (2002). In 2007, she edited, together with Silvia Martínez–Falquina, the collective volume *On the Turn: The Ethics of Fiction in Contemporary Narrative in English.* She has also published several articles and book chapters on David Lodge, Jean Rhys, Doris Lessing, and Tim Winton. Her current field of research is postcolonial literature and criticism, with special emphasis on the relationship between literature and the intimate sphere. She is a member of the research group "Contemporary Narrative in English," funded by the Spanish Government, and is currently working on the literary representations of trauma.

MERLINDA BOBIS, a Filipino-Australian academic and author–performer, writes in three languages: English, Pilipino, and Bikol. She has published novels, collections of short stories and poetry, and has had her dramatic works performed/produced in Australia, Philippines, France, Spain, the USA, China, Thailand, and the Slovak Republic. Her literary awards include the Prix d'Italia and the Australian Writers' Guild Award for her radio play *Rita's Lullaby* (1997); the Steele Rudd Australian Short Story Award (for the Best Published Collection of Australian Short Stories); the Philippine National Book Award for her collection of short stories *White Turtle* (1999); the Philippine Balagtas Award, a lifetime award for her poetry and prose in Pilipino, English, and Bikol; and the Carlos Palanca Memorial Award for Literature for *Peopleness*, which was published as her first poetry collection, *Rituals* (1990). Her first novel, *Banana Heart Summer* (2005), was short-listed for the Australian Literature Society Gold Medal, and her poetry collection *Summer Was a Fast Train Without Terminals* (1998) for *The Age* Poetry Book Award. Her other novel, *The Solemn Lantern Maker* (2008), is an exploration of a family's trauma in the context of Philippine politics and the global war on terror. A third novel, *Fish-Hair Woman*, will be published in 2012. Her most noted work as writer–performer is the *Cantata of the Warrior Woman Daragang Magayon.* Published in both English and Pilipino (1993, 1997), this epic poem has been performed by Bobis over nearly fifteen years (1992–2006) in its various versions with traditional Philippine chanting and dance. Bobis is Senior Lecturer in Creative Writing at the University of Wollongong, Australia, and is Poetry and Fiction Editor of the online journal *Postcolonial Text.*

Currently she is researching the 'transnational imaginary' and strategies for 'localizing the global' in cultural production with partner investigators in the Philippines and Spain. Author's website: http://www.merlindabobis.com.au

DONNA COATES is an Associate Professor at the University of Calgary, where she teaches courses in Canadian, Australian, New Zealand, and American responses to the First and Second World Wars, and the Vietnam War in fiction and drama. She is currently completing a book on Australian women's responses to the Great War, the Second World War, the Korean War, and the Vietnam War. She has published numerous articles in journals such as *Brno Studies in English, Antipodes, LiNQ* (*Literature in Northern Queensland*), *Australian Studies, Southerly, Canadian Literature, Australian Literary Studies,* and *Australian and New Zealand Studies in Canada.* She has also published numerous chapters in books such as *The Cambridge Companion to the Literature of World War II* (2009); *Focus India: Postcolonial Narratives of the Nation* (2007); and *Back to Peace: Recrimination and Reconciliation in the Afterwar Period* (2007). With Sherrill Grace, she has selected and edited plays for *Canada and the Contemporary Theatre of War* (2010) and *Canada and the Theatre of War: Eight Plays on the First and Second World Wars* (2008); and, with George Melnyk, *Wild Words: Essays on Alberta Literature* (2008). She currently sits on the editorial board of *Antipodes.*

MARC DELREZ (MA Adelaide; PhD Liège) teaches literature in English (new and established) as well as comparative literature at the University of Liège, Belgium. In the postcolonial field, his publications include articles on Salman Rushdie, Randolph Stow, David Malouf, Robert Drewe, Nicholas Jose, Richard Flanagan, Andrew McGahan, and Janet Frame. His monograph on Janet Frame, *Manifold Utopia*, appeared in Rodopi's Cross/Cultures series. He is currently working on another book on Frame.

MAITE ESCUDERO lectures in the Department of English and German Studies at the University of Zaragoza, where she obtained her PhD. Her research interests centre on the field of trauma studies, feminist criticism, and queer theory. She has published widely on the representation of identity categories, such as gender, sex, sexuality, and race in cultural manifestations and in contemporary narratives in English. Her latest publication is *Long Live the King: A Genealogy of Performative Genders* (2009).

ISABEL FRAILE is a Lecturer in English and English Literature in the Department of English and German Philology of the University of Zaragoza (Spain), where she graduated with honours in English. She is currently teaching English as a Second Language and English Literature in the Faculty of Arts in Zaragoza, working on postcolonial and Australian studies, and writing her doctoral dissertation, "The Re/De/Construction of an Australian Identity in Janette Turner Hospital's *The Last Magician* and *Oyster*." Her published research includes work on classic film noir, Hollywood comedy, Oscar Wilde, and Australian literature. She belongs to a competitive research team now working on the representation of trauma in contemporary fiction written in English, and her latest publication is "Self-Responsibility and the Articulation of Identity as Reflected in Janette Turner Hospital's *The Last Magician* and *Oyster*" (2007).

AITOR IBARROLA–ARMENDÁRIZ lectures on American Studies at the University of Deusto, Bilbao, where he teaches courses in US literature, ethnic relations, and film adaptation. He completed his graduate degree at Deusto and did postgraduate work on nineteenth-century naturalist fiction at the University of Pittsburgh. He has published articles on minority and immigrant narratives, the pedagogy of literature and cinema, and processes of cultural hybridization. He has also translated some classic works of American prose fiction and poetry into Spanish and Basque. Currently, Ibarrola–Armendáriz is Director of the MA Programme in Migration, Conflict, and Social Cohesion at the University of Deusto. He has been a Fulbright Scholar at the University of Texas and has taught at the universities of Middlesex, Pittsburgh, and Manchester. He has also edited several volumes: *Fiction and Ethnicity in North America* (1995); *Entre dos mundos* (2004); *Migrations in a Global Context* (2007).

SUSANA ONEGA is Professor of English at the University of Zaragoza, and is the head of an Excellence Research Team currently working on Ethics and Trauma in Contemporary Fictions in English. She has written numerous articles and book chapters on contemporary British literature and narrative theory. She is the author of *Análisis estructural, método narrativo y "sentido" de "The Sound and The Fury", de William Faulkner* (1980), *Form and Meaning in the Novels of John Fowles* (1989), *Peter Ackroyd: The Writer and his Work* (1998), *Metafiction and Myth in the Novels of Peter Ackroyd* (1999), and *Jeanette Winterson* (2006). She has edited *"Telling Histories": Narrativizing History/Historicizing Literature* (1995); edited and translated into Spanish John Fowles' *The Collector* (1999); and co-edited *Narratology: An Introduction* (with J.A. García Landa, 1996), *London in Literature: Visionary Mappings of the Metropolis* (with John A. Stotesbury, 2001), *Refracting the Canon in Contemporary Literature and Film* (with Christian Gutleben, 2004), *George Orwell: A Centenary Celebration* (with Annette Gomis, 2005), *The Ethical Component in Experimental British Fiction since the 1960s* (with Jean–Michel Ganteau, 2007), and *The Ethics of Trauma Contemporary British Fiction* (also with Jean–Michel Ganteau, 2010). She is at present co-editing a book (with Jean–Michel Ganteau) on *Traumatic Realism and Romance in Contemporary British Fiction*.

CHANTAL ZABUS holds the Chair of Comparative Postcolonial Literatures and Gender Studies at the University Paris 13 and the University of Paris 3–Sorbonne Nouvelle, and is a Senior Scholar at the Institut universitaire de France, Paris. She is the author of *Between Rites and Rights: Excision in Women's Experiential Texts and Human Contexts* (2007); *The African Palimpsest* (1991; rev. ed. 2007); and *Tempests after Shakespeare* (2002). She has also edited *Fearful Symmetries: Essays and Testimonies on Excision and Circumcision* (2009); *Le Secret* (with Jacques Derrida, 1999); *Changements au féminin en Afrique noire* (2000); and *Colonization or Globalization? Postcolonial Explorations of Imperial Expansion* (with Silvia Nagy–Zekmi) (2010). Her personal website can be accessed at www.zabus.eu

The Editors

DOLORES HERRERO is Senior Lecturer of English Literature in the Department of English and German Philology at the University of Zaragoza. She currently teaches an undergraduate course on Victorian literature and another on postcolonial literatures in English; and two MA courses on postcolonial literature and cinema. Dolores Herrero is a member of a competitive research team currently working on the ethical and traumatic component in contemporary fiction in English under the directorship of Susana Onega. She has published articles and book chapters on Victorian and postcolonial literature – in particular Australian and Indian authors such as Mudrooroo, David Malouf, Peter Carey, Merlinda Bobis, Roberta Sykes, Janette Turner Hospital, Gail Jones, Satendra Nandan, and Meena Alexander, to name but a few – and film and cultural studies. She has co-edited, together with Marita Nadal, the book *Margins in British and American Literature, Film and Culture* (1997). She was also the editor of *Miscelánea: A Journal of English and American Studies* from 1998 till 2006.

SONIA BAELO–ALLUÉ is a Lecturer in the Department of English and German Philology at the University of Zaragoza, where she teaches American literature and English. She is a member of a competitive research team currently working on the ethical and traumatic component in contemporary fiction in English under the directorship of Susana Onega. Her current research centres on trauma literature and 9/11 fiction. She has published widely on blank fiction writers, the concept of intermediality, and the representation of violence in literature. Her recent publications include the monograph *Bret Easton Ellis's Controversial Fiction: Writing Between High and Low Culture* (2011).

◄❖►

Index

⟨❖⟩

Lightning Source UK Ltd.
Milton Keynes UK
UKOW050626210911

179031UK00001B/17/P

9 789042 033887